AF394420

The Migrants

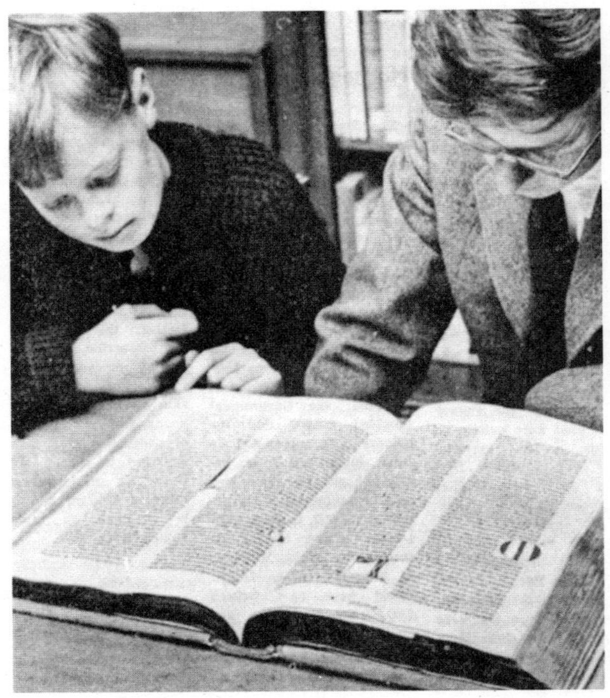

The author on the left, aged 13, with his brother Michael, looking at a Bible of 1472 in the Dunedin Public Library in September 1964.

The Migrants

A Memoir with Manuscripts

CHRISTOPHER DE HAMEL

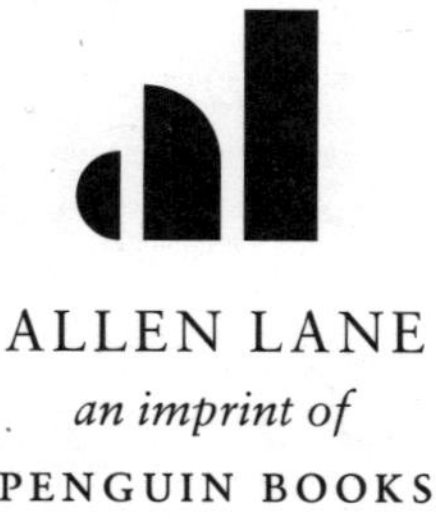

ALLEN LANE
an imprint of
PENGUIN BOOKS

ALLEN LANE

UK | USA | Canada | Ireland | Australia
India | New Zealand | South Africa

Allen Lane is part of the Penguin Random House group of companies
whose addresses can be found at global.penguinrandomhouse.com

Penguin Random House UK
One Embassy Gardens, 8 Viaduct Gardens, London SW11 7BW

penguin.co.uk

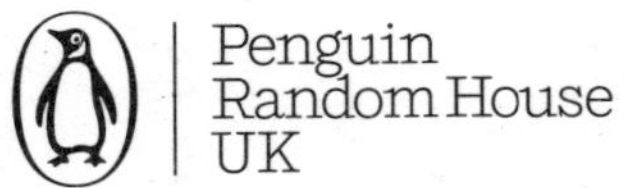

First published 2026

001

Copyright © Christopher de Hamel, 2026

The moral right of the author has been asserted

Penguin Random House values and supports copyright.
Copyright fuels creativity, encourages diverse voices, promotes freedom
of expression and supports a vibrant culture. Thank you for purchasing
an authorized edition of this book and for respecting intellectual property
laws by not reproducing, scanning or distributing any part of it by any
means without permission. You are supporting authors and enabling
Penguin Random House to continue to publish books for everyone.
No part of this book may be used or reproduced in any manner for the
purpose of training artificial intelligence technologies or systems. In accordance
with Article 4(3) of the DSM Directive 2019/790, Penguin Random House
expressly reserves this work from the text and data mining exception.

Set in 12.8/16pt Dante MT Std
Typeset by Six Red Marbles UK, Thetford, Norfolk
Printed and bound in Great Britain by Clays Ltd, Elcograf S.p.A.

The authorized representative in the EEA is Penguin Random House Ireland,
Morrison Chambers, 32 Nassau Street, Dublin D02 YH68

A CIP catalogue record for this book is available from the British Library

ISBN: 978–0–241–67012–5

Penguin Random House is committed to a sustainable future
for our business, our readers and our planet. This book is made from
Forest Stewardship Council® certified paper.

Contents

List of Illustrations

Every effort has been made to contact copyright holders. The author and publishers will be pleased to correct in future printings any errors or omissions brought to their attention.

Black and White Images

Frontispiece: The author aged 13 with his brother Michael, looking at a Bible of 1472 in the Dunedin Public Library, 1964. Photograph by the *Otago Daily Times*.

Colour Plates

from Boethius, *De musica*, *c.* 1163. Wellington, Alexander
Turnbull Library, MS R-05, fol. 27v, detail.

21. Opening initial and Canterbury identification symbol from
the Boethius, *De musica*. Wellington, Alexander Turnbull
Library, MS R-05, fol. 1v, detail.

22. Blacksmiths striking an anvil, coloured diagram from
Boethius, *De musica*. Wellington, Alexander Turnbull
Library, MS R-05, fol. 8r, detail.

23. Upper cover of an incunable of 1481 bound in Oxford by
the 'Rood and Hunt' Binder, who strengthened his sewing
folds with strips of printed indulgences. University of
Otago Library, Shoults/Ic/1481/B, ref. S25-553e.

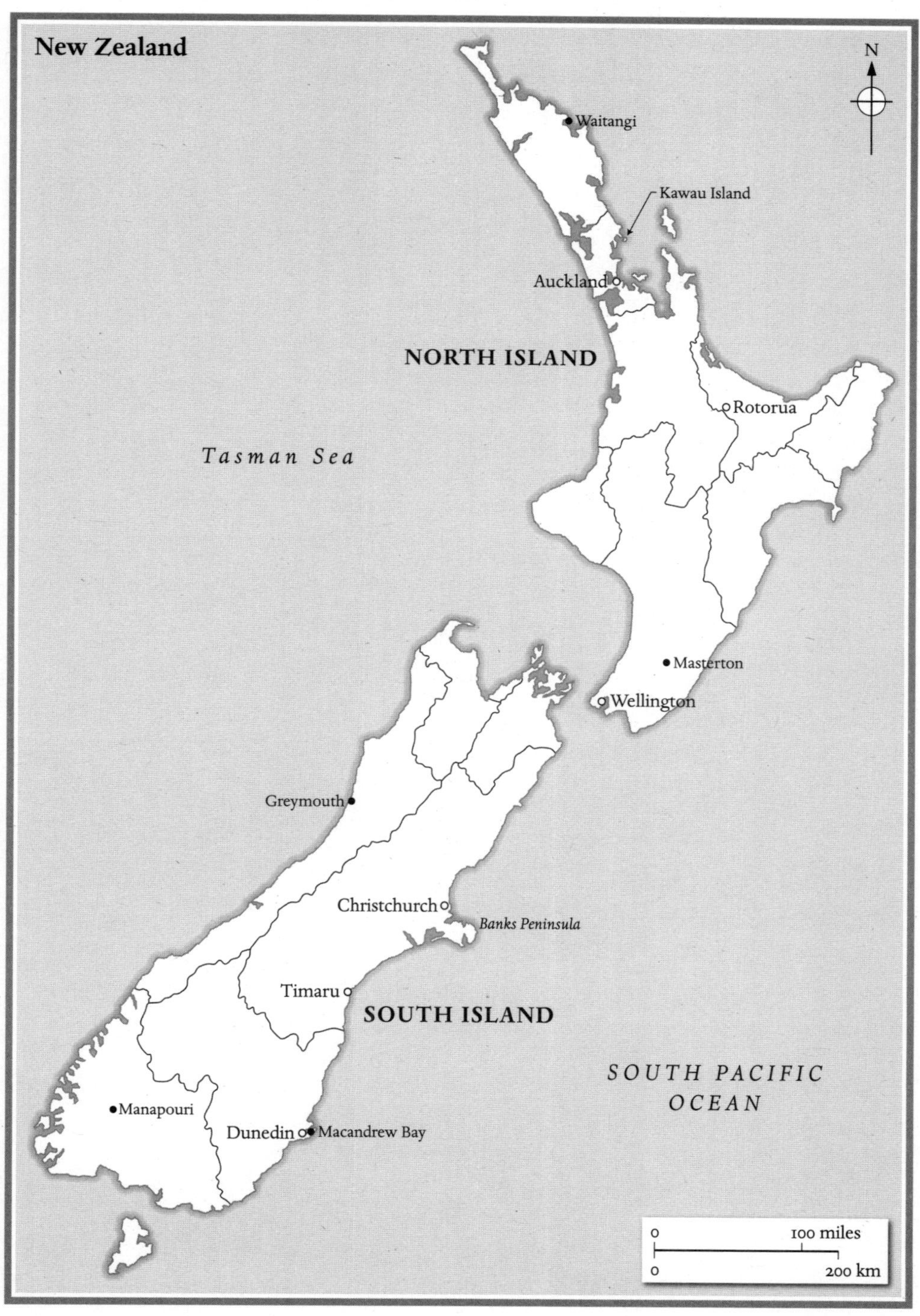

New Zealand
N
Waitangi
Kawau Island
Auckland
NORTH ISLAND
Rotorua
Tasman Sea
Masterton
Wellington
Greymouth
Christchurch
Banks Peninsula
Timaru
SOUTH ISLAND
SOUTH PACIFIC
OCEAN
Manapouri
Dunedin
Macandrew Bay
0
100 miles
0
200 km

Introduction

I think I can truly say that I love all aspects of medieval manuscripts, even when they have no script. There is an immense fifteenth-century genealogical roll in the library of the University of Canterbury in Christchurch, New Zealand, recounting the history of the kings of England. When I saw it last, it was unrolled on a long table the entire length of the room. It traces the unbroken line of royal descent and chronology from Noah in the Old Testament down to the early 1420s, when the manuscript was written. However, history never stops moving onwards. The passage of time continues, and the roll was extended and updated some forty years later. The new medieval scribe then helpfully left a further space of about two feet of blank parchment at the end, in the expectation that future owners might one day want to complete the narrative by filling in all subsequent historical events between the 1460s and the end of the world, whenever that would be. That big uninscribed white area at the end was never used. It has a sublime symbolic beauty, like the most perfect poem or an utterly satisfying scientific formula: it represents infinite possibilities. All historians should have a copy of it pinned up above their desks, for absolutely everything is comprehended within its silence. The moment we begin writing down history, there are gaps and faulty memory, and a narrative can never be more than a small selection of what actually happened.

This book is not a conventional memoir in that much of it takes place now, but it does try to address that eternal and usually puzzled dinner-party question, 'What got you started on that?' It is a blend of inquiry and personal memory of childhood. Like most history, it seems to have happened long ago. In my case, the past really is a different country. If I did not know when I was born, which I do, I might think I was older than I really am. How many Christmases or summer holidays have I had? More than a hundred? It could easily seem so, at least. When the authors of Genesis interviewed Noah and he said he was 950, maybe he thought it possible, gazing back over his life. His distant memories of the Ark would appear as far off as the steamship *Rangitoto* which took our family out to New Zealand in 1955. Life in Christchurch in the 1950s and early 60s seems to me now as remote from our modern world as the fifteenth century. My first little publication on medieval manuscripts, called *Books of Hours*, came out in Dunedin in 1970, almost sixty years ago. To put the timespan in context, that period is more than 10 per cent of all passage of time since the Middle Ages.

I was in fact born in London in November 1950, the second of five children, all boys. When I was four, my father accepted what was intended to be a temporary job in New Zealand, over a month away by ship. The story here is one of growing up. It ends in 1972 when I was twenty-one and returned by aeroplane to England for postgraduate work, having already decided that happiness lay with medieval manuscripts. I have lived back in Britain ever since, mostly in London. New Zealand was then (and still is) the most distant country from Europe in any direction. The manuscripts in this book have travelled further than any have ever done or could do, without venturing into space. (If there is one thing we were wrong about as children in imagining the future, it is that we thought we would all have rockets and be routinely visiting other planets.)

New Zealand was the last major country on earth to be settled by humans – by Māori migrants from Polynesia, perhaps from the thirteenth century, and by Europeans only since the nineteenth. I need to acknowledge from the outset the place and accepted precedence of the Māori citizens of contemporary New Zealand. In my time there as a child, New Zealand was for all practical purposes a European and almost entirely British nation, especially where we lived in the South Island. There were some Māori placenames – 'Otago' is a corruption of one of them – all pronounced in those days in an English manner, rather as Churchill spoke French. Traces of former Māori occupation were familiar and discoverable through archaeology, but did not come into our daily lives any more than, say, evidence of Viking settlement impacts much modern life in Britain today. There was no macron accent on 'Maori' and the plural was 'Maoris'. We were taught that a corner of the coast of New Zealand was first found in December 1642 by the Dutch sea captain Abel Janszoon Tasman and that the country was properly discovered and charted by James Cook on the *Endeavour* from October 1769. Captain Cook was the national hero, shown on banknotes, like the Queen. We learned that there were some European settlers by the early nineteenth century, often rough and unscrupulous plunderers of seals, whales and timber, with a few overworked and well-meaning Christian missionaries in the far north. We were told that the magnanimity of England introduced a bilingual treaty on the beach at Waitangi in February 1840, to protect Māori people from unprincipled exploitation and to bring New Zealand into the security of the British empire and to prepare it for orderly colonization. This document was itself a calligraphic

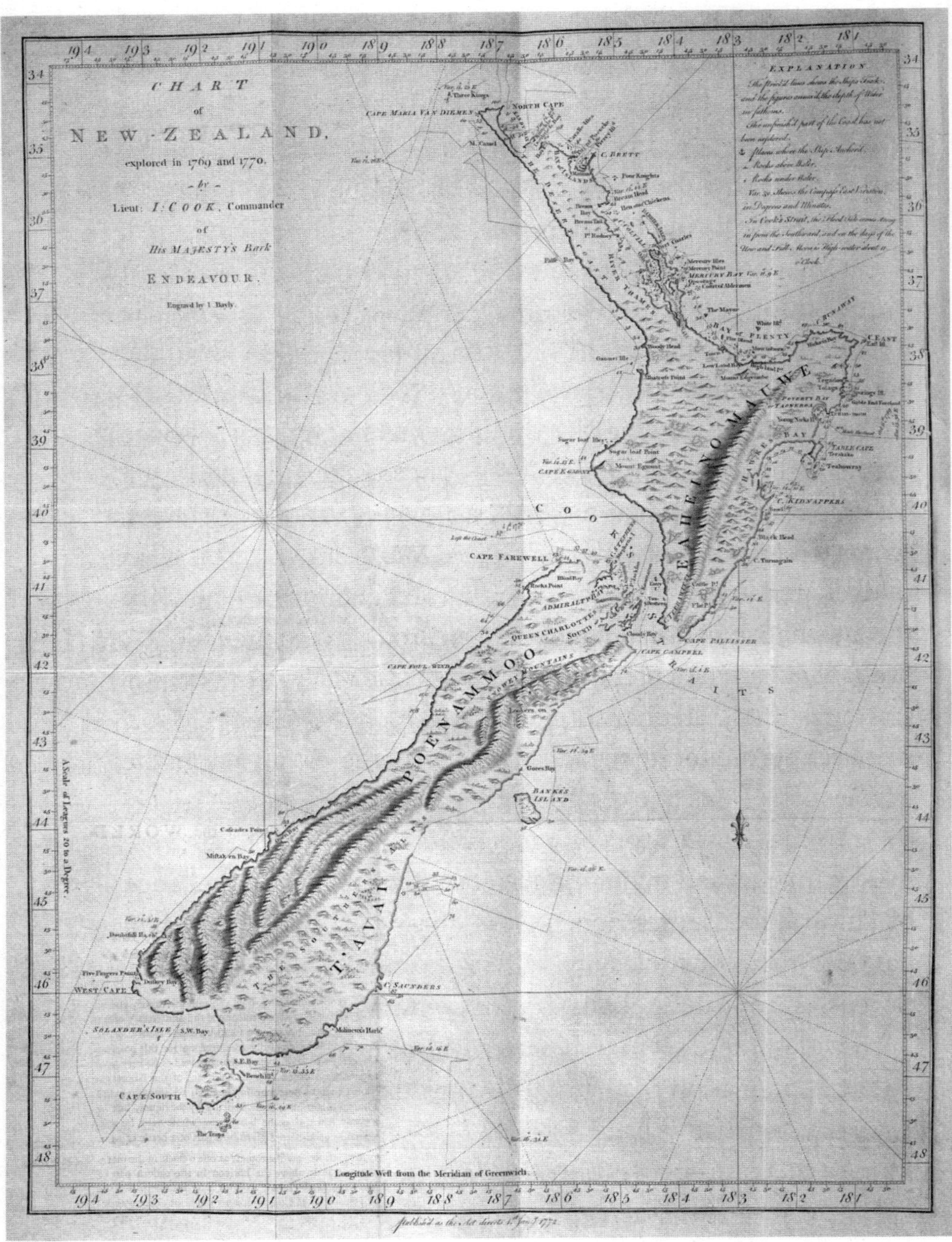

New Zealand as surveyed by Captain Cook in 1769 and 1770,
published in London in 1773.

manuscript on parchment; 6 February was celebrated annually as Waitangi Day, the nation's birthday. That was the standard interpretation throughout the period I lived there, 1955–1972, and the setting of this book must be understood within the parameters of those years. To pretend otherwise would be to misrepresent history.

New Zealand today feels very different. Considerable recent immigration from the Pacific, as well as from Asia and the Middle East, has altered the Eurocentric focus, especially in the big cities. The diversity of the modern New Zealanders' ancestries is brought together by the undeniable fact that all have come to settle in a land which was once occupied solely by a Māori population. That, more than a once-shared Englishness, seems to be what unites them. The old Māori language has been rejuvenated and is now consciously used and promoted, with the alternative national name of Aotearoa ('long white cloud', probably a late nineteenth-century invention, perhaps even by an Englishman, Stephenson Percy Smith). There are no Māori manuscripts or literate records. What is so interesting within the framework of this book is that during my childhood, the collections of medieval European manuscripts in New Zealand were mostly unused and under-appreciated. Today, for all the change of cultural focus, every one of the libraries I knew there then has been rebuilt with facilities for safekeeping and exhibition of rarities. European book history is now taught in New Zealand universities, there seem to be medievalists everywhere, and the public appreciation of the treasures of their libraries is apparently greater than it has ever been. This book documents one stage in this transformation.

There are several themes which run throughout. The biggest is migration, both of people and manuscripts, over immense distances. The puzzled follow-up question at dinner parties is, usually, 'How did manuscripts come to be there at all?' Their stories are as much part of the history of colonization as those of human immigrants. The first settlers in New Zealand (and many of the finest manuscripts) arrived on sailing ships, after cramped and creaking journeys of many months round Cape Horn and across the vast Pacific, or down the coast of Africa and over the Indian Ocean. On arrival, some assimilated and settled; others came back to Europe – manuscripts as well as people. Chance plays a large part, but there were also motives of idealism and the creation of utopia.

There is a delight in seeing manuscripts in largely untouched medieval libraries in Europe, in places such as Durham Cathedral or St Gallen, for example, but these books are in some way virginal and innocent. People who have had a life are often more fascinating to talk to than those who still live with their parents. The manuscripts in New Zealand have travelled the world, have entered and left libraries, passed through salerooms and bookshops, and have met and interacted with many and very different owners often in far more important ways than some volume that has never left its medieval shelf. Many immigrants would say the same about their stay-at-home cousins. Sun-wrinkled faces and experienced eyes make for better conversation.

In Europe, children can be inspired by the Middle Ages from seeing medieval houses and churches and castles still in the landscape. There is nothing comparable in New Zealand and, in reality, there are no visible Māori constructions of any notable antiquity. The touchstones of history there are artefacts which can be transported across the world, and for me these were manuscripts. I still know of no greater thrill than cradling an original medieval book in the hands, as people did centuries ago, turning its pages, looking at the decoration and (occasionally and sometimes almost unconsciously) even reading the text. These are no reproductions or modern substitutes. The knowledge of their absolute and tangible authenticity is essential to the experience. Manuscripts can still speak to us face to face from the Middle Ages, even so far from their native habitats. The tales here stray (but only just) into late medieval printing, including the discovery of some unknown pieces by William Caxton.

I am a medievalist, accustomed to research and judgements on people and events from a distant past. It is not so easy when the subject is partly my own time *et quorum pars magna fui* (a phrase we learned from struggling with the *Aeneid* at school). During its early drafts, this book was known as *The Life of Clive*, for a reason which will appear in Chapter 4, an initial suggestion of the editor who told me it might be easier to write if I could pretend to myself that the childish protagonist was another person, some naïve little boy, part of history, long ago. It can be read as a universal story of migration, and of an alien family sometimes failing to acclimatize in its new environment. That is probably the crucial factor in opening up medieval manuscripts to me. It would almost certainly never have happened in England. I have endeavoured to recapture here something of that electrifying joy of suddenly encountering manuscripts for the first time, silent upon a peak in Darien, and what the discovery meant to me then, in New Zealand. In alternating chapters I will try to tell you what those same manuscripts really are, looked at again a lifetime later, and we will venture together in Europe, back to where they began their migrations up to almost nine hundred years ago. It is a travel book as well as a memoir and we will share the different journeys.

As with previous books, this one too owes its inspiration and encouragement to Caroline Dawnay, literary agent, and to Stuart Proffitt, editor and friend at Allen Lane. It is especially indebted to Lieve De Kesel. My four brothers, Michael, William,

Richard and Quentin, have all answered questions and made precious contributions, but none of them so far has read the entire text and so blame for faulty memory or variant interpretation of what we experienced as children rests only with me. In New Zealand, my greatest debts are to Donald Kerr, with whom I stayed when re-visiting Dunedin, Julian Smith in the Reed Collection, Anthony Tedeschi in Wellington, and Jane Wild and her husband Philip Clarke in Auckland, and out to Kawau. I had valuable conversations in Christchurch with Chris Jones, who died suddenly in 2024, aged only forty-seven. Richard Linenthal, Davina Honess, Sir David Skegg, Scott Schwartz and Nicolas Barker have all read and corrected chapters. My whole life would of course have been impossible without my late parents, Francis and Joan de Hamel, to whom I owe it all, and I wish they too could read it.

I

Kawau Island

'G'day, my name is Caleb and I'll be your skipper,' says the catamaran pilot, in dark glasses, shorts and tramping boots. He will be taking us out to the most remote place on earth where medieval illuminated manuscripts have ever been kept. All of New Zealand still feels a very long way from Europe, and even their nearest neighbour Australia is about as distant from New Zealand as London is from North Africa. We are going today six miles off the east coast to Kawau Island in the Hauraki Gulf. I have been driven by my hosts up State Highway 1 north from Auckland, turning off at Warkworth to the seaside holiday resort of Sandspit. At this time of year, in the winter month of August, it is distinctly out of season, and there is a chance of rain. Beyond the marina is an empty car park. There is an information and ticket office, offering fishing bait and excursions to Kawau, either aboard the regular 10.30 Royal Mail Run cruise boat or, for smaller parties such as today, on the 'little cat', as they call it, the *Explorer*, which is bobbing in the sea at the end of the jetty.

You can sit inside or stand out on the back deck, as the salty wind tangles your hair. The sea is deep green, the colour of the damp native ferns or the purest greenstone jade of the ancient Māori, once their most precious natural commodity since they had no use for gold later found in New Zealand rivers. Our catamaran rushes out past islands and promontories of the mainland, either still covered in the impenetrable thatch of dark bush coming right down to the water's edge or shorn by Europeans of their trees and now instead the palest green of pasture. Eventually one island bigger than all the others appears in our sight, with substantial sand-coloured cliffs and vegetation dotted with white specks of houses. This is Kawau, or *Te Kawau-tu-maro*, which, Caleb tells us, means 'the motionless cormorant' in Māori, in honour of the statuesque seabirds regarded by the earliest New Zealanders as sacred for silently retaining ancient wisdom. The cormorants have lived here for ever. The island was also occupied by successive and competing Māori tribes, until it was abandoned after a particularly violent skirmish in the 1820s. There was a short period of manganese and copper mining by Europeans in the 1840s and 50s. As we get closer, we can see a number of buildings and holiday houses along a fringe of beaches with anchored pleasure boats. There are no roads on Kawau. Our catamaran moves round the island anticlockwise, pulling into landing-stages at Vivian Bay and North Cove, dropping off supplies and passengers, before eventually docking at a jetty in front of what is now called Mansion

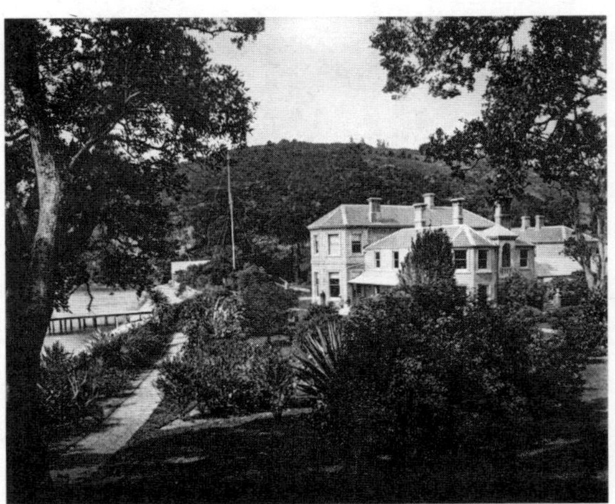

Sir George Grey's house on Kawau Island, *c.* 1868, during Grey's residency there with his medieval manuscripts.

House. This is a broad, two-storey, white Victorian house with a slate roof and a slightly later double-height veranda wrapped around the left-hand frontage of the building. This is our destination and where the world's most displaced manuscripts were brought from Europe in the nineteenth century.

The house was owned and greatly enlarged from an original mining manager's cottage by Sir George Grey (1812–98). He remains a mighty figure in the early history of New Zealand and British colonial administration. He was governor of South Australia (1841–45), New Zealand (1845–53), the Cape Colony (1854–61) and New Zealand again (1861–68), and then became premier or prime minister of New Zealand from 1877 to 1879. His reputation is controversial today, when imperialism is deeply unfashionable. There are those who admire him greatly, as I

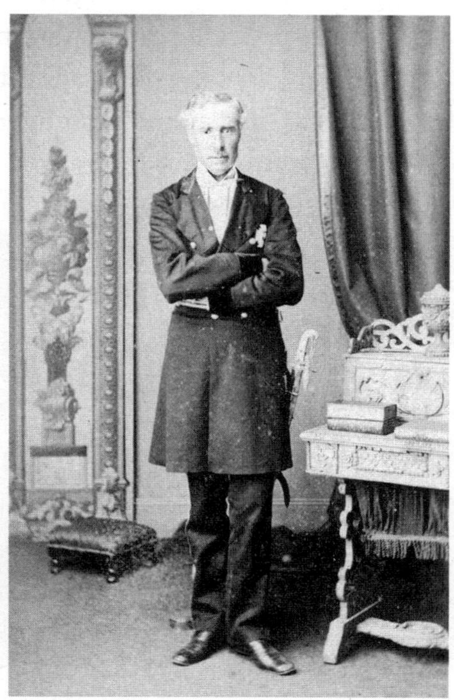

Sir George Grey, in a photograph of 1867.

do, for his book and manuscript collections and literary philanthropy, while there are many others who now find it impossible to forgive his high-handed response at a time of Māori resistance to colonial settlement. In November 1862, Sir George Grey personally bought the entire island of Kawau. It cost him £3,700 and about another £5,000 to remodel the house and landscape. Here he built himself a private paradise, a Garden of Eden in the South Seas, a Prospero's island. Kawau is about five thousand acres in size, or nearly eight and a half square miles, a substantial private kingdom about ten times the size of Monaco.

Kawau is mostly very hilly, but Mansion House lies at the head of a long valley stretching inland between woods on either side. The area around the house was cleared and laid out as lawn or parkland. In what feels like a conscious re-creation of images of Eden in European imagination, Grey then brought in exotic animals to adorn his island Arcadia. He had zebras, monkeys, antelopes, donkeys, elk and deer of various kinds, Cape sheep, kangaroos and wallabies. There are no animals indigenous to New Zealand, and all were necessarily imported on logistically complex journeys. There are, however, an immense number of native birds, some very beautiful, and for centuries before Grey's arrival the bush of Kawau would have been alive with their daily symphonies of songs and competing calls – the incessant three or four piano notes of the tui, the tinkling staccato of the bellbird, the chuckle of native pigeons, the bark of the morepork, the babble of tiny fantails like the trickle of water, and noises like the squeaking of unoiled wheels from parakeets high in the treetops. There are even kiwis on Kawau. To this native parliament of fowls, Grey also added decorative emus, kookaburras, coloured parrots, cassowaries, magpies, blackbirds, jackdaws, jays, goldfinches, geese, partridges, pheasants, swans and many other birds from Europe and elsewhere. In the streams and ponds of Kawau, he introduced trout, goldfish and carp. There is a long tradition of art collectors owning private menageries, including Henry of Blois in twelfth-century Winchester, the duc de Berry, and several Rothschilds of the nineteenth century.

The forests and native bush of New Zealand have many extraordinary plants. The landmass was so cut off from its neighbours for infinite millennia that it developed its own unique species. Early settlers from Europe often commented on the dramatic scarlet flowers of the indigenous rata and its cousin the pohutukawa, or New Zealand Christmas tree, a large shrub of the myrtle family. The pohutukawa can live for hundreds of years. It too has a place in Māori mythology, as having supposedly received its bright red colour from the spilled blood of an early warrior who had climbed to heaven and was dashed back to his death on earth. It gives its name to the Pohutukawa Trust, which I read about from a signboard in Sandspit while waiting for the catamaran, dedicated to ridding Kawau of all its inappropriate and now unwanted foreign species, some shockingly from Australia (a particularly distasteful word in New Zealand), to allow the island to return to its native state. In addition to animals and birds, Grey had embellished his paradise with magnolias, Brazilian palms and rhododendrons around the house and, further back, oaks, elms, cedars, cypresses and poplars, and groves of figs, strawberries, pears, walnuts, limes, guavas, oranges, bananas, cinnamon, camphor, olives, grapevines and mulberries. Some of the actual trees planted by Grey as seedlings are still alive, now grown to massive giants, such as his monkey puzzles and the huge Australian Moreton Bay fig trees. Grey exchanged plants with Kew Gardens, sending local specimens back to London and receiving instead species entirely new to the colony. It is no wonder the Pohutukawa Trust dreams of a little botanical ethnic cleansing.

There is a certain irony in interpreting Grey's Kawau as a Garden of Eden reborn, since, until the arrival of European settlers, New Zealand had probably been as near to primordial creation as anywhere then left on earth. Before the landing of the first Māori migrants from Polynesia in perhaps the thirteenth century, no human had ever set foot in the country at all. Each of the two civilizations brought some desecration of paradise. The Māori imported dogs and fire and sweet potatoes, and they relentlessly ate to extinction various conveniently flightless species of bird. The Europeans in turn, especially after 1840, unpacked and unleashed many of the movable accompaniments of their former lives and they cleared land for farms and housing. As far as vegetation is concerned, it is estimated that before 1840, only a few dozen exotic kinds of plant had ever been brought into New Zealand, mostly for food; by 1870, there were almost three hundred introduced species, and by the 1930s, more than a thousand, two-thirds of which arrived in the second half of the nineteenth century. The numbers for animals are more extreme, as primeval New Zealand had until then had none of its own.

Grey's zoological and botanical importations to Kawau were not mere vanity or a rich man's playthings. The journalist James Grattan Grey (no relation) described Kawau in 1879 as 'a kind of acclimatisation depot . . . for subsequent distribution throughout the Colony.' The governor was testing compatibility to New Zealand of animals and plants which might one day be useful to the settlers, for food, medicine, timber or sport. Wallabies could provide meat; even the zebras were harnessed to pull his carriage. He did not bring koalas or giraffes (no use at all) or bears or leopards or others from picture-book Gardens of Eden or toybox Noah's Arks. (Perhaps, strictly, even in Eden, animals and plants were there only for their usefulness to humankind – Genesis 1:29–30.) Grey considered badgers for Kawau but rejected them as of no value. The decorative peacocks, currently strutting near Mansion House, are not from his initiative. Grey was a close correspondent of Charles Darwin and other Victorian natural scientists then studying varieties of environment. Not every arrival, like not every human immigrant, took to life in New Zealand at all. Of imported British garden birds, sparrows, blackbirds and thrushes thrived and bred, and their fertile families have now lived throughout the country for more generations of their own than any human population. Blue tits, robins and chaffinches did not survive. Grey's zebras both died. On the other hand, the wallabies escaped, and their happy descendants still live on Kawau, to the distress of the Pohutukawa Trust. Their breed is rare in Australia now, and I learned from a Kawau information board that when some were recently reintroduced back into their ancestral homeland, they died, for their families had become accustomed to better lives as New Zealanders. Most of the fruits cultivated by Grey are now common in New Zealand. He gave samples of a new grapefruit, *Citrus paradisi*, to a nurseryman in Warkworth on the mainland, and from there it has become the most widely grown variety in New Zealand, sometimes called the poor man's orange.

Bearing all this in mind, let us now walk back towards Grey's residence down by the shore. It was known as Big House in his time but has taken on the more dignified name of Mansion House. It is owned by the Department of Conservation and administered by the Mansion House Foundation. I am fortunate that our party today includes not only Georgia Prince and her successor, Jane Wild, of the Grey Collection at the Auckland Public Library, but also Jane's husband, Philip Clarke, who is a trustee of the Foundation and drove us up to Sandspit this morning, and Sarah Macready, its current chairman. It transpires that Sarah is a cousin of my cousin in Auckland. New Zealand is like that. A few minutes into any conversation, even dangling your legs over the edge of the gazebo during a picnic lunch on Kawau, and they are asking, 'Didn't your parents buy their house from my driving instructor's uncle?' or 'I think your brother's wife once shared a flat with our daughter's godmother.'

You enter Grey's house now on the left-hand side, if approaching it from the beach, which must have been the kitchen door in the nineteenth century. Turn right into a shaded drawing room, which extends to the front, looking out towards the sea through tall narrow windows. The walls are dark burgundy and there is a wooden fireplace against the inner wall. This room appears in various nineteenth-century photographs of the house, then with hanging pictures in massive gilt frames, oriental pots crowding

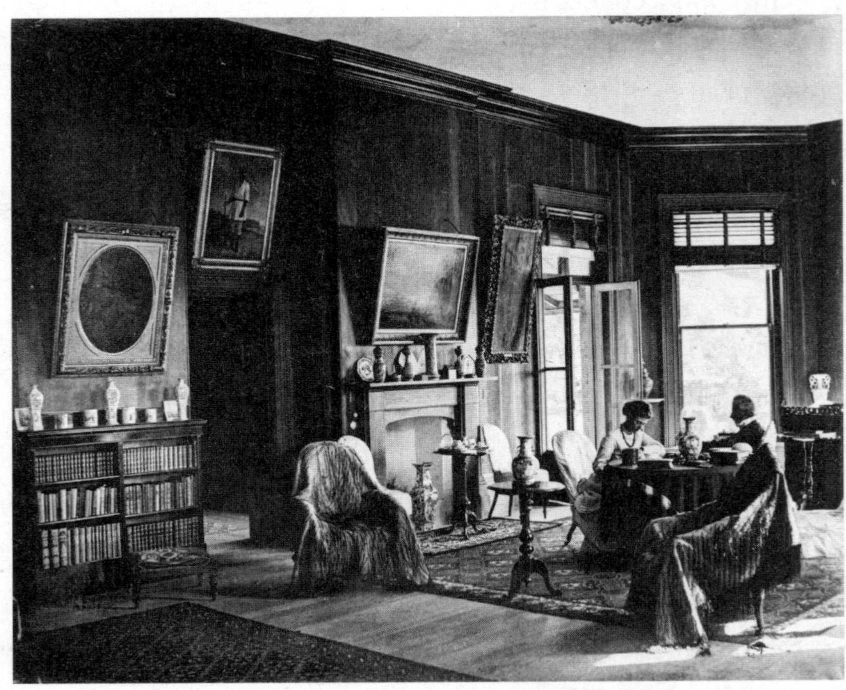

Sir George Grey with his niece Annie Matthews
in the drawing room of the house on Kawau, *c.* 1868.

the mantelpiece and the top of a bookcase, rugs on the floor and armchairs draped in textiles. In the photographs, Grey is sometimes shown seated reading at a table, opposite Annie Matthews, daughter of his late half-brother – for Grey, like Prospero, shared his island with a young Miranda, adopted by Grey a year after he had abandoned his wife. Through the door to the left of the fireplace was Annie's day room, with a fine view of the bay and the late afternoon sun, and through that again is the house's original entrance hall, with access to the dining room and the main staircase. The bedroom at the top on the right is very doubtfully identified now as the location of Grey's library. It is more likely that the library was in the larger space above the drawing room, which would explain the pillars added to that room by Grey, probably to strengthen the floor above for the weight of books.

Grey was a collector all his life. His first medieval manuscript was offered in 1841 by the London bookseller H. G. Bohn, for £2.10s. It is an elegant little Florentine Petrarch signed by the well-known Florentine scribe Gherardo del Ciriagio in 1455. If Grey acquired it in 1841, which is not entirely certain, he probably had it with him in South Australia. It is generally said that the first medieval manuscript to reach Australia was bought by the Public (now State) Library of Victoria as relatively late as 1902. The presence of the Petrarch would predate it by more than sixty years. By the time of his first governorship of New Zealand in 1845–53, Grey was ordering books massively from London, including a request for fourteen 'Missals and Illuminated Manuscripts' from Bohn in 1848. This was only eight years after New Zealand became a colony. He was also buying great quantities of early printed books, international literature, wide-ranging scientific and reference material and, importantly, extensive material relating to Māori and Pacific languages. His intellectual thirst is deeply impressive, and characteristically nineteenth-century.

Grey's considerable collection was moved from New Zealand on Grey's transference to the Cape Colony in 1854. He then added African languages to its scope and greatly increased his acquisition of medieval manuscripts, not only Bibles and Books of Hours but also classical texts – Livy, Caesar, Lucan, Valerius Maximus, Boethius – and copies of Petrus Riga, Mandeville, Guido delle Colonna, the *Roman de la Rose* and another Petrarch. These were the kind of European manuscripts easily available in Britain following the wholesale dispersals of monastic and aristocratic libraries after the French Revolution and the Napoleonic upheavals in Italy and Germany. Grey's best books by modern standards were a late Carolingian Gospel Book with canon tables and evangelist portraits, a fourteenth-century Dante from the library of the Marchese Antaldi of Pesaro (sold at Sotheby's in 1857), and an entire Hebrew Bible, probably of the fifteenth century, in a contemporary *mudéjar* blind-stamped box binding, apparently bought from Bohn for only £8.8s. Grey was forming the idea of enriching the British Empire with representative treasures of old Europe.

In September 1859, when Grey was back in London, he visited Sir Frederic Madden, Keeper of Manuscripts at the British Museum. We have Madden's account in his unpublished journal. Grey, probably already accustomed to exchanging plants with Kew, suggested giving the British Museum modern African and Australasian books they lacked in exchange for 'duplicate' rare books which could be sent out instead to the colonies. Madden was appalled:

Of course such a proposition is out of the question . . . I think Sir George Grey has taken a very foolish step in laying out a large sum of money in purchasing Manuscripts and rare printed books, all of which he destines for a library in

Australia! I would have thought *a century hence* would be time enough to send them such objects of (to them) mere curiosity. Among other MSS he had purchased, he mentioned one of the Antaldi Dantes, for £79, and a Book of Hours executed for Margaret de Valois. I am vexed to think that MSS of this class should be sent to the other side of the globe. It is not the act of a sensible man.

It would be interesting and unexpected if Grey really said Australia, but this may have been Madden's inference. (The donation actually went to Cape Town.) However, while the very idea that illuminated manuscripts should be sent to the southern hemisphere was deemed absurd, the Museum had no trouble with accepting 118 Māori artefacts from Grey himself in 1854, or with acquiring the finest royal Ethiopian manuscripts for Madden's department from the British sack of Magdala in east Africa in 1868.

Grey boasted to Madden of Margaret of Valois (1492–1549), a credulous fantasy for a medieval Book of Hours in a late sixteenth-century gilt binding on which he had misunderstood the common sacred monogram of 'M' and 'V' (*Maria virgo*). Grey, trusting what booksellers told him, rejoiced in supposed provenances and the connections they brought. In a meditation written on Christmas morning in 1860, he contemplated another Book of Hours in the language of prayer: 'I sit here at the base of a lofty mountain in South Africa . . . Dear old book that has now for nigh four centuries presented these and such like words of comfort, to so many men, in so many lands . . . in City, and in desert, in Palaces . . . Dear old friend of mine, how I too love thee.'

Grey presented almost his entire first collection, including 114 medieval and Renaissance manuscripts, to the new South

African Public Library and Museum in Cape Town. He seized the chance of a visit by Prince Alfred, son of Queen Victoria, to have him inscribe a Greek Gospel Book and declare the library open to the public on 18 September 1860. The building overlooks the public botanical gardens, and in that it slightly resembles Kawau, where imported and indigenous species of plants, birds and books were brought to live together. The Dante and the 'Margaret of Valois' Book of Hours are now part of the Cape Town campus (as they call it) of the National Library of South Africa, with Grey's other manuscripts and incunabula and his African collections. It is difficult to know whether the early European books were ever much appreciated in South Africa. I have spent several periods in Cape Town, looking carefully at every medieval manuscript. No one I met even knew they were there. All are in the condition they were in 1860, unthumbed if they were pristine then or with broken or loose bindings if that is how they arrived. Many are still in nineteenth-century brown-paper packages tied with string, presumably by Grey himself. Slightly cool and ambiguous endorsement was given by Anthony Trollope, who visited the collection in 1877:

> But why a MS of Livy, or of Dante, should not be as serviceable at Capetown as in some gentleman's country house in England it would be hard to say; and the Shakespeare folio of 1623 of which the library possesses a copy . . . is no doubt as often looked at, and as much petted and loved and cherished in the capital of South Africa, as it is when in the possession of a British Duke.

By November 1861, Grey was back in New Zealand. He had retained a few books from his library, including a huge two-volume Bible manuscript presented to the Dominican nuns of Wijk bij Duurstede in 1419, which carried a preposterous assertion that it had been the actual exemplar used by Gutenberg in Mainz for his first printed Bible of the 1450s (Plate 1). Grey had acquired it in 1855 and had perhaps been reluctant to pass over so touching a relic. In 1862, as we saw, Grey bought Kawau. From here, he began collecting all over again, receiving catalogues and writing to booksellers, mainly in England. He ordered six medieval manuscripts from Henry Boone in 1863, of which the most expensive – at £14 – was one volume (of two) of a twelfth-century *Moralia in Job* by St Gregory, trumpeted – as inaccurately as the claims for Margaret of Valois and Gutenberg – as having once been owned by Henry V, king of England 1413–22, following a grotesque misreading of the Gothic letters 'h. n' on its sixteenth-century stamped binding ('n' looking slightly like a 'v'). Others from the same purchase included an early fourteenth-century Aristotle (£2.10s.) and a tall Florentine humanistic manuscript of Josephus (£9). Many of Grey's manuscripts are truthfully rather dull copies, good texts and usually complete, but often without the sparkle and

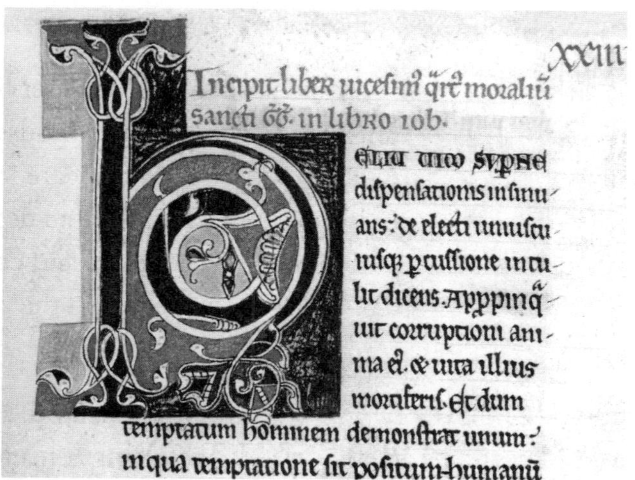

Gregory, *Moralia in Job*, England, twelfth century, wrongly believed by Grey to have been bound for King Henry V.

tactile delight that a practised connoisseur might have selected if allowed personal access to the bookseller's shelves. This is a reality of all collections assembled by post, usually unavoidable from the furthest ends of the empire. Later in 1863, Boone was confident enough of his client, and trusting of the international postal system, to send several major manuscripts from London to Kawau on approval, enabling better purchases for larger sums of money than Grey might have chanced unseen. They included two of his most spectacular acquisitions: the Rossdhu Book of Hours with twenty-five miniatures, made in Flanders but used in medieval Scotland, and the splendid two-volume Missal from Besançon, which forms the subject of Chapter 3 below.

Prospero in Shakespeare's *Tempest* tells Miranda that a kindly friend had 'furnished me, from mine own library with volumes that I prize above my dukedom'. Grey, governor of all New Zealand in times of increasing civil unrest, comforted himself with rare books on Kawau and immersed himself in their company. He also took opium for the same purpose, differently but equally addictive. He signed his name in ink on many of the manuscripts' first leaves, and some have annotations by him. Grey was himself of a moderately good Irish military family but not of noble lineage. He was unrelated to other more aristocratic Greys in politics, such as Earl Grey, prime minister (1830–34) and tea drinker. There is an element of aspiration to a self-image perhaps more patrician than he had enjoyed at home, as so often in the history of colonial administration. In Cape Town there is a humanistic manuscript of Caesar's *Commentaries* in which Grey had his own recently acquired coat of arms inserted into the medieval decoration. He clearly saw himself as an educated statesman enjoying his library as a private relief from a tumultuous public life, like a modern

Cicero or Cosimo de' Medici in the fifteenth century or George III in the eighteenth. Grey's almost exact contemporary William Gladstone gathered and used a very similar library, kept at St Deiniol's in northern Wales. It may be that especially in New Zealand, where every Māori had a known ancestry and tribal identity, and every European immigrant was suddenly cut off from all family background, old books and manuscripts had a value in connecting to the past. They speak reassuringly of long ago, like cormorants.

In acquiring exotic natural history for Kawau, Grey had sourced specimens he already knew from previous residences. Almost without exception, the animals, birds and plants came from Grey's earlier experience in Britain, Australia or southern Africa. Similarly, in selecting rare books and manuscripts for the house on Kawau, he opted for what was familiar to him, duplicating what he had done for Cape Town. He brought to New Zealand a second humanistic manuscript of Petrarch and examples of Cicero, Valerius Maximus, Boethius, Petrus Riga, Guido delle Colonna and Boccaccio, as well as two Greek Gospel Books, and Bibles and medieval liturgy, and (at the very end of his life) another First Folio of Shakespeare, all of which were represented in the previous library. The collection in Cape Town was three times the size of that on Kawau, but they were close cousins. In the passage of even a decade or so, the availability was drying up for European manuscripts disgorged by revolution, and prices were rising. One difference is that for his earlier library Grey had acquired a number of manuscripts in the Dutch language, including liturgy and the romantic voyages of Mandeville, perhaps in acknowledgement of the Afrikaans-speaking population in southern Africa; there were almost no Dutch settlers in New Zealand, and there were no manuscripts in that language in Grey's collection on

Kawau. There are several Hebrew manuscripts too in the bequest to Cape Town, coinciding with a time of considerable Jewish migration there. There is nothing comparable in New Zealand. Instead, Grey bought two Bohemian books, a Psalter and the romances of the Trojan War, both in the medieval Czech language. The extraordinary rarity of these is perhaps not even now recognized by the librarians of Auckland. Their purchase might have been with an awareness of the arrival in 1863 of an entire village from Bohemia, settling in Puhoi on the mainland, only about ten miles across the sea from Kawau. It suggests that Grey was already considering a collection for future New Zealanders, as he had for the European immigrants to the Cape Colony.

Grey must have known that the response to his benefaction in Cape Town was underwhelming. One can imagine him using the library on Kawau like the acclimatization trials on plants and animals, testing their suitability by the reaction of people to rare books in so unusual a setting, before releasing them into New Zealand. All collectors will assure their families that books can self-propagate and multiply. If the bulk of Grey's increasing library was upstairs out of sight, the best of the rarities were probably kept in the drawing room on the ground floor, where they could be seen. The photographs of the room show a broad bookcase of three shelves, with bulky and apparently old books on the lower tiers. A female visitor in 1879 described bookcases as being on either side of the fireplace, filled with volumes, 'some 300, some 500 years old', such as a manuscript of 'Pope Gregory (1413)', she remembered. This must be the *Moralia* and what Grey proudly told her about its supposed provenance, since Henry V became king in 1413. She also mentions a library and bedrooms upstairs, a different location. Another guest that year saw 'old illuminated missals' and 'the handiwork of the monks done centuries ago'. The only actual Missal was the luxury pair of volumes from Besançon. The French-born Roman Catholic bishop of New Zealand, Jean-Baptiste Pompallier, had an enjoyable visit to Kawau in 1866, and it is inconceivable he was not shown it. In 1868, Prince Alfred, who had opened the library in Cape Town, came out to Kawau in a private capacity, including some shooting (a reason for importing wildlife); he too must have seen manuscripts.

One account of Kawau was the visit of the English writer J. A. Froude in 1885. He crossed on the weekly steamer, a bit like my catamaran, dropping off deliveries and passengers at various destinations before finally berthing at Grey's house on Kawau, where he and his son stayed for several days as guests of the former governor. Grey was an attentive host:

> In the evening he showed us some of his treasures. Library treasures were produced chiefly – I suppose in compliment to me, for he had all sorts. There were old illuminated missals; an old French MS. of the fourteenth century, which had belonged once to Philippe le Bel and afterwards to Sully . . . Besides these was a precious MS. of the four gospels which had come from Mount Athos . . . All these he had himself collected, and he had agents all about the world looking out for him.

This tells more about Grey and what he displayed and said that night than about what was actually on Kawau. The French manuscript is a fifteenth-century copy of an anonymous French translation of Boethius, with a supplementary prologue by Jean de Meun, co-author of the *Roman de la Rose*, addressed originally to Philip IV (Philippe le Bel), king of France 1285–1314. It is a graceful manuscript, but more than a century too late to have been the dedicatee's own copy (Plate 2). It belonged much later to Marie-Caroline de Bourbon, duchesse de Berry (1798–1870), who sold it on her bankruptcy in 1837. It has her bookplate of the Château of Rosny-sur-Seine, where she lived after her husband's assassination at an opera in 1820. Grey supposed this bookplate referred to the royal courtier Maximilien de Béthune, duc de Sully (*c.* 1559–1641), also of Rosny but two hundred years earlier. Both wrong identifications involved sophisticated knowledge of French history: they are not primarily mistakes of ignorance but isolation, unchecked conclusions of a proud owner living infinitely far from fellow collectors and scholars who in Europe might have gently steered him to wiser interpretations.

There is no reason to suppose that either of Grey's Greek Gospel Books was ever actually on Mount Athos, the Kawau of the Aegean (an epithet no monk of Athos has probably ever thought of). The older of the two manuscripts, perhaps the one shown to Froude, had been catalogued in 1862 by Bernard Quaritch as being 'from a Monastery in the East. It was selected by an English officer, as one of the most precious books in the library there, and obtained under very peculiar circumstances.' Today that would make it unownable, not only because disposal by a monastery and export from Greece or the Levant would be illegal, but especially for the explicit suggestion of military looting and sharp practice. To Grey, an officer of the 83rd Regiment of Foot and son of a lieutenant-colonel, such cavalier provenance was both romantic and patriotic, and in boasting of the story it had become Athos itself.

Froude also described how boatloads of local excursionists used to come out from Auckland and were allowed by Grey to wander freely through the house and library. 'They did no harm,' he said. 'They perhaps learnt a little.' Especially popular were trips by steamer on Boxing Day and New Year's Day, for five shillings return, including refreshments and a brass band on board. An account published in 1935 quoted the recollection of an elderly man who as a young boy on one of these excursions had

> penetrated unbidden into a book-filled room [and] was there found on his knees before a volume of rare prints, too fascinated by its beauties to hear the step which paused beside him, until the gentle pressure on his shoulder made him look up abashed into the blue eyes of the owner of this treasured room. Soon he was telling Sir George Grey of all the books he had read and the difficulties of getting more. He followed his host from one bookcase to another, while quaint old volumes . . . were spread open before him. Manuscripts gilded by the patient hands of cloistered monks, who had become dust hundreds of years before New Zealand had ever been heard of, were put into his hands, and their beauties pointed out with winning simplicity.

Occasions like that, possibly no more than this one, decided Grey that his rare books on Kawau were by now acclimatized to a life in New Zealand and were ready for the public. In 1883, he announced his intentions in a speech at the Theatre Royal in Auckland, mentioning both the Besançon Missal and a Greek Gospel Book. He declared how future citizens of New Zealand could all profit from such books: 'Let them consider how much we owe to the men who devoted their lives to industry of this kind.' Grey's unlikely library on Kawau was slowly dismantled and boxed up towards the end of 1886, and between 29 December and 23 March the next year was transported down to Auckland on the *Rose Casey*, the same steamer as had brought Froude to the island. The Auckland Free Public Library was formally opened in Wellesley Street adjacent to the art gallery on a humid 26 March 1887, with eight thousand volumes including twenty-seven medieval manuscripts and twenty-four incunabula. Flags fluttered from every building and the Auckland Choral Society performed part of Mendelssohn's *Lobgesang*, which had originally been composed to celebrate the four hundredth anniversary of Gutenberg's invention of printing.

Not everyone was happy. Annie Matthews, Grey's island Miranda, had married her Ferdinand and become Mrs Seymour Thorne-George. She had witnessed her half-uncle's every order for rare books from London and had shared the excitement of unpacking countless shipments unloaded onto the jetty on Kawau. She knew or had been told so often how much of Grey's wealth was tied up in his library, wealth which might in other circumstances have remained in the family, and she wondered if anyone appreciated what had been sacrificed: 'The people here do not, & never can be educated up to it', she wrote to a friend in 1898; 'Those who can afford to interest themselves in those sorts of things would not live in Auckland.' About a third of Madden's estimated hundred years had now passed, and his prediction was holding up so far.

The experiments of Kawau had all run their course. In May 1888, Grey sold the island for £12,000 and moved south to Parnell, to join Annie and her husband. Acclimatization takes different forms and is not always predictable. Annie settled, had seven children, and died in her mid-eighties, still in Auckland, in 1938. Grey drifted, uprooted and mostly now bookless, and in March 1894 he left Wellington for England on the SS *Gothic*. He died in South Kensington four years later and is buried in the crypt of St Paul's Cathedral. His monument there was erected by the government and people of New Zealand.

As for me, we took the 2.05 catamaran back to Sandspit, and I was home in London less than two days later.

2

Christchurch

Archives New Zealand has a website from which you can search the passenger lists of immigrant ships for the first century or so of the country's European colonization. It is used mainly by people researching their family histories. I typed in my own name and there I am, duly recorded as disembarking in Auckland from the RMS *Rangitoto* on Friday, 17 June 1955, aged 4, child, with Francis de Hamel, aged 32, medical practitioner, Joan de Hamel, 31, 'd. d.' (initials accorded to most wives, perhaps 'domestic duties' or 'direct dependant'), and my two brothers, Michael, 6, child, and Geoffrey William, 2, child, all rightly written down on arrival as born in England. I have a photograph from earlier that day too, taken by my mother. We are seen from behind standing on the deck of the ship, gazing out in wonder at the heads of Auckland harbour along the skyline, our first sight of land in several weeks. My father is in the middle, tall, in sports jacket and baggy trousers, hands in pockets. At his left side is Michael, his hands clasped behind his back, like an officer inspecting the troops. I am in shorts, bending down to look under the rail, for I am too small to see over it. At the far right is William, then still called Geoffrey, dumpy and apparently not interested.

The migration of people, or manuscripts, is often almost entirely chance or a casual decision of a moment with

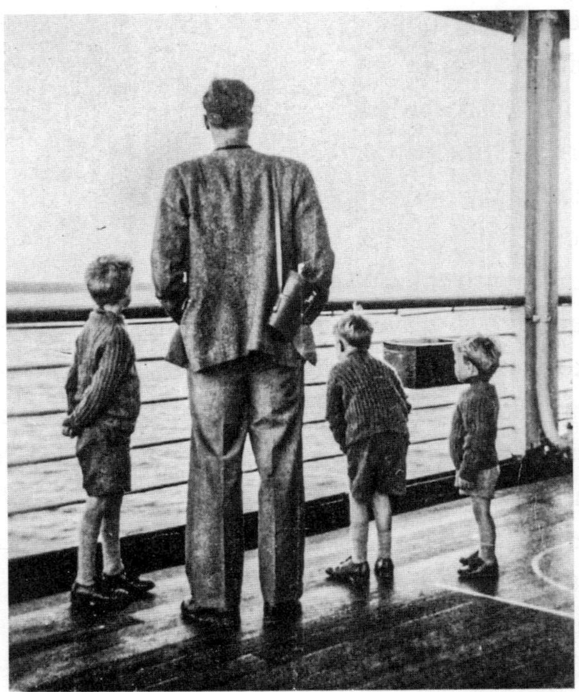

The first sight of New Zealand from the *Rangitoto*, 17 June 1955: the author (bending to look under the rail) with his father and two brothers.

consequences which can last for centuries or millennia. I once persuaded both my parents to write down for me the reasons why we happened to be going to New Zealand at all, and they gave me a series of individually minor but cumulative circumstances. They had married when hardly into their mid-twenties in 1948, far too young, as their own parents always believed. My father's medical training was delayed by service in the Royal Air Force and an uncanny knack of failing examinations, and we children were born in London hospitals where he was assigned at the time – Guy's in my case. By the early 1950s his annual salary was £240 as a house surgeon in the Royal Hampshire County Hospital in Winchester. The rent for our cottage south-east of Guildford was £200 a year. My father aspired to a consultancy in chest diseases, but in the newly formed National Health Service such positions required a minimum age of thirty-two, usually much more. Post-war Britain was economically exhausted, and there were still uncleared bombsites and rationing well into my own lifetime. My parents reasoned that Michael and I still had several years before being sent off to preparatory school (how the fees came into their projection I do not know) and the baby was old enough to travel. A finite, perhaps two-year job somewhere exotic might be an adventure and add a new dimension to career prospects, but it would have to be soon. The Amazon and Brazil were apparently both mentioned, partly for the joy of any name with a 'z' in it; Zanzibar would have been irresistible. The dreams dragged on, and we children pottered contentedly through our unaffected lives in what was called Holly Cottage in a country lane considered unsuitable for cars.

One day my mother extracted a recent but damp-stained medical journal from the bottom of the box where the gumboots were kept and noticed an advertisement for an urgent but short-term position as a medical registrar in somewhere called Rotorua in New Zealand, offering only a modest salary but including free passage by ship for the appointee's family, there and back. It triggered the imagination. They could perhaps go out through Panama and back through Suez, right round the world, and be home in time for our schooling and a proper job for my father. An application was sent off. As was my father's form in jobs as with exams, he had no success. However, the New Zealand health service kept his letter, and some time later sent a telegram asking if he would be interested in a better paid but three-year contract in Christchurch, setting up a mass X-ray programme there and on the West Coast, for monitoring tuberculosis (subject to interview at the New Zealand High Commission in London). Three years was longer than had been envisioned, but he accepted. I am sure my mother encouraged him, but it was a time when a wife's choice was as irrelevant as the children's. I remember exactly where I was standing in the hall in Holly Cottage when I was told, and asking if we would need to learn a new language.

Preparations for departure were probably much as they would have been in the nineteenth century: 1955 was nearer in time to Sir George Grey on Kawau than it is to the date of writing this. We divided our luggage into 'Hold' and 'Wanted on Voyage'. My nonagenarian great-grandmother, who had been born in Australia, told us we must see the phenomenal Pink and White Terraces near Mount Tarawera, which had impressed her so much on her own childhood visit to New Zealand. (Unknown to her, the marble terraces were lost when the volcano there erupted in 1886.) Our grandparents drove us to Tilbury docks. Their car had a puncture on the way, adding unneeded stress to the timing of an already very emotional day. As the engines began and ship's horn finally sounded, the hawsers were released and the *Rangitoto* began to edge outwards into the Thames. Paper streamers were thrown from the deck down to the quayside, where tearful relatives waved to families they assumed they would never see again. This was a last chapter of the old way of things, for we were, in effect, government-assisted passengers on an immigrant ship. The disembarkation lists record the occupations of all our fellow travellers – surveyor, tractor driver, stenographer (26, single), boiler operator, carpenter, librarian, farmer, and others, going to new lives.

The RMS *Rangitoto* of the New Zealand Shipping Company was built in 1949, with a full capacity of 416 passengers. It had a single pale-yellow funnel. Our family all shared a tiny cabin with bunks and a porthole. For boisterous children, a ship is a prison, with all its delights exhausted before we had entered the

English Channel, while our parents had deck quoits and afternoon beef tea and, later, cocktails with tiny paper umbrellas and dinners with decorative menus printed on board each day. They stood entranced for days on end with field-glasses at the ship's stern watching storm petrels and albatrosses and shearwaters along the white tail of wake slowly diffusing into the distance. For them, it was precious time together. Life on land came to seem far away and hard to remember. There was a fancy-dress competition for children, and I and my brothers were paraded as the Three Wise Monkeys, with crêpe-paper fezzes and tails attached to our swimming trunks and our hands over eyes, ears (me) or mouth, no doubt baffling to most of our fellow passengers. The ship refuelled in Curaçao, off the coast of Venezuela (another 'z' there). We bought enamelled tin cereal bowls in the market, used at breakfasts for the rest of childhood, and little dusty rubber figures of people under palm trees, which fell apart. We stopped in Panama City at the far end of the canal and again in the shallows of Pitcairn Island, still the most inaccessible place I have ever been. A bearded and probably rather drunk King Neptune appeared on board the day we crossed the Equator, as half-believable as Father Christmas. There was an incident I remember only dimly, of answering a distress call from a Russian trawler in the Pacific to transfer a very ill sailor across to our ship. The whole voyage took exactly a month.

We had brought a car with us from England, which seems an odd thing to do, but cars were coveted possessions and ours had been a present from my mother's parents. We drove down from Auckland to Wellington, stopping to see the geysers and volcanic mud pools of Rotorua, with their distinctive smell of sulphur and thrilling proximity of danger. The main road from Auckland to Wellington, part of that same State Highway 1 as I travelled on up to Sandspit some seventy years later, had then only recently been tar-sealed the whole way, reported proudly to my parents as a great advance and novelty. Rural and side roads were still gravel and sent up clouds of dust in the summer. For much of my childhood you still waved if you passed another car, even on the highway. We took the overnight ferry MV *Maori* from Wellington to Littleton, the port for Christchurch, on the east coast of the South Island. My father used to recount how the Health Department had telephoned him by the shore-to-ship radio on the ferry at 10 o'clock at night, to welcome him to his new job. That impressed him immensely.

My father loved New Zealand. Like some of the imported species on Kawau, he took to his adopted surroundings and flourished. Although medicine was his job, his passion was for birds and plants, as it had been in his childhood in the countryside near Tamworth, and New Zealand has unusual varieties of both in great abundance. Within three weeks of arrival, his work for the new X-ray unit had taken him by overnight railcar through the Southern Alps to Greymouth on the West Coast, a former goldrush town on the Grey River (both places named after Sir George). It was then known for its uninhibited frontier life and was as far from the stifling inhibitions of urban England as my father could ever have wished. He considered himself a socialist, loosely at least. He revelled in the West Coast and welcomed the equality of all fellow migrants. He was captivated by the unexplored wilderness and New Zealand's little-studied natural history. Even in the second half of the 1950s it was still possible for the kakapo, for example – a kind of chunky prehistoric-looking ground parrot, assumed to be long extinct – to be re-discovered still living unnoticed in the South Island bush. In 1957–58, my father contrived to be part of the Trans-Antarctic expedition in which Edmund Hillary and Vivian Fuchs crossed the continent to the South Pole for the first time since Captain Scott's ill-fated mission of 1912. He was both medical officer for the party at Scott Base, and assistant biologist, tasked with documenting Antarctic seals and penguins. 'Exactly like English winter weather', he told a reporter from the Christchurch morning newspaper cheerily on his return. He was fundamentally a shy and self-centred man, but imaginative and quick-witted, which passed for intelligence in his own estimation and in that of the often-uncompetitive society of 1950s New Zealand. It all suited him very well. He was devoted to my mother, who flattered and reassured him, never for a moment daring, even secretly to herself, to question the emperor's clothes.

She, however, like Sir George Grey's zebras, did not adapt quickly to the new environment. She was from a well-established intellectual family of lawyers and doctors in London. The men had all been to Trinity College, Cambridge, since the early nineteenth century. My mother had an MA in modern languages from Oxford (Lady Margaret Hall), not so common for women then, and she had taught French and art history in London. A suburban house in Christchurch in the 1950s with three children for company was unthinkably far from the National Gallery, which she knew intimately, and the classically furnished libraries and drawing rooms of an upbringing in South Kensington. The distances were enormous. Letters from Britain came by ship; blue aerogrammes, recently introduced, took a week. There was no international airport in New Zealand at all until 1950, mainly because it was still further than a passenger plane could safely stay aloft over empty ocean. Telephone calls to England, booked weeks or even months in advance, cost a week's salary for a few distorted and unsynchronized minutes, mostly shouting 'Can you hear me?' Births and deaths were reported across the world by telegram.

We acquired a house built in 1923 on a steep site above a terraced street in the suburb of Cashmere on the adjacent Port

Hills, with a spectacular view from its main windows across all of Christchurch laid out far beneath us. On clear days you could see beyond the city out to sea one way and to snowy mountain ranges on the horizon ahead and to the west across the Canterbury plains. At other times it showed a hazy vista of an endless town grid of almost identical cream-yellow wooden bungalows with red corrugated-iron roofs and verandas and tiny gardens with rotating washing lines. In the middle was the spire of the nineteenth-century Gothic-revival cathedral, no bigger in reality than many English parish churches, like a stage-set re-creation of an Englishness no one had seen. Conversation in those days, as far as my mother could tell, seemed limited to sport, pavlovas and child-care (there was no television until the 1960s). The biggest news of 1956 was the three-matches-to-one victory of the All Blacks over the Springboks. My mother cheerfully accepted all this as part of the deal, but it is in her wistful nostalgia for a probably unrealistic lost world of old Europe that I trace the genesis of my life among illuminated manuscripts.

I began school at Cashmere Primary, walking distance downhill from home. I could already read and learned to dissimulate with *Janet and John* in class while actually reading *Moomintroll* at home. I have school photographs from 1956 and 1958, tiny girls in the front row, myself somewhere behind staring out solemnly, with very straight sun-bleached fair hair. In both pictures I am wearing a tie, which almost no other boys are, and, since I could not have put it on myself, I suppose my mother had tied it for me that morning. We were always slightly different. The important point is that my father had a three-year contract, and we all knew from the outset that we would then be returning home to England, where we could attend proper British schools and slip back into our expected place in the system. Our parents took a conscious decision – probably wrong, I think,

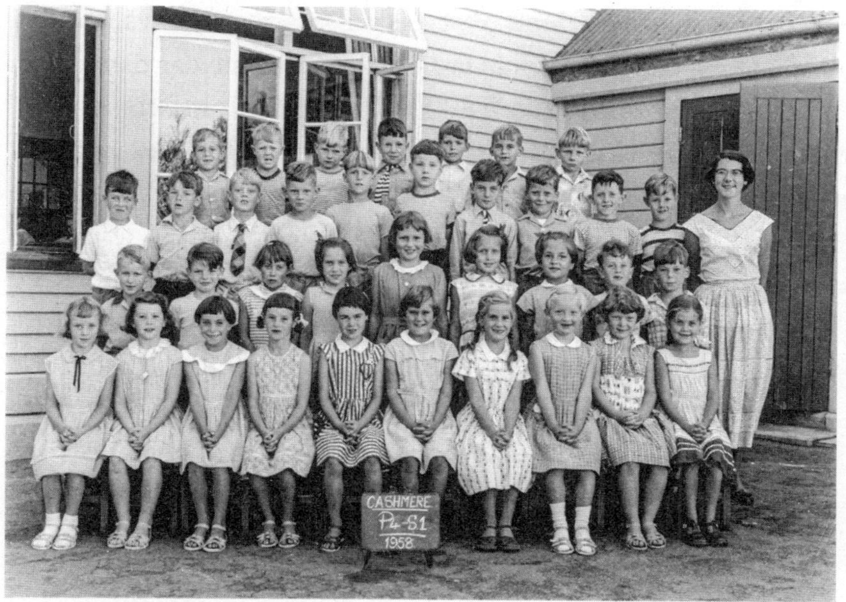

Class photograph, Cashmere Primary School, 1958: the author is in the second row from the back, third from the left, wearing a tie.

although times were different then – that little boys with New Zealand accents and habits would never be acceptable on our planned return. My father made a list of local words and idioms which amused or puzzled him, including a handle, posties, bach, two-tooth, dag, biddy-bid, euchred, ripple-control, a jug, crook, the bot, toot, hogget, backblocks and boohai, number 8, the lurgi, bush-lawyer, shingle roads, and many others. I was right in my childish assumption in Holly Cottage that we might need to learn a new language, and I do not recognize some of these words taken from his notes. My parents were entertained by the novelty of it all and would gleefully tell one another tales of misunderstanding the New Zealand accent or vocabulary, chuckling with joy tinged (I regret) with a certain superiority. When such stories were then shared with New Zealanders, they were heard in silence. We children were corrected if we ever used a local vowel sound or stress on an unacceptable syllable. William, who was persuaded to change to his middle name from an easily mispronounceable Geoffrey ('Jeef'), simply ignored them and carried on. Michael and I were mocked and teased at school even by teachers every time we opened our mouths to say anything. This tended to make him silent, and I developed a stammer, sometimes crippling. This is not some anguished lament of miserable childhood (for it was not at all, and we were a secure and happy and self-contained family), but integration was out of the question. We were always told that New Zealanders do this, but we do that; we are not quite like them. We did not acclimatize.

There were family outings and expeditions, mostly based on natural history, including regularly to Lake Tekapo and over to Stony Bay beyond Akaroa on Banks Peninsula. My father tried to stuff a dead penguin they had found there; it became extremely smelly and had to go. From his visits to the West Coast, however, he brought back an already stuffed and mounted grey spotted kiwi, given to him by a logger, and, on another occasion, a live black-and-white goat, caught in the wild. We called her Minty and she lived in our garden for several years, eating flowers and disconcerting neighbours with her satanic horned face peering through the bushes. Other people did not do that in Christchurch.

Finally, when my father's three-year contract reached its end, he was offered a further term in an even better position within the Health Department. My parents had more decisions to make. They had absolutely promised their own parents in England, now advancing into white hair (or none at all), that we would all be back by 1958. My father hoped to undertake a diploma in public health at London University. A deal was proposed: the Department would sponsor him for a year's absence on full pay, a kind of sabbatical, if he agreed to return to Christchurch again for another three-year contract from the end of 1959. I suspect my father liked the idea more than my mother did. Again, our parents reasoned, counting on their fingers, Michael would be only thirteen in 1962 and I would be almost twelve, both still just in time to get back home for proper English schooling after all, especially with a year's prep school in England in the meantime. William would be nine by the end, and all would be fine. We rented out the house and left from Wellington on the *Rangitoto* again on 23 August 1958, bound for Southampton.

I wish I could have said that I discovered medieval manuscripts in that year back in England from the age of seven and a half to nearly nine. We did, however, become immersed in historical sights. We visited Stonehenge and early British hillforts, where Michael and I filled our pockets with sherds of Roman pottery picked up from molehills and little segments from the stems of eighteenth- and nineteenth-century clay pipes. We were taken to the National Gallery (we liked Holbein and Pieter de Hooch, or were told we did), St Paul's Cathedral with its Whispering Gallery and Westminster Abbey, where an irreverent ancestor had once carved his name on the Coronation Chair, Hampton Court, Nelson's *Victory* in Portsmouth, the Roman springs in Bath, the ruins of Glastonbury Abbey and Corfe Castle, and across the Channel to Bruges, with an outing by bus to Ghent to see the Van Eyck altarpiece. My mother was not going to miss her chance to put us right. Not all worked out quite as planned, for my father was seriously ill for much of the time, and Michael and I stayed with my mother's parents in Surrey while we attended Desmoor School in Ewhurst for a year. It was reassuring to find we were part of an ordinary family with cousins our own age in Wiltshire, where we spent the long summer of 1959. However, like Persephone, we had a pact with the Underworld, and our time to go back down came round inescapably. We departed in late October that year on the SS *Arcadia*, a P. & O. passenger ship on the London to Sydney route through the Suez Canal. We stopped at Port Said, Aden, Bombay, Colombo, Freemantle and Sydney, and from there had our first experience of an aeroplane, back over the sea to Christchurch.

This time, the necessity to maintain our Englishness for the second three years was, if anything, more intense, for there would now be no margin for error at the end, and we children had a clearer idea of what awaited us. We were all three sent to the Cathedral Grammar School. This was (and is) a private Anglican preparatory school on the English model, founded in 1881 initially to train choristers for the cathedral in the centre of the city. We wore grey jackets and had dark red caps decorated with a bishop's mitre. I started Latin, taught by Mrs Muir, which seemed to the class a no more pointless foreign language than any other, since even French had no speakers nearer than New Caledonia or Tahiti, which no one was likely to visit. It would have been unimaginable at that time to have learned Māori. We were taken one day over to the Classics Department in the University nearby to see the collection of Greek and Roman pottery, given in 1957 by Marion Steven, in memory of her late husband James Logie. I remember realizing with awe that the people who used these items actually spoke Latin, or maybe Greek, and that in carefully holding a vase we were only one touch away from witnessing the classical Mediterranean at first hand. It is the same experience that manuscripts can give, even, or even especially, so far from their source. A child in Italy, for example, with bits of antiquity on every street corner or in the basements under houses, would never quite feel that same tingle of suddenly crossing a magic portal in time and distance. Another formative moment, almost shameful in comparison but which had a huge impact on my outlook, was the epic film *Ben Hur* (1959), starring Charlton Heston, which I saw on a schoolfriend's birthday outing. I thought it utterly mesmerizing, the Roman and biblical worlds re-created before my eyes, and for months I was obsessed, replaying every moment in my memory. It even had pottery like that in the Logie Collection. Very many years later I met Charlton Heston himself at Sotheby's in New York, a place I would probably never have been anyway without one tiny cog in the wheel of fortune having once been unwittingly placed there by him.

At home, we had reproductions of English and French paintings round the house, especially by Christopher Wood, my mother's favourite artist, after whom, I suppose, I had been named. The books bought for us or borrowed from the library were all set in the northern hemisphere, in England, or Narnia, or Moominland, and later in Middle Earth, years before that became identified with filming in New Zealand. Michael was serious and wore glasses and preferred Arthur Mee's *Children's Encyclopaedia* to fiction. William blithely trotted bookless through life. He had some schoolwork to learn the names of the medieval kings of England. My mother, who painted quite well, drew up for him what was in effect a kind of illuminated manuscript scroll of mnemonic text and amusing pictures with captions connecting Edward I through to Henry VII, which hung on the back of the bathroom door for years. I do not suppose William learned much from it, but I cannot really recall ever not knowing the reigns of the English kings.

Unknown to us, there was in fact the fifteenth-century English manuscript scroll chronicle on almost exactly the same subject in Christchurch, mentioned in the Introduction. Until 1966 this was the only medieval manuscript in the province, and it is still one of only two (and a few fragments). It is usually called the Maude (or Canterbury) Roll, owned by the university (Plate 3). It is in Latin, on parchment about 18 feet long by about 13½ inches wide. It tabulates the descents of the successive kings of England, with marginal paragraphs on important or interesting events of their times. It was made initially as far as the reign of Henry V (1413–22), with the addition of his infant son Henry VI, born in 1421. It reflects national events of its time. By 1455, England was split into factions by the Wars of the Roses, and the manuscript roll was then adapted and extended to endorse the Yorkist claims of Edward IV (white rose), crowned in 1461. He was the eldest descendant, but through a female link, from the second son of Edward III. The Lancastrian Henry VI (red rose) came by an entirely male line but only from Edward III's third son. Morally, the rival claims were fairly evenly divided. The Christchurch manuscript was altered to dismiss the accession of Henry IV in 1399 as illegal usurpation. The chart my mother made showed the deposed Richard II sitting glumly with his head in his hands in Pontefract Castle, saying, 'And I did so well with those revolting peasants in 1381.'

However, the Maude Roll goes back a great deal further than the Middle Ages. Like this chapter – and much of the history of New Zealand, both Māori and European – it opens with a ship and epic tales of migration and assimilation. At the top of the manuscript is an image of Noah's Ark (now partly overpainted with a Tudor rose). It assumes that everyone in the Middle Ages already knew the Bible and the genealogy from Adam and Eve to Noah (Genesis 5). It takes up the family tree from that moment on. There is a red line from Japhet, one of Noah's sons, through five generations to Saturn and his son Jupiter, who married the daughter of King Atlas the giant, and to Jupiter's great-grandson Troius (with a branch off sideways to the dynasty of Hector and the kings of Troy), and in the main stem down to Anchises and Aeneas, with a marginal digression on the latter's voyages and arrival in Italy in 1157 BC, and on to the great-grandson of Aeneas, Brutus. His name is surmounted here by a huge crown. The text tells of his exile through the Greek islands and into Gaul, where he established a Trojan city in Tours, and up to the island of Albion, eventually renamed Britain in his own honour, where he fought giants and founded New Troy, or London. I hope this is all true. His line continues in the manuscript, still unbroken, eventually to King Lear and his three daughters (adding a story not in Shakespeare that Lear's father learned to fly and fell to his death in a temple of Apollo), and, much later, to King Lucius and Constantine the Great, both also written in red, and their descendants including Vortigern and King Arthur and, slightly to the side, King Egbert, in red too, and through to King Alfred and Edward the Confessor and at last to Edward I, from which point my mother's version can take over. Parallel to this on the left is a green line of descendants from Japhet's other son. (It is nothing if not all-inclusive.) This branch goes down at length to King Boerin, ancestor of the nine races of the North, and on through Woden, the god of Wednesdays (it says so), and to the Welsh and Celtic kings, eventually rejoining the red line at King Egbert. These legendary connections are not unique but here they are wonderfully exhilarating and graphic.

What is interesting about such a manuscript being in New Zealand is that its mythologies of ancient migration and genealogy are curiously paralleled by those of the Māori, who care immensely about such things, and the digitization of the roll in 2017 was supported by the Ngāi Tahu, the principal Māori clan of the South Island. By contrast, scholars of European descent in New Zealand tend now to dismiss the roll's acquisition in

1918 as a piece of patronizing colonialism. Its subject, even from six hundred years ago, is deemed by some to carry unfashionable connotations of entitlement and elitism. In that sense, the roll has not acclimatized comfortably to its life in New Zealand, whereas Christchurch's second manuscript, a little Renaissance Sallust bought in 1966, is clearly quite innocuous. Canterbury University paid £50 for the roll, much more than its value at the time, from Sibylla Maude (1862–1935), founder of a well-known Christchurch nursing scheme. Half the money came by public subscription, the first such instance in New Zealand, and half from a government grant. Nurse Maude said the scroll had been in her family in England for many generations, dismissed by the modern anti-colonialists as further snobbish pretension, but in reality very likely. Such secular manuscripts did generally survive in family possession, especially more than a century ago, and the scroll has none of the common marks of transit through the saleroom or book trade, such as lot numbers or dealer codes. When I first saw it in the 1960s, its ends were nailed to rollers fitted inside an old-fashioned varnished wooden box, lettered in gold like a head prefects' board in the school lobby. The box had a crank handle which you turned, and the scroll rattled rapidly past a viewing aperture. This was disassembled for conservation reasons and the box seems to have been lost in the Christchurch earthquake of 2011. We knew none of this, of course, when we lived there.

As a child, I was fascinated by dates. Children easily remember telephone numbers (ours was Christchurch 35079), car licence plates and birth dates, in a way I never can now. However, I could see the passage of time in a very linear shape, along which we moved, out to the left as far as 1900, when the line turns sharply to the right and then moves downwards from 1800 backwards. It flattens out in the seventeenth century and dips again at 1500. I could visualize a historical date as being at a clear place on that line. Remembering a date in history was simply a matter of seeing where it was. Some readers will know exactly what I am describing; to others it will be incomprehensible. I collected things which were exactly dated, like bus tickets, and would tear out and keep the dated headings from newspapers, watching how they went within a day from being now to becoming history. Every passing moment added to the length of the line extending behind us, like the wake of the *Rangitoto*, moving ever further into the distance.

On 6 September 1960, I decided to collect stamps. Mock if you wish, but it became immensely important to me in those childhood years. Philately is full of firmly anchored dates, in its commemorative issues for anniversaries, its postmarks and first day covers, and the necessity of sorting and classifying sets into chronological order. Michael soon joined me and we both had albums, which occupied countless happy hours and patient effort. Issues with animals on, with which I began, soon gave way to specializing in New Zealand and Great Britain, and in time to gathering British and then Victorian stamps only. Our pocket money was spent foraging for unnoticed treasure from Mr Savill in the New Zealand Stamp Company opposite the joke shop in Chancery Lane, a walking passage off the north-west corner of the Cathedral Square, now vanished in the earthquake, and in the Armagh Street Book Shop, which had an alcove with stamps displayed at what seemed to us bargain prices to the right of the entrance. The sums we spent were tiny. We used the bright red 1958 Stanley Gibbons catalogue: the 1841 imperforate penny red-browns were listed there at three shillings each (they currently price none under £55), and most variants of the 1858 penny reds were fourpence or sixpence. It may be that in nineteenth-century New Zealand, where every letter from home was precious and likely to be kept, some higher denomination stamps were relatively more common than in Britain, and I am sure we never spent as much as three shillings on anything.

Defenders of stamp collecting will tell you what a lot it can teach children about geography and history, the local names of Finland and Hungary, when Australia became a commonwealth, that the Gold Coast is the same as Ghana, and even when the currency in Ceylon changed from sterling to rupees and cents (between 1868 and 1872). More than that, however, as a book historian now, I realize how much Michael and I must have unwittingly absorbed even at that age about different printing and engraving techniques, watermarks, typographical variants, reprints and forgeries, the use of catalogues and the value of condition. We could assign approximate dates to most stamps we had not seen before by familiarity with evolving style, much as one does with manuscripts. Stamps, like any other artefacts, are products of their time. The jaunty British jubilee definitives of 1887 have the colours of musical hall and gaiety; the George V sepia Britannia half-crown stamp of 1913 speaks of ponderous empire and naval certitude.

Stamp collecting, like rare book collecting, is very private. Acquisitions are not put on display, like paintings or most antiques, where motives for purchase may be mixed with demonstrations of wealth or taste, but hidden in albums, usually seen by no one else unless perhaps one's elder brother, and collections are generally expected to be silently dispersed again eventually with no record of achievement. It is pure collecting, and I rejoiced in it. For Christmas 1961, our grandparents in Surrey sent Michael and me each a penny black on its original envelope of 1840, the best presents we could possibly imagine. I still have mine. It was the year from which philatelic time began, but also the year of the foundation of the colony of New Zealand with the Treaty of Waitangi. Anything earlier than 1840, by both references, was effectively prehistoric.

Two crucial things happened in our family life. One is that in early 1960, my mother found she was pregnant again, and our brother Richard was born in Christchurch in August that year, followed by Quentin in 1963, making five boys in all, two of them now native-born New Zealanders. My parents were happy their eldest was a boy; the rest of us were disappointments. The second is that around the end of 1962 or early 1963, when the current three-year contract in Christchurch was reaching its end, my father was offered the permanent position of Medical Officer of Health in Dunedin, running his own small government department. The fantasy of going home to England was over. Apart from brief visits, my parents never came back. My mother died in New Zealand in 2011 and my father there in 2014.

Most people can remember the first event of international significance they were ever aware of. I can just recall the excitement of standing in the street in London with my grandfather to watch the Coronation procession in June 1953. He had brought a stepladder from home so that Michael and I could see over the crowd. The earliest political event I followed moderately closely and mentioned in my schoolboy diary was the Cuban Missile Crisis of 1962. I was dimly aware of trouble in Suez in 1956, principally because it affected a possible visit by our grandparents to see us in New Zealand. In 1957, we ascended by ladder (again) to the flat part of our house's roof to witness the first Russian sputnik passing over. They all shouted, 'Look! There it is! See there!' and I could not make it out, as it orbited overhead and out of sight; I was taken back down in tears of disappointment. Oddly, one event our whole family came to know about was the Hungarian Uprising of November 1956, crushed by the

Soviets. Suddenly, displaced refugees fled across the world, sent anywhere the aid agencies could find passages. Following a plea from our local Anglican church, my parents offered to take one in, remembering the diaspora from Germany in the late 1930s and thinking it would be good for the children to see another culture. We were assigned Janoš (which became John) Udvardi, who was probably aged around thirty-five. We were told he had been a cine-projectionist in Hungary but I recall him seeking work as a French polisher. He was also a good cook, an entirely new experience in our household. He spoke no English or any language my parents knew, and he was profoundly emotional and scarred by his ordeal. Instead of attempting English, he preferred teaching us phrases of Hungarian instead, *jó éjszakát*, 'good night', and *bobs*, the creamy white beans he would prepare for us in a rich sauce, and *madzsik*, 'it's magic', when he brought out some dish which had taken him six hours to cook, by which time we could hardly stay awake or care. If we said, *Csókollak draga apu*, which means approximately, 'I kiss you, dearest father', he would cry and go into deep depression. He was lost, lonely and frightened, unimaginably far from his elderly mother, with whom he had lived in Budapest. He was a Roman Catholic, the first I had ever met. I remember him going to Mass in the local Catholic church, which my parents tolerated with rather the regrettable distaste they might feel in having to feed live mice to a pet owl. However, John Udvardi came home sobbing with happy emotion, for the service was still in Latin, as it always had been throughout the world before 1962, and he recognized every word of it.

3

Besançon

There is a miniature about halfway through the second volume of Sir George Grey's manuscript Latin Missal which would have puzzled visitors to Kawau in the nineteenth century, and doubtless even Hungarian Roman Catholics at church in 1956. Describe it or, better still, show a photograph to any over-confident medievalist. Probably not one in a thousand will know what is depicted (Plate 4). It shows a stout priest in a pink robe riding on the back of a devil high over a landscape of hills and rivers. He is holding reins which he has looped around the devil's neck. The priest looks serenely confident and in control, whereas the brown and gold devil is clawing the air in fury as he reluctantly carries his passenger on their flight through the pale blue sky of medieval France. The priest is St Antidius, supposedly bishop of Besançon in the early fifth century. Two hymns in the Missal here describe how even devils were impressed with the bishop's moral care of his flock. One day, it was revealed to Antidius that the pope was committing fornication. He persuaded a devil to fly him at once to Rome, where the pope was about to say Mass on Maundy Thursday. Antidius called the pontiff aside and charged him with the sin, which the pope tearfully admitted, whereupon Antidius said the Mass himself and afterwards gave confession and absolution to the penitent pontiff, before returning to Besançon, presumably by the same means of transport. He was later martyred by the Vandals.

Grey's Missal is now in the Central City Library in Auckland. The present three-storey triangular building, just off Queen Street, the principal thoroughfare running up from the harbour, was opened in November 1981. To reach Special Collections, you take the escalator to the top floor, emerging towards the front of the building into a spacious lobby with a seminar room called the 'Whare Wānanga', decorated with Māori carvings. This – but in no other way – resembles Grey's island house on Kawau, where visitors would have seen native artefacts in the hall before passing on to the European collections in the drawing room. Here in Auckland, you go through glass doors on the left into an exhibition area, which includes little portable steps so that small children can see into the cases (a good idea), and from there on again into the secluded rare books room itself. Readers sit on the right around big pale-yellow tables. On the shelf behind is a modern bust of William Shakespeare contemplating a globe. The playwright may not have known of New Zealand, but he must have assumed lands beyond Prospero's island. (The 'brave new world' of *The Tempest* is in reality not some new-found continent, as popularly supposed, but Miranda in exile first rediscovering Europe.) The staff of the library in Auckland seem to be occupied mainly with patiently helping the public with questions on family history and immigration, but you could ask for Grey's illuminated manuscripts or his First Folio, if you wished, migrant treasures from the Old World.

The two volumes of the Missal, when they are brought over and removed from their cloth-covered boxes, are bound in eighteenth-century dark blue leather, each with the gilt title 'MISSALE' on the spine, parts I and II. Open up the first volume. You naturally pause for a moment, as everyone has probably done since the books first arrived in New Zealand, on the small printed description from Boone's sale catalogue of 1863, snipped out and pasted onto the flyleaf. Medieval manuscripts usually have no title-pages and so this is the first identification we have, and, unlike the text inside, it is mostly in English. It begins,

> MISSALE AD USUM ROMANUM. A SUPERB MANUSCRIPT ON VELLUM, written in the XV. Century in a large Gothic hand, with Music of the Chants. It is divided into 2 volumes, each with a Calendar and a Canon of the Mass: both contain two large and highly finished Miniature Paintings, occupying an entire page . . . There are likewise (in the 2 vols.) 63 very delicately painted Miniatures, measuring about 3 inches square . . . There are, moreover, 163 highly ornamental large Initial Letters, besides a profusion of smaller ones . . . This fine Manuscript is presumed to have been executed for a Bishop of Besançon . . .

There are actually sixty-four of the smaller miniatures, although I have not counted the initials. Adding up the number of illuminations became common in nineteenth-century catalogues, as a useful means of quantifying the relative richness of a manuscript, like grading the size of a house by its number of bedrooms. Four full-page and sixty-four column-width pictures is indeed exceptional, especially for a Missal. (There are two other medieval Missals in New Zealand, both of them with only a single small historiated initial each.) The pages here sparkle with colour and burnished gold, and this is everything people expect an illuminated manuscript to be. The borders include birds and flowers. It is obvious why this glittering book was a favourite for Grey to bring out to show impressionable guests in paradise. In the handlist of the rare books in Auckland published in 1908, it was described as 'the finest illuminated MS. in the Library', and, by implication, in all of New Zealand.

A Missal is the service book used at a Catholic Mass. In the time of Sir George Grey, an orthodox Anglican, Roman Catholicism in England still carried a residual whiff of sedition or even ungodliness unforgiven since the Reformation, and never more so than in performance of the Mass. Even cautious tolerance of the old faith was still recent and controversial. The Catholic Emancipation Act was passed in 1829, on the day before Grey's eighteenth birthday. Owning a manuscript Missal still made some English book collectors uncomfortable and gave others a pleasurable frisson of dabbling with wickedness, like taming a devil for a new purpose. The Library in Auckland also owns a gilded frame inset with small oval cuttings trimmed from an Italian manuscript Missal of the early sixteenth century, attributed to the illuminator Antonio da Monza, showing priests performing Mass. They had been given to the city Art Gallery in 1927 but have now been transferred to the Library. They depict priests in exquisite vestments performing different stages of the Mass, including consecrating the wine and blessing the congregation. They resemble the confections of excessively Catholic manuscript fragments assembled and brought to England for sale by the former priest Luigi Celotti (1759–1843), who proudly boasted that they had been cut from the service books of the Sistine Chapel, when Catholic liturgy was still both shocking and deeply fascinating to Anglicans. If the biography of a manuscript matters, this is part of the inescapable legacy a medieval Missal carried with it at one period of its long transit through Protestant history.

For many people in the Middle Ages, a Missal was the only book they ever saw in their lives, even if from a distance and in the candlelight of a dark church. However, it challenges all our conceptions of the definition of a book. It is not a text which carries information or recounts a story. A Missal's pictures do not illustrate any narrative. The volume was not made for a library or for an individual's or community's interest or pleasure, like most books now, and it was not kept on a shelf or consulted at a table, as we do today in the Auckland Central Library. Its intended audience, as with all prayers, was ultimately divine, not human at all. Even during a Mass in church, a Missal was probably hardly used at all, because priests would know its principal texts more-or-less by heart, from endless repetition, day after day. Its Latin language was incomprehensible to many who witnessed a Missal in use. The most sacred words of Christ when breaking bread at the Last Supper, '*Hoc est corpus meum*', on which so much theology and interpretation depends, may have sounded to people unlettered in Latin as mumbled hocus-pocus. The words occur here in volume I, folio 160v, and volume II, folio 126r.

A Missal was part of the liturgical paraphernalia of an altar. It was stored in a sacristy, not a library. In duplicate in the centre of each volume in Auckland is the text of the Canon of the Mass, including the words of consecration of bread and wine recited by the priest every time a Mass was celebrated. The pages here are made of parchment that is thicker than elsewhere in the manuscript, in expectation of heavier use, and the script is larger. Each is accompanied by two spectacular full-page miniatures, the first showing the Crucifixion and the second, God enthroned in majesty in the heavens, with the emblems of the evangelists in each corner (Plate 6). These are the openings usually exhibited when the manuscript is on show, perhaps unfortunately, because they convey religiosity more than charm. Their status as works of art is complex, for these are not illustrations of text as one might find in any normal book. They have a practical function in liturgical performance. The crucified Christ becomes a visible manifestation of the body and blood of the eucharist, to be venerated. The liturgy requires kissing the Cross. Because this might damage the illumination, second simpler gold crosses have been pragmatically inserted in the manuscript's lower margins, which could be touched instead with equal efficacy. The image of the Father is to be adored as the priest recites, 'Holy, holy, holy, Lord God of hosts, heaven and earth are full of your glory.' In the Auckland manuscript, these full-page pictures are all executed on double thicknesses of parchment laminated together. This is partly for strength during constant use, but also because the presence of liquid could cause unsightly cockling, or wrinkling. The picture of God in volume II is indeed splattered with spots of damp, quite possibly from consecrated wine.

The use of gold in a Missal was not merely decorative, for it was made to catch and reflect the light, contributing to the supernatural atmosphere of a Mass. This is what the word 'illuminated' means. A library table with electric lighting is the wrong setting to study a Missal. Half-darkness and flickering candles would be more appropriate. Once, many years ago, I found a thirteenth-century manuscript Missal in a Belgian castle, dusty and unopened for centuries; I shook it open and for a fleeting moment – and never again – I released the haunting smell of medieval incense trapped between its pages. That is the world these books grew up in, not libraries.

A daily Mass was part of the larger context of annual liturgy. The Christian Church year has two orbiting and intersecting sequences. One, which is called the Temporal, celebrates anniversaries of events in the life and ascension of Christ, many of them movable feasts anchored to before and after the variable date of Easter. That is the first cycle. The second is the Sanctoral.

These are the saints' days, which are fixed by the calendar and never vary in date, but can happen to fall on any day of the week. The different sequences overlap. The Mass celebrated on any day might include elements of both cycles – Pentecost in 1469, for example (the probable date of the Auckland manuscript, as we shall see), was also the feast of St Germanus of Paris, 21 May. Anyone using the book on that day would need to keep bookmarks in both pages, as well as following the unvarying words of the Canon. The first volume in Auckland comprises the texts needed for November to Easter, and the second volume those from Easter to November again. In medieval Europe these would be called the winter and summer volumes of a Missal, but it becomes reversed in New Zealand where Christmas is at midsummer and Easter in the autumn. The duplication of the Canon meant that each six-month volume could be used on its own, while the other was in storage.

The complexities of these various and sometimes simultaneous texts for any one day render a Missal quite difficult to navigate. That is what the pictures were for. They do not primarily illustrate the text: they have a practical purpose in rendering the manuscript easier to use. Almost all major festivals in the Auckland Missal are introduced by images which would have been immediately recognizable by the medieval priest quickly riffling through its pages. The opening of Advent, for example, which begins with part of the psalm 'To you I have lifted up my soul', is illustrated by King David the psalmist in a medieval French landscape, his harp hung on a tree, praying to God in the sky (Plate 8). Palm Sunday is at once locatable by finding the picture of Christ entering a Gothic gate of Jerusalem on a donkey; the feast of Pentecost, in turn, is found quickly by recognizing the Virgin and the apostles kneeling in a vaulted room; and so on. Major feasts in the Sanctoral are similarly easy to identify from seeing distinctive and familiar iconography of the principal saints. Their attributes were like trademarks or shop signs in the streets. Everyone would recognize them, such as the unforgettably flying St Antidius, and could thus locate the necessary feast days without an index or page numbers.

Each volume opens with an identical liturgical calendar, listing the days of the months by their respective feasts or saints' days, graded into importance by use of black or red ink ('red-letter days'). To us, as medievalists now, calendars are invaluable in localizing a manuscript to a particular region. Ignore the well-known festivals of the universal Church and look instead for obscure and local names. It was doubtless because of its two distinctive calendars that this Missal was already by 1863 rightly ascribed to the diocese of Besançon. The city is the capital of Franche-Comté in eastern France, not far from the Swiss border. The feast of the aeronautical St Antidius would have been a clue. As well as his picture in the Sanctoral, he is here in red ink in both calendars too, on 17 June, accorded the maximum number of nine lections. Another is the feast day of Saints Ferreolus and Ferrucio in red on 29 May, also with the nine lections. These were the first evangelists of Franche-Comté, said to have been sent by St Irenaeus of Lyons in the late second century and martyred in 212. They also appear here in the text of the Missal itself, with a miniature showing two priests standing side by side in a church interior, neatly decapitated and holding their own heads in both hands before them, one still wearing its bishop's mitre. I recall being intrigued by this image when I saw it first as a teenager, for the saints' haloes hover over their truncated necks, rather than remaining above the heads, as I would have imagined. The feast of the finding of the relics of Saints Ferreolus and Ferrucio also occurs in the manuscript's calendars, on 5 September, nine lections, and in the Sanctoral (without a miniature). Their remains were reputed to have been discovered in the late fourth century in a cave near Besançon by a soldier whose dog was chasing a fox, and were brought back to the cathedral and enshrined by our airborne Antidius. Ferreolus and Ferrucio are still venerated as the patron saints of Besançon. All this makes the manuscript's origin very clear. If it was owned by a bishop – as was suggested in 1863 and to which we will return in a few moments – then it is likely to have been made for use in Besançon Cathedral.

When all seemed neat, however, it now becomes complicated. Almost uniquely in Europe, late medieval Besançon had one bishop but two cathedrals. It had been a Roman town, with several Christian churches from a very early date. One, just inside the Roman wall, was on the site of the present cathedral of

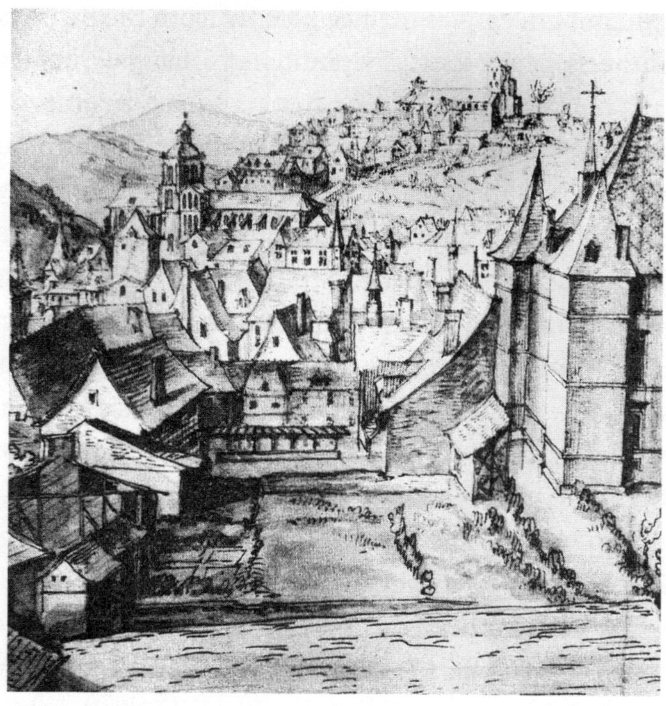

An early seventeenth-century drawing of Besançon, with the cathedral of St-Jean in the foreground and the rival cathedral of St-Étienne on the hilltop in the distance.

Besançon, eventually dedicated to St John the Evangelist, as it still is. There was another cathedral on the top of the hill, however, which came to be dedicated to St Stephen, the first Christian martyr (Acts 7:54–60), for it owned one of the most important relics of the saint. There is a very fine miniature of Stephen in the Auckland Missal, raising his arms as his murderers begin to throw stones. There is also a very unusual miniature of the discovery of the bones of St Stephen near Jerusalem in the fifth century, marking the festival of his relics on 3 August. It shows the priest Lucian asleep with his head on his right hand, dreaming of Gamaliel, the rabbi recorded as the teacher of St Paul (Acts 22:3), who points to a bier on the tiled floor where Stephen was buried. With the miraculous precision of those who uncovered the remains of Richard III beneath a car park in Leicester in 2012, Lucian and his colleagues then dug on the spot indicated and discovered the bones of both Stephen and Gamaliel himself. The saint's right arm, apparently with marks from his martyrdom, was eventually brought to Besançon. In the mid-eleventh century, Bishop Hugh of Salins had the hilltop church entirely rebuilt in honour of St Stephen and persuaded the pope himself, Leo IX, to install the precious arm relic beneath the altar. This event too was given a special commemorative Mass in the manuscript, *In dedicatione altaris sancti stephani bisuntinensis* (naming Besançon in Latin), with a picture of a pope in a triple tiara kneeling in a chapel before an altar. To endorse the new church, Bishop Hugh asked the pope to elevate it to the status of co-cathedral, equal to the older church further down the hill and sharing the right to elect bishops (later archbishops), who as primates of the diocese were responsible for both cathedrals.

As should have been anticipated, this was unwise. It led to intense rivalry between the two cathedral chapters. In 1092, the canons of St-Étienne claimed that theirs should be declared the primary cathedral of the archdiocese. Their site was better, their church almost certainly larger, and St Stephen was a martyr of infinitely greater status than their competitor's two unmemorable and headless founders. The canons of what was now St-Jean countered that their church was older (doubtless true) and that Saints Ferreolus and Ferrucio were disciples of St Irenaeus, who was a disciple of St Polycarp, who had been ordained by St John, their cathedral's dedicatee and the beloved disciple of Jesus himself, whom Stephen-come-lately had never even met. That direct chain of pupil to master meant a great deal. The arguments persisted up and down the hill for centuries until the pope finally ruled in favour of the primacy of St-Jean in 1254. Both churches remained as cathedrals in a grim truce, sharing a single archbishop. The calendar and Sanctoral here include the feast on 5 May, with three (not nine) lections, *Dedicatio matricis ecclesie sancti iohannis evangeliste*. Note the triumphant – or grudgingly conceded – word *matricis*: 'the dedication of the *mother* church of St John the Evangelist'. The miniature depicts a bishop outside a church which bears negligible resemblance to the actual cathedral, but it does show a free-standing bell tower, which it had (it fell down in 1729). After the French conquest of Besançon in the seventeenth century, the basilica of St-Étienne was closed and entirely demolished in 1668–73 to build a citadel instead, on the summit of the hill. There is now only one cathedral.

The Auckland Missal may have been used in either cathedral, or both. There is a curious detail which might tip the balance slightly towards St-Étienne. The miniature for Epiphany, or the feast of the Magi, is very unusual. Instead of showing the three kings kneeling with their gifts in Bethlehem, as would be expected in most medieval art (including Romanesque carvings in the cathedral of St-Jean), the scene here is of the Magi on horseback, first meeting and greeting one another in the wilderness, before proceeding on to Judea together. Prominently in the foreground is a small black boy in a gold cloak accompanying a (white) king in a turban (Plate 5). This must reflect an annual religious procession unique to medieval Besançon. According to a local ceremonial of 1629, the journeys of the Magi were formerly acted out each year in the basilica of St-Étienne during the office of Terce on the feast of the Epiphany, 6 January. Three deacons were dressed as kings and three small choristers as pageboys wearing Persian costumes. They would process around the various chapels of the cathedral, the youngest in front, chanting music and Gospel readings. The unusual instruction is that the boy attending the king of Nubia was to have his face and hands blacked up to resemble an African. It borders on pantomime. Here the boy is shown in the manuscript, a character straight from liturgical drama evidently familiar to the illuminator or the patron.

At this point, for we are all in need of a break, Jane Wild, librarian of the Grey Collection, takes me over to lunch in the nearby Auckland Art Gallery, with Sophie Matthiesson, curator of international art there. We speak of Grey and Kawau and migration to New Zealand. Afterwards, I return to the Library's reading room.

When I first looked at the Missal in my late teens, the Public Library was still in the old building in Wellesley Street, attached to the southern end of the Art Gallery, as opened by Grey himself in 1887. I remember sitting at a table in a long Victorian room with pillars down each side, a bit like the nave of a church. To my unpractised eyes, the miniatures of the Besançon Missal were utterly magical. I gazed past saints straight into landscapes of the fifteenth century; the dusty New Zealand cabbage trees and trolleybuses of that hot Auckland summer vanished as I was transported into blue hills and cool rivers and forests of medieval France.

Since that bookseller's description of 1863, the manuscript Missal had always been said to have been made for an unknown bishop of Besançon, a statement repeated but not followed up in accounts of the manuscript published in 1908 and 1955. The borders of many illuminated pages in the first volume once included a coat of arms, now carefully erased, superimposed over a gold episcopal cross. In volume II, the (erased) arms are often accompanied by the letter 'C', sometimes also within initials or on its own, again with the cross. (Although we might now identify a bishop's arms by a crozier, this would usually have been reserved for an abbot in medieval heraldry: a cross indicates a bishop, or archbishop.) In some instances, a slightly later attempt has been made to rework the illumination to adapt the cross or initial into nondescript leafy ornament. Despite this, enough remains of the original arms, either in shadowy traces or offsets, to detect the original outlines and spots of red colour. I made drawings of these in 1970. The Library preserves a letter from me in 1972 identifying the patron for the first time as Charles de Neufchâtel, archbishop of Besançon 1463–98. It was not difficult to do, even for an inexperienced and amateur student, but evidently no one had attempted this before, and I was rather proud of myself.

Charles de Neufchâtel was born in Brussels in 1442, the son of Jean II de Neufchâtel, seigneur de Montaigu. The arms here are those of Neufchâtel (*gules*, a bend *argent*) quartered with Montaigu (*gules*, an eagle *argent*). The family was prominent both in the court of Burgundy and in the archdiocese of Besançon. Charles's mother was *demoiselle d'honneur* to Isabella of Portugal, wife of Philip the Good. He and his brothers were named after dukes of Burgundy. Charles was appointed as cantor to the chapter of Besançon in 1452 at the age of nine.

Perhaps he too, as a junior choirboy, once played the part of the black servant in the Epiphany processions, which may be why the detail appears in his manuscript. He was elected to the archbishopric in 1463. This was a secular as well as religious post, for it included the civil administration of Franche-Comté, an independent but fragile county between Burgundy and the Holy Roman empire. Charles was only twenty on his appointment, too young for ordination and while still at university in Louvain. He assumed his full office as prince-bishop in 1469. He initially supported the popular Burgundian factions in Besançon, which endeared him to the citizens, and he acted as ambassador for Mary of Burgundy in Switzerland after the death of Charles the Bold in 1477. However, as Louis XI attempted the gradual occupation of Franche-Comté in the late 1470s, Charles de Neufchâtel changed allegiances, probably primarily to protect his family's properties, and he joined the French cause. This was regarded as betrayal by Besançon. In October 1479, he was forced into exile from his archdiocese and fled to the French court. Following the death of Louis d'Harcourt, the bishop of Bayeux, in December that year, the king appointed Charles de Neufchâtel instead, technically as acting administrator of the diocese in Normandy since he was still archbishop of Besançon, to which he never returned. He died in 1498.

Charles owned a number of manuscripts, both commissioned by him and acquired second-hand. In addition to many liturgical books, he also had two manuscripts of Virgil with the commentaries of Servius, both now in Paris, and a copy of Boccaccio, *De claris mulieribus*, with his arms in the border of its first page, with an episcopal cross. By an entirely different migration, the Boccaccio was in Australia from 1946 until 2001 and I secured it for another collection in Australia in 2024 (Plate 7). These could have been texts familiar from Charles's student days.

The Missal must date from after his appointment as archbishop in 1463, and, in historical likelihood, before his enforced departure from Besançon in 1479. It is the work of two artists, distinguished by slight differences in style. The most prolific painted all forty-seven small miniatures and the two large pictures in volume II, together with six of the small miniatures in volume I. His general style is characteristic of manuscript illumination in central and eastern France, especially Burgundy, including huge rocky hills which jut out and overhang perilously. He usually executes saints' haloes as discs of burnished gold, like coins. The second artist uses a softer and more painterly technique: his haloes are generally shown as faint gold orbits, with stylistic echoes of manuscripts from Savoy and the southeast. He painted eleven small miniatures and both large pictures in volume I. It was a close collaboration. Sometimes the artists worked in the same gatherings (quires 23 and 26 of volume I) and may even have both contributed to the miniature of the Conversion of St Paul, which seems to show the facial types of one but the colouring of the other. It is slightly unexpected to find two illuminators together in the first volume of a manuscript and only one in its second half, although there could be explanations, including illness, death or quarrelling. There is another possibility. Perhaps they made the summer volume first. There is no reason why not, since both parts are self-contained. It would be imaginable that the main artist finishes the summer volume with forty-nine pictures, and realizes he is running out of time; he and the scribe reduce the miniatures in the winter volume to nineteen and they bring in an assistant to help meet the deadline.

The hand of the principal illuminator has now been found in a number of Books of Hours made for use in Besançon, which must also have been illuminated locally. Because of the patronage of Grey's Missal, the artist is now known to manuscript historians as the 'Master of Charles de Neufchâtel', a sobriquet which gives me quiet pride every time I see it mentioned. One Book of Hours in his style (and probably hand) is still in Besançon; its miniature for Terce, which in most Books of Hours would be the Adoration of the Magi in Bethlehem, shows the Magi on horseback on their procession to the Holy Land, as in the Missal, although without a black servant.

Come with me now to Besançon itself, to see where the Missal began its own migration. Bring your car to meet me off the Eurostar in Lille and we will drive across France together. The old city is enclosed within a great loop in the River Doubs so that it is almost an island, rather like Durham. At the neck of the peninsula is the high hill, now with the citadel, descending steeply on three sides down to the encircling river far below. The edge of the Roman town around a hilltop fortress can be envisaged by the survival of a second-century city gate crossing the Rue de la Convention. Walk uphill through this arch and you are suddenly right up against the walls of the cathedral of St-Jean, tucked sideways into the edge of the hill. Unlike many French cathedrals, which dominate their landscapes or present striking porticos rising up across open squares, St-Jean is quite hard to find, approached only through narrow streets offering no vistas. It has rounded apses at each end and is oriented (unusually) with its high altar at the western end. It is entered through a neoclassical door in a corner between the downhill side of the cathedral and the adjoining diocesan buildings. Inside, the nave is stately and Romanesque, and was already ancient in the time of Charles de Neufchâtel. In a few moments, we realize we are in a setting where the familiar Missal in New Zealand was entirely at home. The chapel of Saints

Ferreolus and Ferrucio is at the far left, now with a baroque altar-piece depicting their preaching, by Charles-Joseph Natoire (1700–1777). Late Gothic statues of these saints, holding their heads in their hands, as in the Auckland Missal, are across the nave, brought here in 1674 from the demolition of the cathedral of St-Étienne. A far greater monument transferred from St-Étienne is the actual altar dedicated by Pope Leo IX in 1050. This is in a side chapel opposite the entrance, on the left as you walk up the aisle, now called the 'Rose de Saint-Jean'. It is a circular disc of white marble carved with a graceful Chi Rho monogram within eight radiating petals and a surrounding inscription in Latin. It is now mounted on a single pedestal, like a small tea table in a French street café, quite unlike the oblong wooden tabernacle with altar cloth depicted in the manuscript for the annual feast of the altar's dedication on 3 October. The adjacent chapel is that of St Stephen. The precious relics of all the various saints, once here or brought down from St-Étienne, were scattered at the French Revolution and then quickly regathered up and placed unsorted into an aperture inset behind a grille in the far side of the present high altar, where Saints Stephen and Ferreolus, Ferrucio, Antidius and others are all now jumbled together. Old rivalries are forgotten when your bones are mixed up. The mitre of Charles de Neufchâtel, embroidered with pearls and gemstones and scenes of the Annunciation, is exhibited in the cathedral treasury. There is also a gold chalice dated 1442 and engraved with the arms of the Neufchâtel family. The archbishop doubtless used both when celebrating Mass with his manuscript Missal.

After emerging into the light again, I climbed the steep hill behind the cathedral to the site of the former co-cathedral of St-Étienne, up the road and across a park. It takes about seven minutes uphill, less coming down. There is no doubt that

St-Étienne had a better position and a marvellous view over Franche-Comté and out to the east towards Switzerland.

The following morning, I had an appointment in the municipal library, located down from the cathedral in the rue de la Bibliothèque, as one might guess from the name. There is a small and unremarkable green door off the street leading onto a stone staircase decorated with posters. The little reading room is upstairs, with three rows of wooden tables, like an old-fashioned schoolroom, parallel to the street. It is grey and white, lit by windows looking out across a central courtyard. But for the merest chance, the manuscript Missal might easily have been here, under the gaze of Jean-Baptiste Boisot (1638–94), local abbot and manuscript collector, whose marble bust presides above the invigilators' desk, rather than that of Shakespeare in the rare books room in Auckland.

The first manuscript I asked for was the Missal's long-separated sister, the Pontifical of Charles de Neufchâtel, now divided into three volumes and bound in eighteenth-century red morocco. Opening the manuscript in Besançon is like one of those strange dreams where you find yourself back in a childhood which is nowhere you have ever been and yet is utterly familiar. This and the Missal are almost twins, the same size and shape, and, as far as I can judge, written by the same scribe. A Pontifical comprises services unique to the office of a bishop, such as ordinations and blessings, and its text complements a Missal. The Litany here invokes Saints Stephen, Ferreolus, Ferrucio and Antidius, all now old friends. The style of the illuminated initials and borders is identical to those in New Zealand, with the episcopal cross and arms of Charles de Neufchâtel still intact and unerased. The miniatures are by neither of the Missal artists and may be the work of the Burgundian illuminator known sometimes as the 'Troyes Master' (although he could easily have been employed in Besançon, south-east of Troyes). When I look closely, the arms seem to have been inserted after the first campaign of illumination was completed, for the floral borders and petals have been fractionally adjusted and realigned to make way for the shields. A bishop cannot work without a Pontifical; a private Missal is a luxury, because every church in the archdiocese already owned one. If I had to guess, I would say that the Pontifical was made here in Besançon in preparation for Charles's arrival, around 1463–69, when he was still *electus* but not yet installed, and that it was then updated with his armorial preference on his arrival in the city. The Missal would follow. Its initiation may be documented. There is a record among the archives there that on 14 February 1469, Charles borrowed from the cathedral chapter a Missal formerly owned by his predecessor. An obvious explanation is that this was to serve as the exemplar for his own manuscript and, if so, we probably now, for the first time, have a date for its commencement. A hypothetical 1469–70 suits the artistic style perfectly.

I had supposed, until seeing his manuscripts, that Charles would have left his liturgical books behind when forced to flee his archdiocese in 1479. However, this was clearly not the case. As archbishop in exile, he continued to use and promote the liturgy of Besançon in his own household and from Normandy. We know that he travelled with the Pontifical because it still has his contemporary ownership inscription saying that it belongs to him as archbishop of Besançon and as perpetual administrator of the illustrious cathedral of Bayeux, which cannot have been inscribed before 1480. He arranged the first publication of liturgical texts for the archdiocese of Besançon, including Breviaries in Basel in 1479 and 1480, and in 1485 a Missal; this was printed in Salins, in Franche-Comté south-west of Besançon, but at that time safely occupied by the French. Charles commissioned a manuscript Breviary for himself with the explicit liturgical text for Besançon, now also in the library, which I asked to see too. It is truly enormous, the size of a small suitcase and almost a thousand pages thick. The style is unquestionably Norman, and it was probably made in Rouen, possibly even Bayeux, around 1490. It too has his arms as archbishop throughout and all the saints and festivals of the two Besançon cathedrals, as if Charles had still been in daily residence. He ordered a much smaller Besançon Pontifical, more suitable for travelling, with his arms on the first page, which is now in the canton library in Porrentruy in Switzerland; it is of higher quality than the Breviary but harder to localize: the semi-grisaille borders and initials are certainly consistent with high-end manuscripts from Rouen. To complete the list, he also acquired a richly decorated second-hand Pontifical of the early thirteenth century made for the Use of Beauvais but adapted later for Lisieux and Rouen, both in Normandy, where he must have bought it.

The probability that Charles de Neufchâtel took his Besançon Missal with him into exile, together with his Pontifical, is confirmed by his will, dated 19 July 1498, the day before his death in Normandy. The original is lost but an early and detailed summary survives (unpublished) in the Archives départementales du Doubs. It divides the archbishop's estate (and indeed his body for burial) between the chapters of Bayeux and Besançon. His mitre and silver cross were to be returned to Besançon for use by his successors, and the mitre is still there. Only two books are specifically mentioned in the will: '*Il a donné ses deux missels en parchemin l'un à l'Eglise de St Jean, et l'autre à l'Eglise de St Etienne.*' They both went back to Besançon too, therefore, one to each cathedral. They cannot be the printed Missals of 1485, since those were on paper; these are undoubtedly manuscripts and treasured possessions. The Auckland Missal, by far his most expensive and important surviving book, must be one of the two. It may be that its companion Pontifical, for this purpose virtually a Missal, is the other, especially as it clearly was indeed sent back to Besançon.

They were treated slightly differently. The Pontifical has the archbishop's arms intact. By the late seventeenth century, it had migrated to the library of the seminary of Besançon, built and equipped by the archbishops in the city in 1670–95. That would be explicable if it had been in the cathedral of St-Étienne, which was demolished in 1668–73 and its possessions redistributed. This would mean that the Missal now in Auckland had been assigned to the cathedral of St-Jean. It continued in use there, up to a point. All Charles's coats-of-arms have all been carefully scraped away, probably at an early date, as we can tell because some of their accompanying processional crosses have been skilfully adapted into flowers or leafy stems by a craftsman still capable of manuscript illumination. The last four leaves of volume I are in a sixteenth-century hand, and the book was evidently being made fit for use. In volume II, although the arms are erased, the archbishop's initial 'C' remained untouched. Perhaps it was intended to recondition the manuscript for Claude de la Baume, archbishop of Besançon 1544–84. In the event, it was put aside. It is likely that the manuscript remained in the cathedral until the frenzy of the French Revolution in 1789, which scattered much church property into private hands. By then, luxurious illumin-ated manuscripts had become collectable.

In both volumes is a rococo bookplate of the end of the eighteenth century with a device of a stag and the enig-matic initials P. S. For almost sixty years their identification defeated me. With help from several friends and a database in France, we have finally solved it: the bookplate is that of

Pierre-Charles-Joseph Scherer (1722–1812), born in Lille, died unmarried in Ennetières-en-Weppes, now part of the metropolitan district of Lille. His family, seigneurs de Scherbourg, were of Swiss descent, and Besançon is only about fifteen miles from the Swiss border. Saved by its new credentials as a treasure for a library shelf, rather than as paraphernalia of an altar or cathedral sacristy, the archbishop's Missal had set out on its long journey as a refugee. It came eventually by ship from London on approval out to Kawau Island in 1863, acclimatized, and in 1887, ninety-eight years after the Revolution, it re-settled at home in Auckland.

4

Dunedin

Everything changed when my father told us about Josephine.
We learned on 7 March 1963 that we might be moving to
Dunedin, a slightly smaller coastal city we knew little about in
the southern province of Otago, and my brothers and I hated
the idea. Children, like manuscripts, prefer to be in one place.
We did not want to leave our schools, the house which I had
known since the age of four, and especially the stamp shop in
Christchurch. By late April, my father was spending most weeks
in Dunedin, staying in the Leviathan Hotel near the station and
returning home at weekends. This was when he first revealed
to us the existence of Josephine. She was a nineteenth-century
double-ended railway engine, then parked across the road from
his hotel, with funnels at each end, like a pushmi-pullyu in the
children's books about Dr Dolittle. Now he had our attention. Steam trains to me represented England of long ago and
a frequent part of children's literature, usually as transport to
adventure, and I never forgot being lifted up by my grandfather
to look into the fiery cab of an engine at Waterloo Station. In
mid-May 1963, we all came down for a weekend to visit Dunedin
for the first time. The Starliner bus from Christchurch took
over five hours, a tribulation for my pregnant mother, and we
descended from the hills into Dunedin at 11.30 at night, seeing the
lights of the city stretching out in the darkness. We too stayed

at the pink Leviathan, almost my first experience of a hotel and a leviathan only in the sense that its three modest storeys made it mightier than its neighbours. It had been built as a temperance hotel in 1884. The next morning, daylight revealed Josephine, and another steam engine, as promised, glistening and rusting together in the rain. We ran over to admire, and I drew a picture of Josephine in my diary. She too, like us, was made in England, but was assembled locally in 1872 (as we later learned) for the Dunedin and Port Chalmers Railway. She was dark green with tall black funnels front and back, and on the sides neat red panels with her name in gold and another with the manufacturers' 'Fairlie Patent', which we read as Fairly Patient. It seemed apt for two bleak winter days with estate agents looking dispiritedly at a shortlist of properties around Dunedin where we might live.

Back in Christchurch, our house was put on the market at £5,000 and was sold on 27 May. I began making myself desperate drawings of the local shops, our school, the cathedral and the city square where we had been accustomed to catch the bus home. I was convinced I would never see any of them again, a fallacy not really fulfilled until the Christchurch earthquake of 2011, which did indeed destroy most of them. My last sketch showing the front of our house from the garden was elaborately signed and dated 7 June 1963. The next day, a Saturday, we packed the car, four boys on the back seat, and migrated south to Dunedin. For a day or so, we stayed once again in the Leviathan. With hindsight, the sequence of events that first week is interesting. On the Monday, we joined the Dunedin Public Library. On the Tuesday, it was arranged that I would attend King's High School. On the Thursday, we moved out to our new house. 'Awful muddle', my diary records unnecessarily that night.

Dunedin had been founded in 1848 as a settlement of the Free Church of Scotland, at the inner end of a long but shallow volcanic harbour once used by Māori canoes and, for a time, by European whalers. From almost every long perspective in the city you can still see surrounding hills covered with original native bush, a reminder that urbanization here is a late import into a landscape far older than human arrival. The street plan at the foundation was laid out to remind immigrants of Scotland. 'Dunedin' is the old Gaelic word for Edinburgh. Its central plaza is the Octagon, named from its shape on a quite steep sideways slope, where Princes Street meets George Street end to end, surrounded by an outer halo of Moray Place, all names borrowed from Edinburgh, like the Dunedin suburbs of Corstorphine, Waverley, Musselburgh, Portobello and others. On the upper side of the Octagon is a statue of Robert Burns, turning his back on the Anglican Cathedral and looking pensively downhill towards the Gothic railway station (and Josephine) and, off to the right, in the direction of the Presbyterian First Church on Bell Hill. This resembles a late medieval French cathedral and is a finer building than its chunky and unfinished Anglican cousin at the top of the Octagon. The founding minister of First Church had been Thomas Burns, nephew of the poet, which explains the statue. The earliest settlers from Scotland had never quite forgiven the Highland Clearances and Culloden, and referred to the English in New Zealand as the 'little enemy'. Discovery of gold in Otago in 1861 brought several decades of considerable wealth and migration to the province. For a time, Dunedin was the biggest and most prosperous city in New Zealand. Public buildings in grey stone increased the similarity to the architecture of Edinburgh. Then the gold ran out, as it does. Josephine was shunted into retirement and Dunedin slipped back into its gentle and stately widowhood, which so entranced my parents in

1963 and is still almost unchanged today. Even now, at least from my perspective of living in London, there seem to be almost no pedestrians or traffic in the central city, and it is hard to think how many shops can earn a living. Dunedin retains something of its founders' Presbyterian ethic and the ancient Scottish respect for learning. It has the oldest university in New Zealand (founded in 1869) and some of the best libraries. It has been home to an unusual number of authors. In 2014, it was named as a UNESCO 'City of Literature', another designation it shares with Edinburgh, which received the first award of that title in 2004.

Our new house was in Macandrew Bay, on the Otago Peninsula a few miles out of the city, reached by a narrow road winding along the southern edge of the harbour. As a house, it was dull – a pre-war low-ceilinged wooden bungalow with a corrugated iron roof – and the interior was painted a shocking fuchsia pink when we first moved in. However, the site was stupendous. The house was on a slope with an ever-changing prospect out across the water from its veranda and an illusion of double height when seen from the front. There were substantial areas of trees and shrubs extending through paths and steps right down to the road along the harbour one way, and up beyond the house into bush at the back. My father, like the Pohutukawa Trust, set about rewilding it with native plants. The cacophony of daily birdsong in the trees around us was increased by our conversion of a shed across the courtyard into an aviary for squawking budgerigars, brought with us in cages in the car from Christchurch, and soon joined in Dunedin by tiny chirruping zebra finches. For children, as with birds, the large garden gave endless opportunities for tree houses and secret dens in the undergrowth. Our own shrieks added to the noise. We were not troubled with sight or knowledge of neighbours, although Macandrew Bay was strictly suburban: the drive up to our house was so steep and treacherous that no one attempted it casually. My father, never sociable, could live as remotely as Grey on Kawau, and we were not encouraged to invite people home. My youngest brother was born later that year and we were now five boys, no girls. With a nod to Latin numbering, which we were assured (wrongly) no New Zealander would understand, the new arrival was named Quentin.

Michael, who had already begun secondary school in Christchurch, remained there as a boarder, returning home in the holidays. William went at first to the local junior school in Macandrew Bay. I was entered at King's High School, in south Dunedin, opened in 1936, the year of three British kings but planned for George V's silver jubilee the year before, which is why the apostrophe is where it is. My mother took me to meet the rector, as the principal is called there, Mr Craig, who looked rather like General de Gaulle. After a few questions about what I had learned at Cathedral Grammar School, he conceded that I might jump a class from the final level of the prep school in Christchurch into the middle of the first year of secondary school. One result was that I was always a year younger than most of my form, and I remained so right through to university. In the beginning I was smaller and treble for longer than the rest of them as we all began to lurch into our lanky teens. Another consequence of the leap in mid-year was that the boys in my class at King's High already knew one another when I arrived. My first day, a daunting experience for any child, was 17 June 1963. I was then twelve. We were formally addressed by our surnames at school, and I was presented to my class-mates as 'de Hamel'. They clustered round, all wanting to know what the initial 'C' stood for. Children are strange but for some reason I would not tell them. It may simply have been from fear of stammering on the hard initial, which could without warning suddenly render me inarticulate. At that time there was, I believe, a comic radio show including a ridiculous Eng-lishman named Clive, and someone said, 'I bet he's called Clive' and they all laughed jubilantly, and I still said nothing. 'It is, isn't it?' they crowed; and for five years I was called Clive. It quickly became so normal that I thought nothing of it, and even now, if someone says 'Hello, Clive', I know I must have been at school with him. Five decades later, we gave the name to our cat.

I do not recall for sure when I first set eyes on a medieval manuscript, but it was probably 10 June 1963, the day we joined the Dunedin Public Library. This was on the upper west arc of Moray Place as it orbits the city's central Octagon, at about 10.30 if you imagine Moray Place as a clockface. It was an Edward-ian building in grand Romanesque baronial style, if such a term exists, faced with red brick and Oamaru stone (a local white limestone), ornamented on the outside with panels of Scottish thistle motifs. It had been largely financed by the great American philanthropist and benefactor of libraries – born in Scotland – Andrew Carnegie (1835–1919). Dunedin had applied to him in 1901, emphasizing their Caledonian credentials. The Library

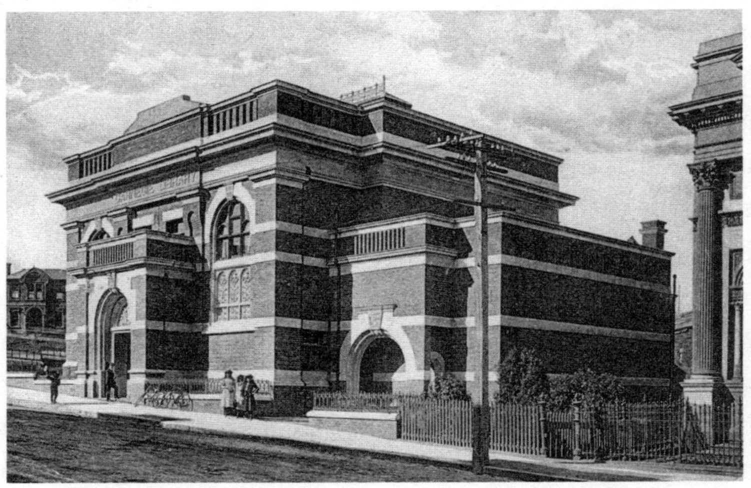

The Dunedin Public Library, *c.* 1910, shortly after its opening.

was opened in 1908 and remained in these premises until 1981. The building's soulless shell survives today, now divided up and rented out to various small businesses, including a Tandoori restaurant, an employment agency and a models and games shop. In the 1960s it was a hub of life and books, now ghosts. One went in through a main entrance into the principal library floor. On the left was a staircase with carved wooden bannisters (still there) which faced back towards the street and turned several right-angles past the librarians' offices on the half-landing and up to the reference floor above. Branching off to the left at the top of the first flight was a low and narrow mezzanine balcony reaching back above the Library entrance. This was the exhibition gallery for the Reed Collection of rare books. There were low glass cases on either side with bookcases beneath, all constructed in 1948, and at the far end down a couple of steps was a small room with further vitrines and wall displays. The gallery has now been demolished, and on my last visit I stood on the bend in the old stairs gazing out nostalgically over an empty space where my entire life became transformed long ago.

The core of the rare book collection was assembled and donated by A. H. Reed (1875–1975), who was as determined as Sir George Grey to introduce early printing and manuscripts to New Zealanders. The principal emphasis was early Bibles and related material. Items on view changed from time to time, but displays might include their portion of a Tyndale New Testament of 1538, or the 'Great Bible' of 1539, once owned by the Wentworth family, earls of Strafford, or one of several Geneva (or 'Breeches') Bibles. At the end on the right was a single framed leaf from a Gutenberg Bible, then the only example in New Zealand, bought in 1954 for £175. There was also a display of English literature, including material on or by Charles Dickens, mostly in the little room at the end. Exhibits were accompanied by sometimes credulous typed notes by Mr Reed. There was usually one of a series of wonderful albums of autograph letters displayed in a separate glass case, mounted and written up in beautiful calligraphic script and neo-Gothic illumination by Reed himself, intended to be changed page by page each day. Above all, at least for me as it turned out, there were usually a number of medieval man-uscripts on exhibition, including one of several small thirteenth-century Latin Bibles, together with a cheerful if gaudy little French illuminated Book of Hours of about 1490 and a Wyclif-fite Gospel Book in Middle English of the mid-fifteenth century. In the wall displays behind the cases, and hanging on the stairs further up towards the top floor, were framed cuttings from man-uscripts and specimen leaves of early printing, including one by Peter Schoeffer of Mainz, labelled by Reed 'A Link with Guten-berg', and another from Caxton's *Golden Legend* of 1483.

Imagine an impressionable twelve-year-old, a schoolboy stamp collector, whose most precious and oldest possession was a penny black of 1840 and whose life in New Zealand until now had been entirely predicated around a sense of the country's immense remoteness from Europe. Reed's autograph letter col-lection already overlapped somewhat with philately but pushed the boundaries back to the seventeenth century. More than that, I could hardly believe I was standing in front of a page of an actual Gutenberg Bible, the penny black of incunabula, printed in Mainz around 1454. I still think it shares the beauty of that primeval stamp, technically unsurpassed from the very first inception of printing in Europe, crisp and black with white margins and an added dash of red rubrication, like the Maltese cross postmark on my penny black envelope. It probably impressed me more than the manuscripts on my earliest visits to the Library. I did not realize, because I did not read the text, that the leaf (Ezekiel 2–3) happens to include one of the few

Ezechiel 106.

ad gentes apostatrices que recesserūt
a me. Patres eoz puaricati sūt pactū
meū usq; ad diem hanc:z filij dura facie z indomabili corde sunt ad quos
ego mitto te. Et dices ad eos. Hec dicit dns deus:si forte uel ipi audiāt·et
si forte quiescant·quoniā domus exa-
sperans est:et scient quia ppheta fuerit in medio eoz. Tu ergo fili hominis
ne timeas eos neq; sermones eoz me-
tuas:quoniā increduli z subuersores
sunt tecum: et cum scorpionibz habi-
tas. Verba eoz ne timeas:z uult eoz
ne formides:quia domus exasperās
est. Loqueris ergo uerba mea ad eos
si forte audiant z quiescāt:quoniā ir-
ritatores sūt. Tu aūt fili hominis audi
quecunq; loquor ad te:z noli esse exasperās sicut dom exasperatrix e. Aperi
os tuū:z cōede quecūq; ego do tibi. Et
uidi:z ecce man missa ad me·in qua erat
inuolut liber:z expādit illū corā me qui
erat script intz z foris:z scripte erāt in
eo lamētatōnes et carmē et ue.

Et dixit ad me. Fili hominis·qd-
cunq; inueneris cōede. Comede
uolumen istud:z uadens loquere ad
filios israhel. Et aperui os meū:z ciba-
uit me uolumine illo. Et dixit ad me.
Fili hominis:uenter tuus comedet·z
uiscera tua cōplebūtur uolumine isto
quod ego do tibi. Et comedi illud:et
factū est in ore meo sicut mel dulce. Et
dixit ad me. Fili hominis uade ad
domū isrl:z loqueris uerba mea ad e-
os. Nō eni ad pplm pfūdi sermonis z
ignote ligue tu mitteris ad domū isrl:
neq; ad ppos multos pfūdi sermonis
z ignote ligue:quoz nō possis audire
sermones. Et si ad illos mittereris ipi
audirent te. Domus aūt israhel no-
lunt audire te:quia nolūt audire me.

Omnis quippe dom israhel attrita
fronte est:z duro corde. Ecce dedi facie
tuā ualentiorem faciebz eoz:z frontē
tuā duriorem frontibz eoz:ut adamā
tem z ut silicem dedi facie tuā. Ne timeas eos neq; metuas a facie eoz:quia
domus exasperās est. Et dixit ad me.
Fili hominis:omnes sermones meos
quos ego loquor ad te assume in corde tuo·z auribz tuis audi:z uade in-
gredere ad transmigratiōe ad filios
ppli mei:z loqueris ad eos:z dices eis.
Hec dicit dns deus:si forte audiant z
quiescant. Et assumpsit me spiritus:
et audiui post me uocem cōmotōnis
magne·benedicta gloria dūi de loco
suo:z uocem alarū animaliū percuci-
entiū alterā ad alteram:et uocem ro-
taz sequentiū animalia·z uocem com-
motōnis magne. Spirit quoqz leua-
uit me z assumpsit me:z abij amar
in indignatione spirit mei. Manus
enim dūi erat mecū confortās me. Et
ueni ad trāsmigratōne ad aceruū no-
uarū frugū·ad eos qui habitabāt iu-
xta flumen chobar:z sedi ubi illi sede-
bant:z mansi ibi septem diebz merens
in medio eorū. Cum aūt ptransissent
septem dies:factū est uerbū dūi ad me
dicens. Fili hominis·speculatorē dedi
te domui israhel:z audies de ore meo
uerbū·z annūciabis eis ex me. Si di-
cēte me ad impiū morte morieris·nō
annūciaueris ei·neq; locut fueris ut
auertat a uia sua impia z uiuat:ipe
impius in iniquitate sua morietz:san-
guinē aūt eius de manu tua requirā.
Si aūt tu annūciaueris impio·et ille
non fuerit cōuersus ab impietate sua
et a uia sua impia:ipe quidē in impietate sua morietur:tu aūt animā tuā
liberasti. Sed et si conuersus iustus a

Leaf of a Gutenberg Bible, Mainz, *c.* 1454, in the Dunedin Public Library.

contemporary descriptions of a double-sided manuscript scroll in antiquity. Mr Reed's typed caption quoted the famous rhetorical injunction of the bookseller Henry Stevens addressed to the customs officers in New York when a Gutenberg Bible was shipped to America in 1872. Reed had copied it out from the essay in A. Edward Newton's *Noble Fragment* of 1921:

> Pray, Sir, ponder for a moment and appreciate the rarity and importance of this precious consignment from the old world to the new. Not only is it the first Bible, but it is the first book ever printed. It was read in Europe half a century before America was discovered. Please suggest to your deputy that he uncover his head while in the presence of this great book. Let no Custom House Official, or other man in or out of authority, see it without first reverently raising his hat. It is not possible for many men to touch or even look upon a page of a Gutenberg Bible.

Extreme and purple prose this may be, but it set my heart racing. Here was one of those defining moments of growing up. Since then, over many years, I have seen (and often touched) about half of all extant copies of the Gutenberg Bible.

On 21 January 1964, I went into town with Michael on a mission to buy zebra finches for our new aviary, from the pet shop at the far end of Dunedin, almost opposite Knox Church. Michael was home for the summer holidays. Our grandparents were visiting from England and had given each of us ten shillings, a rare addition to our pocket money budgets. We wandered into the big and old-fashioned two-storey second-hand bookshop near the corner of George and Frederick Streets. It was like a library where everything was for sale. With a sense of awesome unreality, I bought a volume of French fables printed in London in 1773 and we went home without zebra finches. I

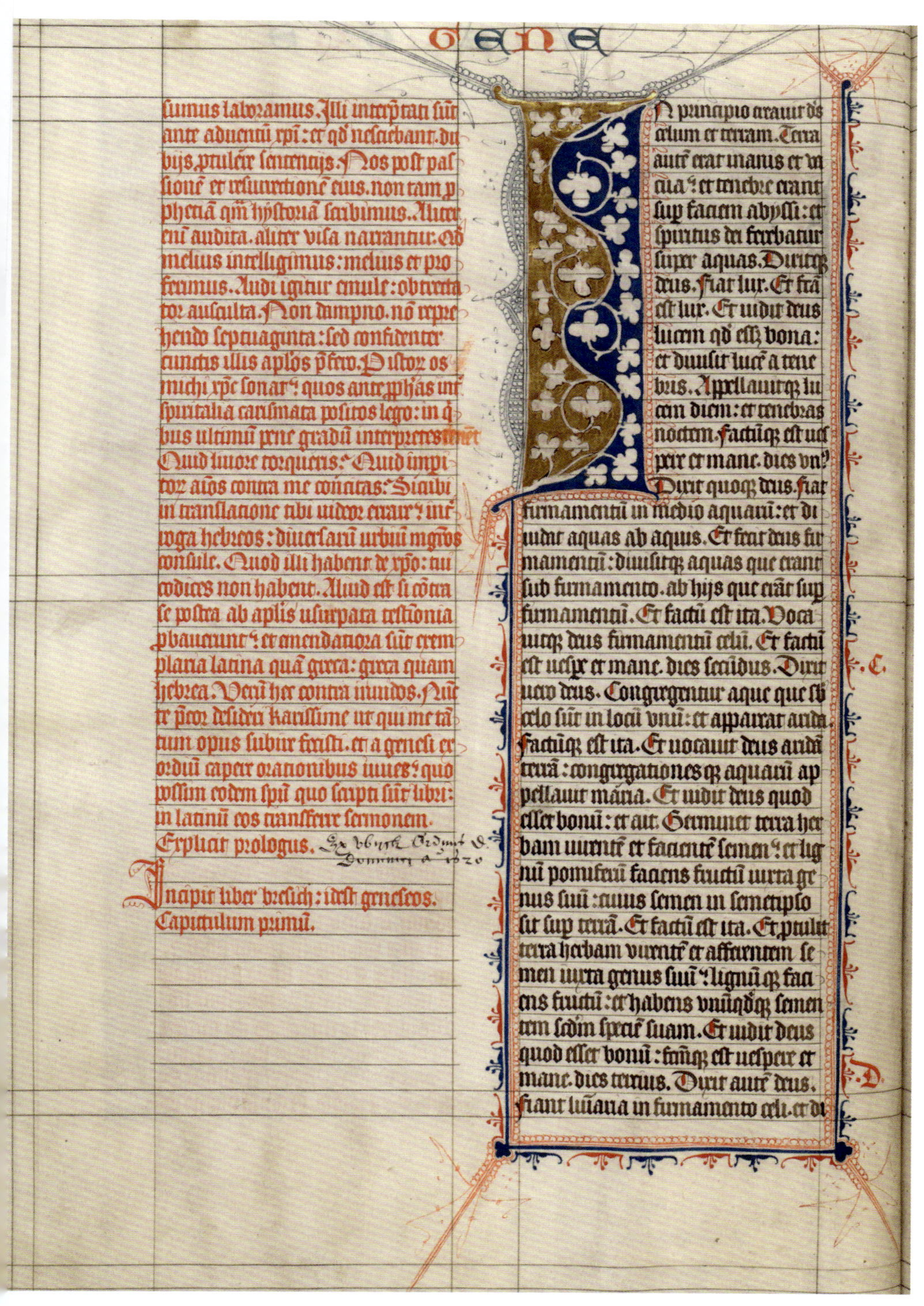

1. The Bible of Wijk bij Duurstede, Netherlands, *c.*1419, bought by Sir George Grey in 1855 in the belief it was the exemplar used by Gutenberg.

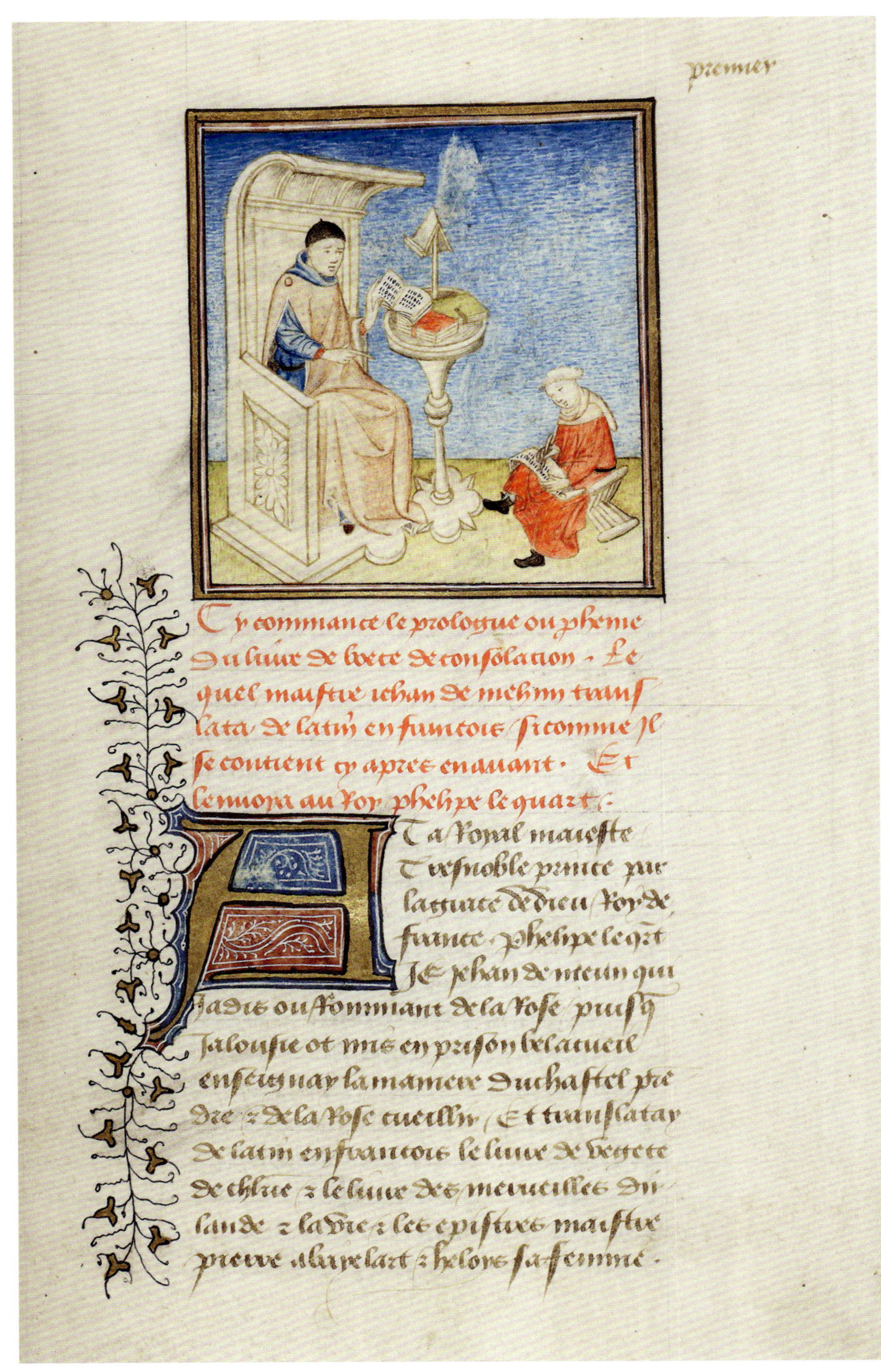

2. Boethius, *Le livre de Boèce de Consolacion* in French, France (probably Paris), early fifteenth century, shown by Grey to visitors on Kawau Island in the 1880s.

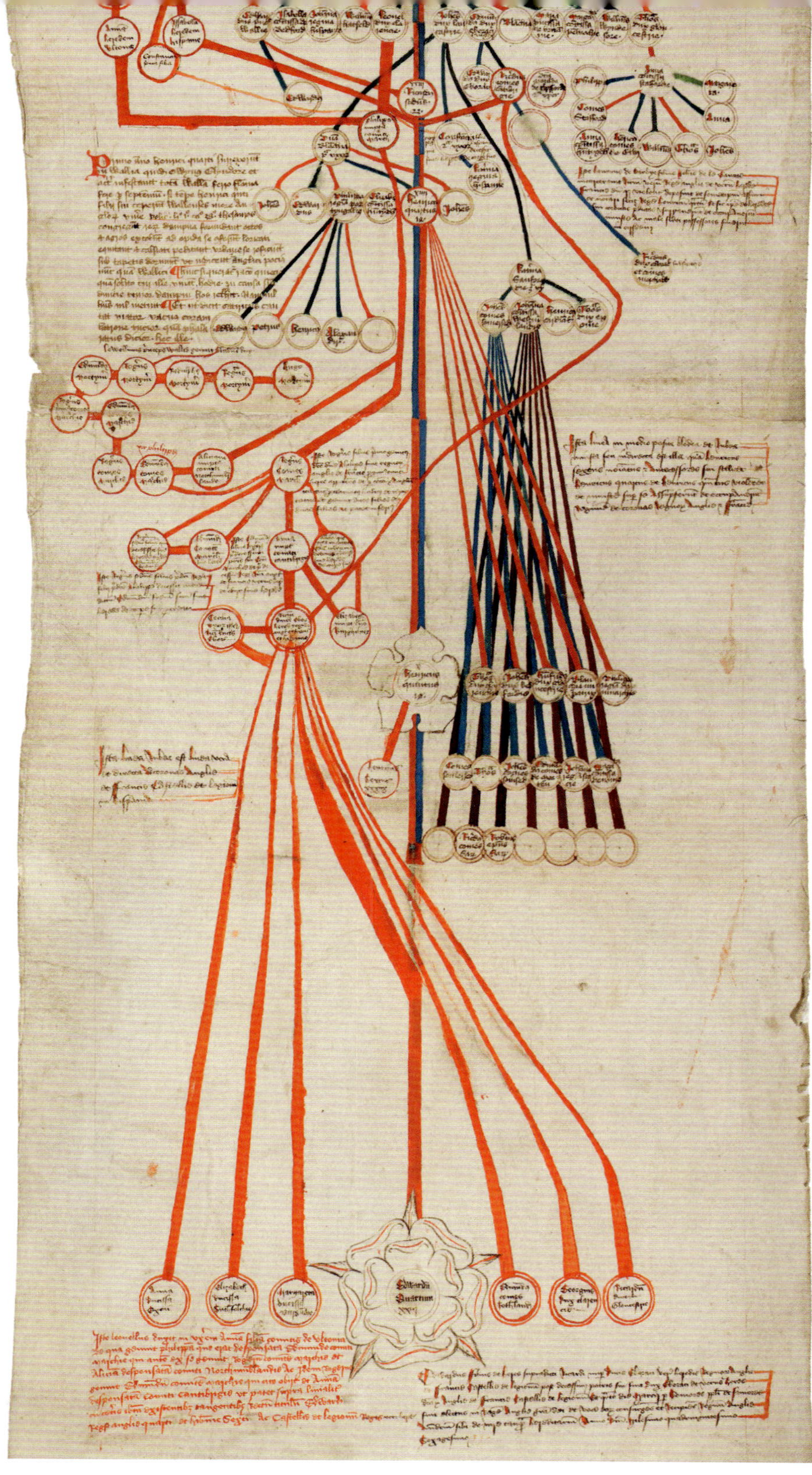

3. The Maude (or Canterbury) Roll, a royal genealogical chronicle, extended to the accession of Edward IV in 1460, England, second half of the fifteenth century bought by the University of Canterbury in 1918.

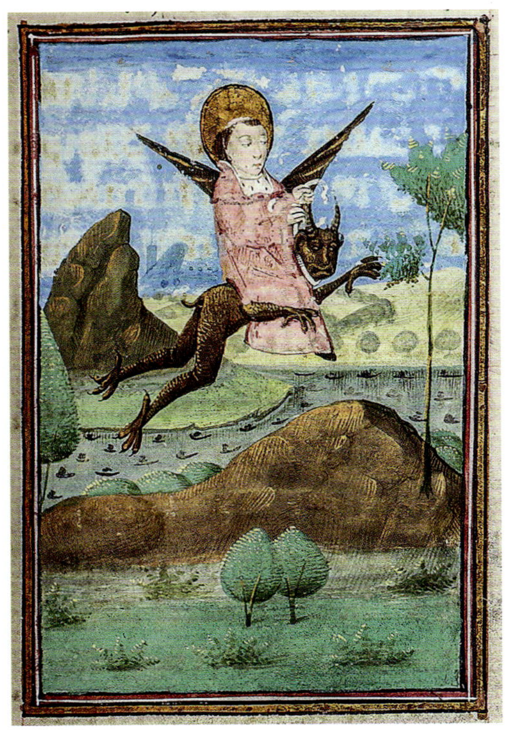

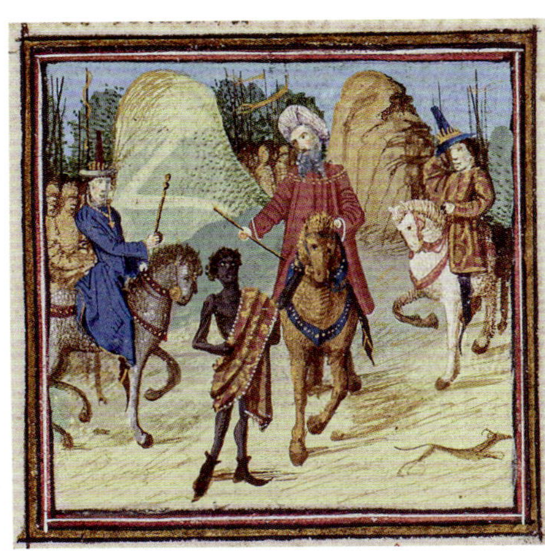

4. (*Left*) Saint Antidius flying on a devil, miniature from the Missal of Charles de Neufchâtel, Besançon, *c.*1469–70, sent out to Grey on Kawau in 1863.

5. (*Above*) The meeting of the Magi on their journey to Bethlehem, miniature from the Missal of Charles de Neufchâtel.

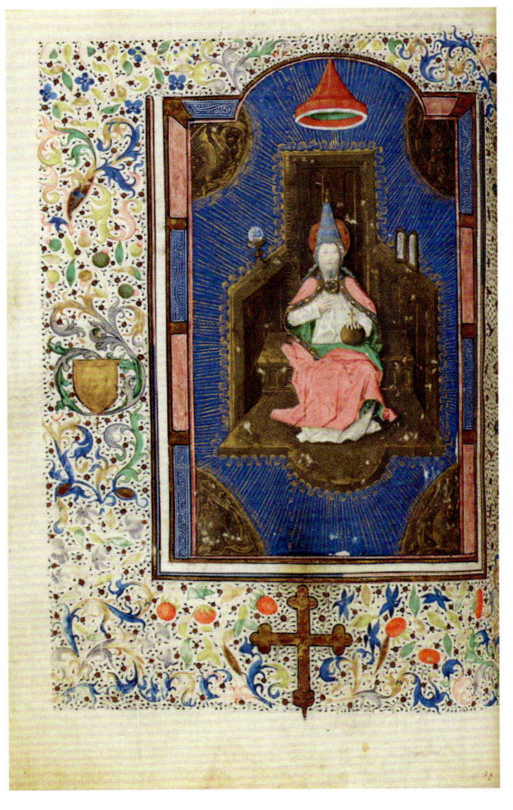

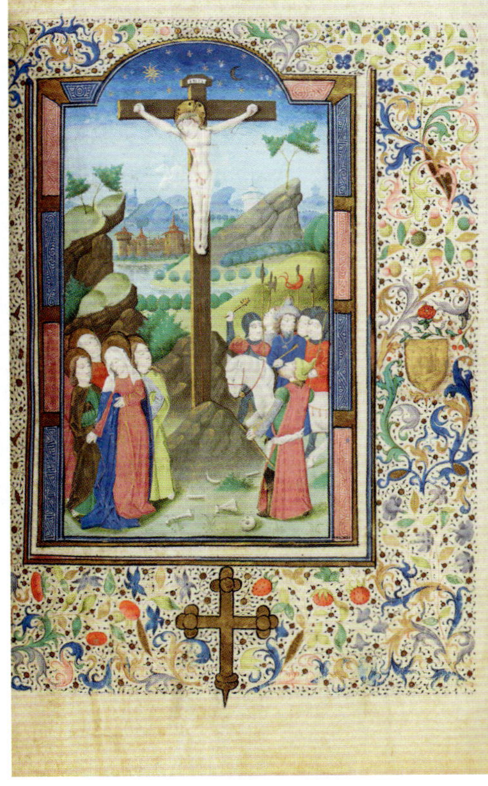

6. God in Majesty and the Crucifixion, miniatures for the Canon of the Mass in volume II of the Missal of Charles de Neufchâtel.

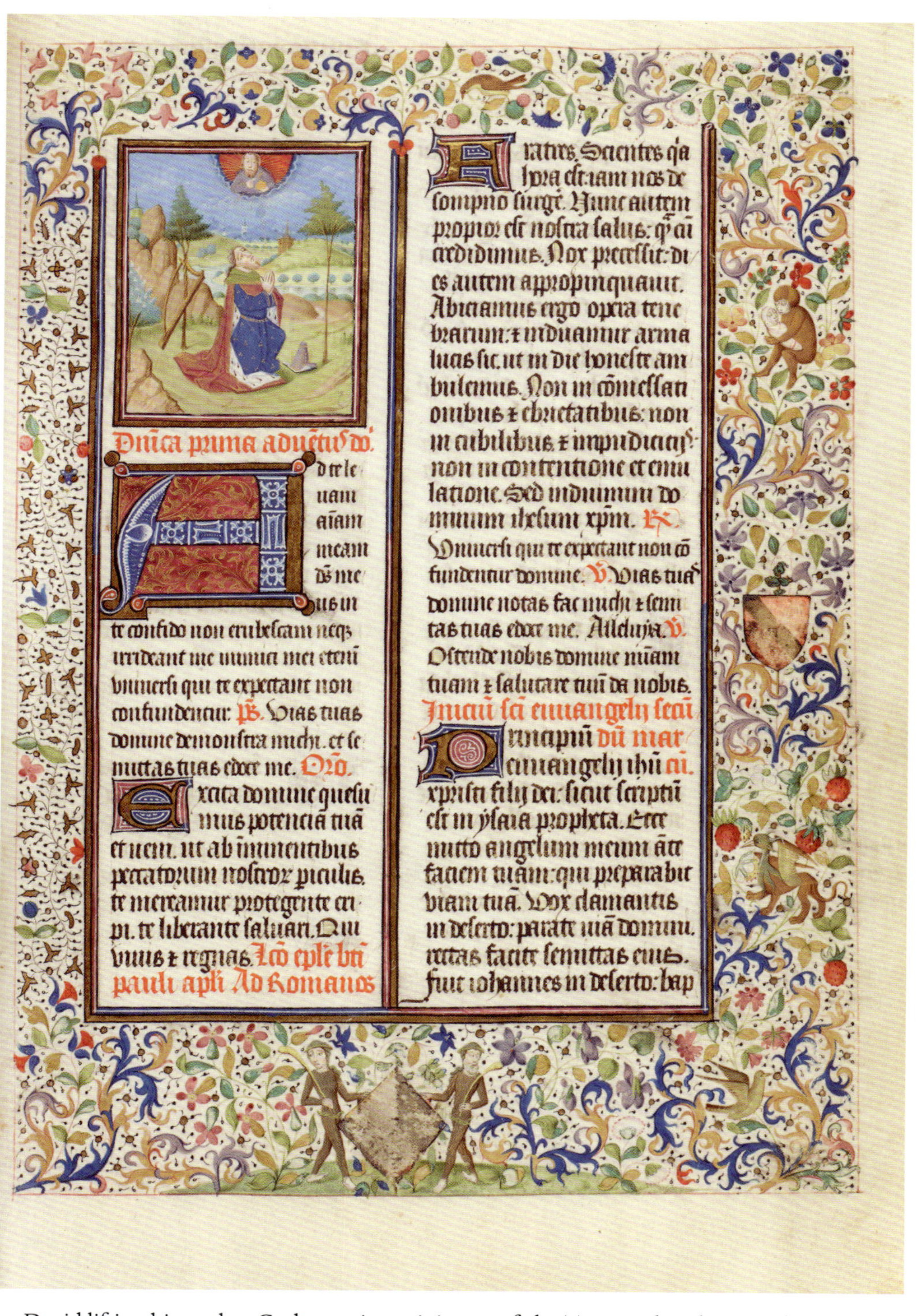

7. David lifting his soul to God, opening miniature of the Temporal in the Missal of Charles de Neufchâtel.

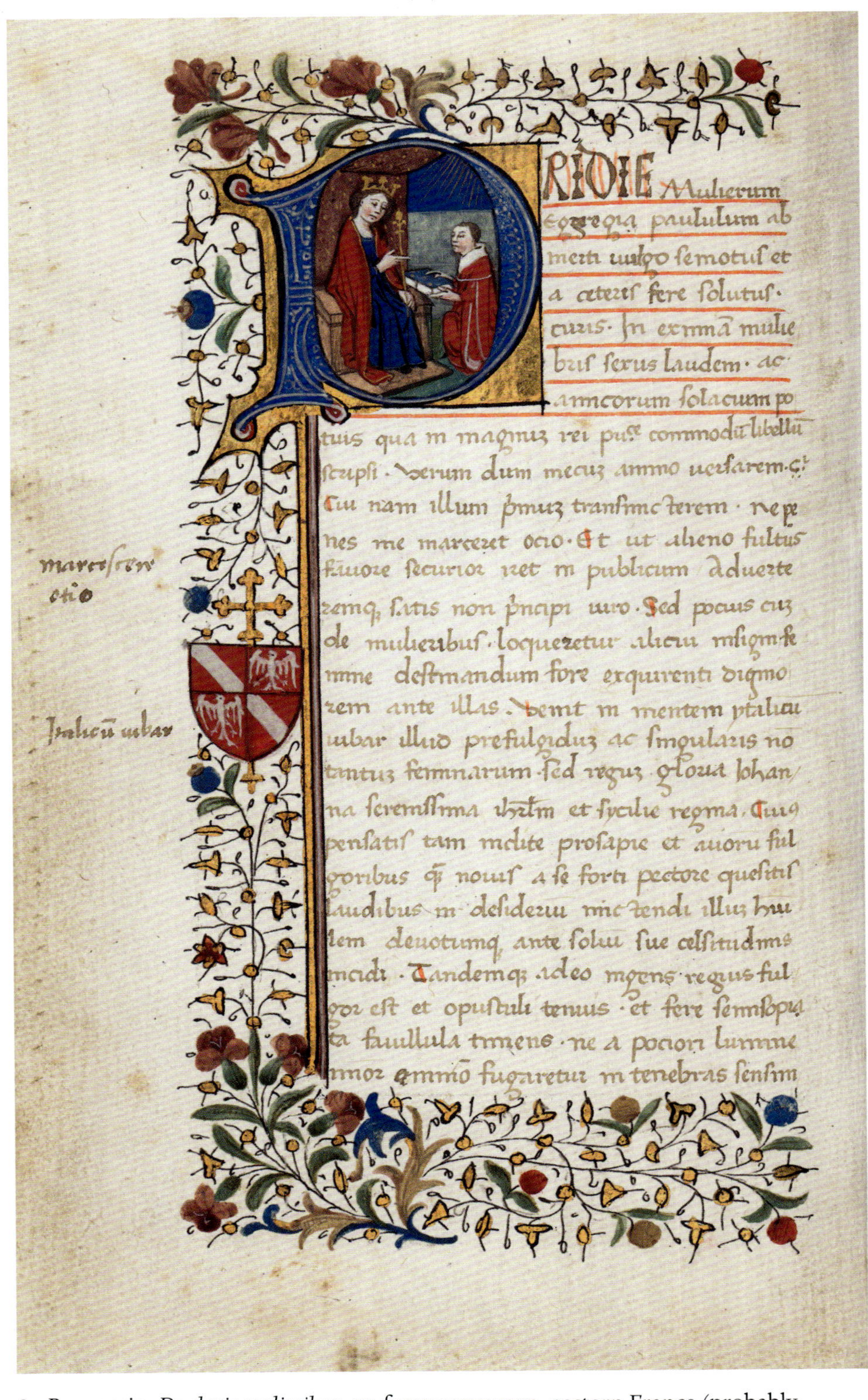

8. Boccaccio, *De claris mulieribus*, on famous women, eastern France (probably Besançon), *c.*1463–70, made for Charles de Neufchâtel with his arms.

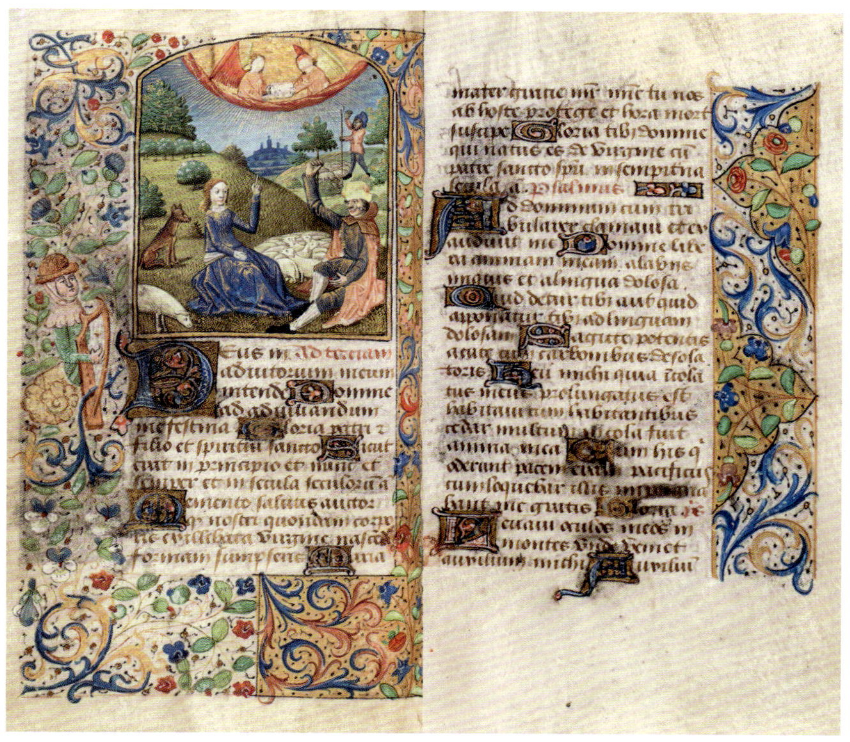

9. Book of Hours, Use of Rome, northern France, late fifteenth century, bought by A. H. Reed in 1949.

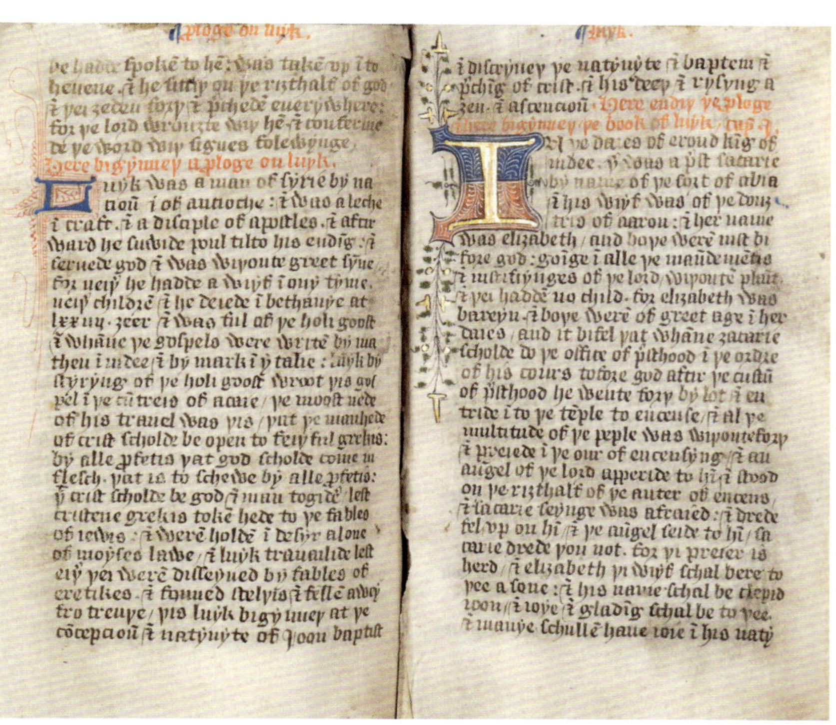

10. Wycliffite Gospels, England, fifteenth century, bought by the Reed Collection in 1956.

11. The Byszewo Bible, northern Poland (Koronowo), *c.*1316, formerly fol. IIIv in the volume as bought by A. H. Reed *c.*1925.

have the book still. It cost me seven shillings, rather a lot I think now. It may have been the largest sum I had until then ever spent on anything, a good if regrettable precedent for later life. On 31 January, ten days later, I ventured back to the bookshop, which was called Newbold's and owned by Dick White (1899–1967), where I risked several more shillings on further books from 1740 and 1664. I did not expect to read them, any more than I expected to use stamps for postage: it was their age and secure dates which astonished me, and their availability in Dunedin – as exciting as stamps but older. Later that same afternoon, my diary for the day concludes 'went to Library, etc.', returning with my purchases to the mothership of the Reed Collection.

Such visits to 'Library, etc.' became increasingly common, on Saturdays or in school holidays. One day, probably in early 1964, I was gazing into the glass cases when old Mr Reed himself appeared. He had doubtless been told by the Library staff that someone was actually looking at his display. He was an easily recognizable celebrity in Dunedin, with his thick white hair and a moustache like Einstein. He was by then in his late eighties and becoming very deaf. 'Do you like what you see?' he boomed, and every head in the Library looked up. 'Oh, yes,' I squeaked, overawed. 'What's that?' he shouted. 'Speak up, boy!' He ordered the librarian to open a glass case and I touched and smelled a medieval manuscript for the first time in my life.

One day later that year I came again with Michael, back in the holidays once more, 'to see old books at Library', as my diary records for 4 September. There were several people in the exhibition area and one of the cases was open. It transpired that they had recently bought a Latin Bible of 1472, the earliest printed copy in New Zealand, and had invited in a photographer from the *Otago Daily Times*, for whom pages of dense Latin type evidently seemed lacking in human interest. He asked if we might be photographed admiring the book. It was carried to a table upstairs in the reference section. The picture appeared in the paper on 12 September 1964 (see frontispiece, p. ii). Michael there looks much more grown up than his mere eighteen months older than me, in a sensible jacket and tie. I am on the left, still small and fair-haired, aged thirteen, in a dark blue jumper – but also wearing a tie, I notice – and I am tentatively reaching out a finger to touch an outer corner of the page. That instinctive thrill of wanting to touch even a margin is something I notice and rejoice in when I show rare books to students now. The Library reprinted the picture on the front of a leaflet they prepared called *A Few Highlights of the Dunedin Public Library's Bible Collection*.

My diaries for those years are filled with all the trivia of family life. Looking at old books was only a small part. There were days when we were taken to beaches over on the far side of the peninsula and scrambled down through the tussock and out over the dunes. It is a big ocean there and far too cold and dangerous for swimming. We would leap from rock to rock along the shoreline, watching seaweed sucked and thrust by the relentless currents. The waves crashed in as they have for millions of years, their first landfall this side of South America. There were comic little penguins bustling up the beach and lazy seals, like old men in club armchairs resentful at being interrupted, and occasional soaring albatrosses, which nested at the end of the peninsula. We were almost always the only people there. The budgerigars at home laid eggs and hatched chicks, all carefully documented by me. There were tragedies when rats tunnelled into the aviary and we learned about mortality as well as birth; little feathered funerals were held behind the house. William was given a cat for his eleventh birthday in 1964 and he went to Pony Club. Michael supervised guinea pigs in a hutch on the lawn. My two youngest brothers toddled and learned to talk. I practised conjuring tricks and could palm cards and make coins vanish. We had a puppet theatre, constructed by my father, and we glued and painted miniature stage props. Fraternization with other people was rare, and there were no audiences for my magic shows or puppetry, except our own family who already knew what was coming anyway.

By 1963 it was clear that we were staying in New Zealand for the duration, and the intense pressure to preserve our uncontaminated Englishness was gradually becoming less acute. My two youngest brothers, born there, grew up with unchallenged New Zealand accents. However, there was always a sense that we as a family were English and therefore different, even special (quite untrue). Sport was not encouraged: that is what New Zealanders did, not us. There were books at home, and my mother had a long set of the little dark blue and gilt Nelson Classics of English literature, most of which I read. Television was not introduced into Dunedin until 1962, and we saw it for the first time at a neighbour's house in August 1963. I volunteered for a local televised quiz show for children called *Top of the Class* in 1964 and won it twice, collecting the huge prize of 25 shillings each time, then the richest I had ever been. My parents did not own a television set until after I had left home. They listened to the news each morning on the BBC Overseas Service, and to *The Archers* once a week, but the wireless (as they called it) was in their bedroom and not for children. They had a gramophone and for a time the only records in the house were Flanders and Swann's *At the Drop of a Hat* (like every member of their generation), and the *Carnival of the Animals* of Camille Saint-Saëns with the spoken verses of Ogden Nash; later *Peter and the Wolf* was added, considered educational, especially for William, who was said to be musical, as if this were slightly unfortunate. Music was not much part of our lives. In June 1964, I joined the excited crowd outside a hotel in Princes Street where The Beatles were staying on a tour of New Zealand, but only because of the (unrealized) possibility of glimpsing famous people from the real world far away, and the idea of any of us attending their concert was never considered, either by me or my parents. Later that year I was given for my fourteenth birthday a record of John Gielgud reading passages of Shakespeare, called *The Ages of Man*, which I listened to so often that I can still recite much of it by heart in his deep resonant voice. It was one of only two records I have ever owned. For a time, Shakespearean England came close to overtaking my passion for medieval manuscripts, but a small part in a school production of *Henry V* in 1965 taught me that my career was not to be in the theatre.

The choice of King's High School was, on balance, a good one. I would catch the school bus from the concrete shelter near the foot of our garden, on the harbour road. Naughty boys sat by self-selection on the back seat and there were occasional incidents of interschool punch-ups and cap snatching. Those of us for King's High got off together where the harbour ended and walked about a mile up Bayview Road, in all weathers, my only regular exercise. In 2023, for the first time since leaving the school, I returned to see it. Not a single building remains from my time, but every house I knew so well along each side of Bayview Road is still unchanged, if smaller than I remember them. King's High was a single-sex boys' state school, which meant it was free, and my classmates were from a wide range of local backgrounds, top to bottom. I remember most of their names, McGoun, Purdie, Morrison, Benson-Pope (who later became a well-known politician), Sargison, Findlater, Moore, Jenner, Hazeldine, Foote, Gibson, and others. We all wore blue and grey uniforms which included dark blue shorts and open-neck shirts and grey pullovers and knee socks, right up to the age of leaving school. The school curriculum was probably old-fashioned even in the 1960s, and we learned Latin, French, English literature and the history of Europe. (These days, Latin has been abandoned altogether by King's High School and there is new emphasis on Māori and Pacific studies.) I hated maths and decided I could not do it. In most subjects I was generally about middle of the class in exam results, but I was a year younger than the others.

This was apparent in 1964, when most of those in my class were already gruff and fantasizing in vain about girls and I was still the little boy of the Library photograph. That was the year our Science master, Mr McCready, gave us his much-anticipated lesson on human reproduction. Of course, I knew where babies came from. My father had a wholesome little medical booklet which he lent to each of us without comment when we got to about twelve, assuring us that all we ever needed to know was there. When Michael received it, he immediately let me see it too, both of us wide-eyed with the unlikeliness of it all. When my turn came to be given the book a year and a half later, I had to pretend it was a surprise. The text explained that, when a couple get married (this was an essential prerequisite), the man has to do this and the woman that, and then there were little diagrams showing how babies eventually grow. I was aware of playground jokes about wedding nights. It all made sense. What absolutely never occurred to me – and the book certainly did not say so – is that this ever happened more than once. I assumed that, by doing what the book assured its readers had to take place after marriage, this somehow sufficed to trigger an on-going process which then resulted in children from time to time thereafter. That was surely how my mother had had a new baby, born the previous October.

On the fateful morning of the lesson at school, there was one hundred per cent attendance and absolute silence. Mr McCready, scarlet-faced, described just what the booklet had explained, including the bit about this being done after getting married. He drew diagrams on the blackboard like those in the book. I had never seen a naked woman and some practical details were vague, but the principle seemed consistent with what I knew. When he had finished, clearly to his relief, and having received more rapt attention than any other class of the year, he asked if there were any questions. Yes! I had one. My hand shot up. Everyone stared, intently curious as to what was coming. 'Why is it,' I asked, thinking of the arrival of my youngest brother, 'that some people end up having lots of children and some only one?' From my perspective of that essential misunderstanding, this was a fair question, and I really wanted to know. Mr McCready turned even more scarlet. 'Well,' he said, 'parents decide how many they want to have.' It absolutely failed to solve the mystery.

Mr McCready was a good teacher. He organized the photography club and I became very keen for a while, enjoying the magic and smell of chemicals in the dark in a tiny room we adapted for the purpose behind the aviary. Michael joined in when home from Christchurch and soon easily overtook me; in later life he became a photographer and then bought and ran his own newspaper. Mr McCready was also an expert on heraldry and had painted the coats-of-arms of famous British authors, beginning with Chaucer and Shakespeare, which decorated the school assembly hall, giving it a chivalric and even medieval air. He drew the school arms with a pale blue lion rampant under a yellow book between two coronets, with the motto *Doctrina vim promovet insitam*, which I looked up one day in the Public Library and found was from the *Odes* of Horace, 'Learning improves natural strength'. When Mr McCready eventually died in 2012, his widow sent me some of his heraldic designs for bookplates. By then I had been married twice and knew more about babies.

Another master who appears often in my diaries was Mr Graham, who taught English but introduced the arts in general into his courses. I have notes of a class he gave us on art history in October 1963 and of school outings to see *Under Milk Wood*, which he was in, and *La Traviata*, which he produced. In July 1963, quite soon after I joined King's High, we were told to choose a poem to learn for homework, any poem, and out of bravado and a certain knack for memory (now long gone), I chose Tennyson's *Lady of Shallot*, twenty nine-line stanzas, and I had to be stopped after five minutes when asked to recite my choice in class the next day. In 1964 there was an occasion that was important for me – and especially for my mother: Kaye Webb came to stay with us for a few days. She was then editor of Puffin Books and a well-known name in children's literature in Britain. She was married to the artist Ronald Searle and my mother had taught their daughter in London in the 1940s. On 21 March we held a literary party at home for people to meet her, the first time I had been allowed to attend an adult function, and we invited Mr Graham too. I remember Kaye Webb telling him that she had been present at the table when Dylan Thomas had announced his decision to write a radio play, which became *Under Milk Wood*; Mr Graham asked if she knew Christopher Fry and she said 'Of course'. She apologized to us the next day for showing off a bit, but her visit was a formative moment in my mother's gradual establishment of herself as a literary presence in New Zealand in her own right, not merely as a housewife living in exile. It also brought Reg Graham, as we learned to call him, into my parents' very rare circle of accept-able acquaintances. He died relatively young in 2007. He was a skilful portrait photographer. In 1966 he took pictures of all of us, including several of me in my room at home. Pinned up on the wall behind me can be seen postcards of the French Book of Hours in the Dunedin Public Library and copies of manuscript pages and an early printed map which I had made myself.

I had become enchanted with making these copies in the Public Library, somehow pretending to myself that they were almost originals. The reference librarian was then Mary Ronnie, who was very Scottish, assisted by tiny Ngaira Mercer, and if they were bemused or irritated by this persistent schoolboy, they showed me nothing but courtesy and kindness. They had both worked in the Library since 1942. They would take manuscripts out of their cases and let me sit upstairs slowly

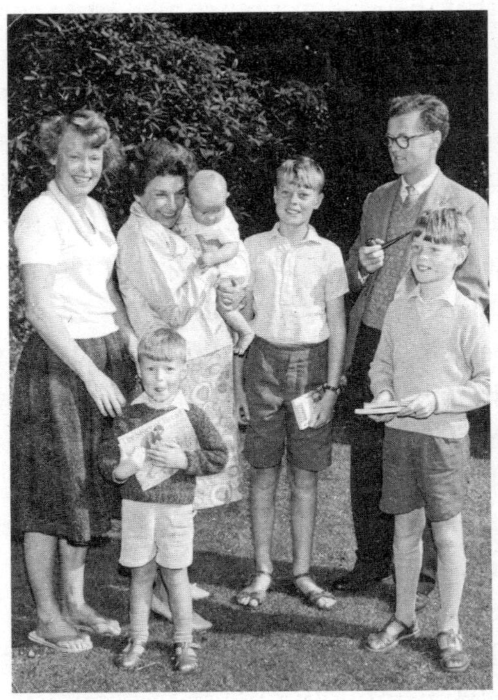

The author's family with Kaye Webb, visiting New Zealand in 1964:
from left, Joan de Hamel, Richard (foreground), Kaye Webb holding Quentin,
Christopher, Francis de Hamel and William.

drawing meticulous facsimiles of script and decoration, using fountain pen ink and carefully labelling my sheets with information about which book each copy came from and its attributed date. As a lesson in how to look closely at a work of art or script, it is hard to beat. If our family had stayed in England, it is unlikely that I would ever have found my way as an early teenager into the forbidding manuscript galleries of the British Museum, not least because an interest in the Middle Ages could easily have been sated by medieval churches and other buildings all across the country; but if I had, it is inconceivable that a boy of fourteen or fifteen would ever have been allowed to handle and copy the precious originals. This was a public library in Dunedin and Mr Reed, in making his benefactions, had always emphasized that the manuscripts should be freely accessible to anyone. The Library offered a loan service for framed pictures, which one could unhook from the walls and check out, like books. I recall asking Miss Ronnie whether this applied also to the fragments from medieval manuscripts hanging in frames on the stairs. There was some discussion, and it was agreed that it might. I came home on the bus one day with a glitteringly illuminated leaf from a fifteenth-century Rhenish choir book, and on another occasion with a bifolium from a Latin Gospel Book of the late ninth century, to the astonishment of my parents. On the back of each frame was pasted the usual library issue slip stamped with the due date of return or renewal. These manuscripts hung on the wall of my bedroom and I lived with them, loved them, and made copies.

I still have some of the careful facsimiles I made. Most are from Bibles. There are red and blue initials with elaborate meandering penwork from a small Bible of about 1270, probably Parisian, bought by the Library in 1952. There are others, rather better, from a Bible made in England around 1240, from the collection of Belton House in Lincolnshire, acquired for Dunedin in 1954. My caption records dutifully that the manuscript had belonged to Gilbert Burnet (1643–1715), bishop of Salisbury and author of *The History of the Reformation of the Church of England*, an attractive connection much emphasized by Mr Reed, but (I now realize) the Burnet bookplate was probably a spurious insertion of recent times. Some of my hand-made copies were taken from printed items, or even from published manuscript facsimiles owned by the Library. There is a map of Elizabethan London in 1563, which I inscribed on the back

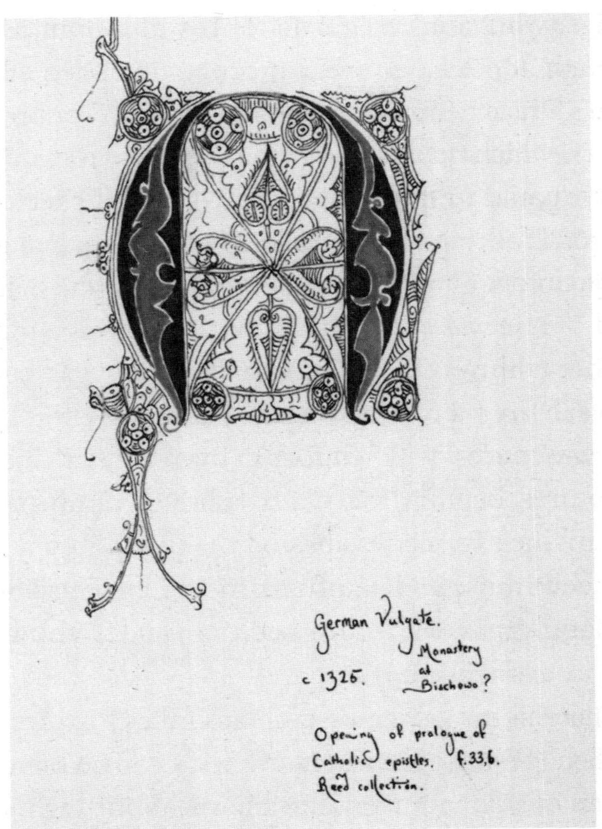

An initial in the lectern Bible in the Dunedin Public Library,
copied by the author as a teenager.

in November 1964 – my Shakespearean phase – and several woodcut initials copied from the Library's Tyndale Bible of 1538, which I can date from my diary to a Saturday in early August 1965. Two weeks later I wrote, 'Spilt black ink over most of my Codex Sinaiticus': among the many frustrations of adolescence, this is an unusual one.

In so far as religion was part of my childhood, we were Anglican, because that is what the English were. We attended St Matthew's Church in central Dunedin, not every Sunday but not infrequently. I went to Confirmation classes there in 1964 and enjoyed my often-animated discussions with the vicar, Maurice Betteridge, who later moved on to Australia. Our assembly at King's High at 9 o'clock every morning included a hymn and the Lord's Prayer. I joined a school Christian group called the Crusaders, which met at lunchtime on Tuesdays, a more interesting alternative to sport or other disagreeable exercise, and for some years I followed short daily Bible readings put out by the Scripture Union. I am not sure how far my interest in the early Bibles of the Reed Collection was anything to do with religion, or whether faith was in any way made more vivid by spending Saturdays in the Library among manuscript Bibles, but neither of these was mutually incompatible. Reasonable familiarity with the Scriptures, begun then, has been a very useful part of my subsequent life as a medievalist.

Mr Reed himself was a fundamentalist Christian from a Baptist family, passing through stages as a Methodist and independent evangelical. His nationwide publishing company, from which his money came in later life, had evolved out of a Sunday School supply business. He wrote, 'The Bible has been the means of giving purpose to life and fortitude in death; of changing men's lives and the destiny of nations.' In a dissenting Protestantism there are no relics and few ancient church buildings and holy sites, and early Bibles are often the touchstone of shared faith throughout history. It is very different from the traditional and patrician bibliophily of Sir George Grey, educated in the classics and High Church Anglicanism. Reed's first antiquarian purchase was in 1907 when he acquired a little 1599 New Testament in English, followed later that year by a sixteenth-century Foxe's *Book of Martyrs*, polemically Protestant. Reed would never have understood wanting a Latin Missal. His most emotionally charged acquisition of all was the fifteenth-century Wycliffite Gospel Book in Middle English, which was bought for the Library in a nail-bitingly close auction at Sotheby's in 1956. His little book on Wycliffe uses phrases like 'morning star of the Reformation'. This mattered to him. The Reed Collection can have no explicit religious agenda in public ownership and it includes much which is not biblical, such as Dickens and Samuel Johnson, but it does not feel out of place in a learned city founded by Presbyterians.

The first medieval biblical manuscript owned by Reed was bought by him in 1925. It is a large Latin New Testament of the early fourteenth century and was usually on exhibition in the Library gallery. I made a number of copies from its red and blue penwork initials, and in 1965 decided to attempt an entire leaf. I began on 8 September in the school holidays; 'copied part of MS at Library', says my diary. On 10 September I went into town with Michael to see the new James Bond *Goldfinger*, which opens with a girl in a bath and features Jill Masterson in a black bikini, who is later covered in gold leaf (like a manuscript), and Pussy Galore in the cockpit and under a parachute. I was evidently growing older. However, after we left the cinema that afternoon, I went back to the Library: 'Did a bit more of the MS'; and on 15 September, 'more MS'.

5

Koronowo

The early fourteenth-century Latin New Testament I was carefully copying in the Dunedin Public Library in 1965 had been brought to New Zealand in the 1920s and was then deliberately cut up by A. H. Reed. It is a shameful story, really. In the belief that seeing and touching even a little bit of a medieval Bible would be an inspiration to students training for the Protestant ministry, Mr Reed carefully took his manuscript apart soon after its purchase and distributed specimen leaves and gatherings to various theological libraries around New Zealand. What remained in the Public Library when I was attempting my facsimile page was less than half of the manuscript as it had been when Reed acquired it. It is odd about Bibles. One might think that the text most sacred to evangelicals would be inviolable and therefore scrupulously venerated intact. Evidently, however, like saints' relics in the Middle Ages, a Bible is infinitely divisible without losing its holiness. The custom of breaking up Bibles into hallowed fragments probably goes back to Free Church piety of the nineteenth century. The two earliest published 'leaf books', specimen pages from rare books prepared for sale to collectors, were both formed from early Bible leaves, issued in 1852 and 1865 by the Quaker bibliographer Francis Fry (1803–86), for fellow Christians. Many others have followed. Sample leaves from old and rare Bibles are commonly found today for sale singly or in sets on religious websites, especially outside Europe, where many librarians of old collections regard dismember-ment as reprehensible or utterly incomprehensible. However, it seems different when viewed from far away. In New Zealand or America, for example, fragments of early Bibles can supply that thrilling sense of shared experience with Christians of long ago which in the Old World is captured by medieval church build-ings and ancient shrines and sacred sites.

Apart from the fact that it is Latin, which Mr Reed could not read anyway, he was right that the manuscript he distributed around New Zealand is an immediately recognizable ancestor of a modern church Bible (Plate 11). The appearance and format of Reed's manuscript could be those of no other kind of book; it is unambiguously a Bible. Its pages are about 17 inches by nearly 12, about the same size as any large Bible one might see being used on a lectern in a church now. The text is in two columns, as Bibles usually still are, each here of thirty-nine lines, and the text is divided into chapters numbered exactly as they are today, opening with big, decorated initials in red and blue. As in a modern Bible too, the names of the books are written across the upper margins of every page, in red in this manuscript. No other text, even in the Middle Ages, looked quite like this. It is conveniently arranged for locating specific passages required for the liturgy or study. The tall columns are narrow, just under 4 inches in width, easy on the eye and suitable for public reading. The manuscript used to be exhib-ited in Dunedin beside the Reed Collection's printed copies of the Great Bible of 1539 and the King James Bible of 1611, both of similarly large size in Gothic script, not unlike this, and 'appointed to be read in Churches'. It served as a graphic and reassuring affirmation of the apparently unchanging and familiar appearance of the Word of God from the past of very long ago and across the world. When I knew it first, I did not realize (or care) that it was only a small residue of what was once a complete New Testament.

However, Mr Reed would have been entirely wrong in supposing Bibles had always looked like this, or had even existed at all as comprehensive texts for much of their history. For most of the first thousand years or more of Christianity, the Bible was not a single book but an assorted collection of texts in different sizes and formats. There are one or two very early 'pandects', as they are called, with the entirety of the biblical corpus in single volumes (such as the fourth-century Codex Sinaiticus in Greek, or the Codex Amiatinus in Latin of *c.* 700), but they are the rarest of exceptions. These famous patriarchs were not ancestors (as Mr Reed supposed) but stately maiden aunts, who died without issue. For most purposes, the forebears of the Bible were multiple volumes, usually copied separately and kept in chests or cupboards from which they could be taken out one by one and used in any order. The Latin word *bibliotheca* meant both 'Bible' and 'library'. The Scriptures were never unknown or unimportant, but even monks and priests would have been most familiar with them from listening to public readings selected for use in the liturgy and from studying biblical commentaries, of which there were many. These were unexpectedly important in the history of Bible transmission. A good example is the twelfth-century monastic manuscript in Auckland of the commentary on the book of Job by Gregory the Great (d. 604) – the manuscript bought by Grey in 1863 in the mistaken belief it was bound for Henry V – which offers its readers layers of practical meaning from the Bible text. This was what most medieval monks wanted to know from the sacred Scriptures. Gregory's commentary was much more useful to them than merely following a repetitive and seemingly pointless biblical narrative of

an old man being unilaterally tested by God in alien circumstances very long ago.

A characteristic early biblical manuscript is a fragment of
three parchment leaves from a Latin Gospel Book, acquired for
the Dunedin Public Library in 1957. It was made in northern
France in the late ninth century, and was the earliest European
manuscript known to be in New Zealand until quite recently
(Plate 12). The leaves used to be framed on the Library stairs
and are among items I sometimes borrowed to take home.
They look nothing like a Bible as we might know it today. The
pages are of medium size, about 11½ by 8½ inches, with thirty
lines in a single squarish block, not in the tall double-column
Bible arrangement familiar now. The script is not some formal
blackletter but a Carolingian minuscule, not unlike the Roman
type you are reading right now. The opening of the Gospel of
Mark, fortuitously present, is preceded by part of a list of forty-
six chapter headings that bear no relation to modern chapter
division. Their purpose is not to subdivide the text but to provide
cross references for matching up parallel passages which occur in
more than one Gospel. This custom goes back to Greek and then
Latin Gospel Books of great antiquity, often tabulated as lists at
the start of manuscripts. One of the Reed leaves has this archaic
number 'viii' in red ink beside the opening of what we would
know as John chapter 4. However, this manuscript was not for
study in private. It was made to be read aloud liturgically in a
church, and we know this because the leaves happen to include
part of the Passion story from towards the end of Matthew. The
different spoken voices of the narrative are marked up with the
symbols '+', 'c' and 's' for performing publicly in the liturgy on
Good Friday, a primitive precursor of Passion plays. Such marks
are common in medieval Missals. They occur in both volumes
of the Missal of Charles de Neufchâtel in Auckland, and in

the fifteenth-century English Missal in the Turnbull Library in Wellington. There are several conflicting explanations of what these symbols originally meant, perhaps once indications of pitch, possibly *celeriter* (quickly) and *sursum* (on a higher note), for example, or conceivably the voices of different speakers in church, such as *cantor* and *sacerdos*. Their use here is evidence that this was not a book for private reading but to be listened to during a service, essentially a record of an oral text.

There were two primary mid-medieval initiatives to gather up the components of Scripture into sets of huge matching volumes. Both were principally to furnish control texts to standardize reading aloud in the liturgy, in the hope that all Western Christendom could listen to identical words when they heard extracts from the Bible in church. The first campaign was under Charlemagne, king of the Franks from 768 to 814 and emperor from 800. Big Bibles in several or many volumes were made probably first in Tours in central France (at least eighteen survive) and then elsewhere across the Carolingian empire, especially in Lotharingia and south-western Germany. The second initiative emanated from Rome in the time of the reformer Hildebrand of Sovana (*c.* 1015–85), pope as Gregory VII from 1073. These Bibles of the second wave were truly vast, known in Italy as 'Atlantic' Bibles, not from the ocean but from the classical giant Atlas, mentioned in the Maude Roll, so huge he could hold up the sky. Copies in multiple volumes were initially distributed from Italy and then, by the late eleventh and early twelfth centuries, were made across Europe, especially for Benedictine monasteries and the newer orders of Cistercians and Cluniacs. They are enormous, heavy to shift, and they vary immensely in the sequence of their biblical texts.

You might think New Zealand would not be an obvious place to discover a Carolingian Bible, or evidence of one. In early 2012, during re-cataloguing of the rare books in Auckland Public Library, the staff there made out traces of inscribed parchment cut into ribbons for use in strengthening the tight inner folds of gatherings of an incunable printed probably in Basel in or soon before 1480. This book had been given to Auckland in 1911 by Henry Shaw, Sir George Grey's bookish disciple (whom we will meet properly in Chapter 8). The Library staff called in the medievalist Alexandra Barratt, of the University of Waikato. She found more pieces and identified them as biblical and Carolingian, with parts of Exodus, Leviticus, Numbers, Ezekiel and Hosea. She then wrote to me in London, and we matched them with other fragments from book bindings now in Munich. In 2023, further pieces of the same Bible were discovered in a binding in University College in Dublin. They are clearly all salvage from the first volume (probably of two) of a Latin Bible of the early ninth century. It was made in south Germany, derived no doubt from an exemplar sent from France, and it closely resembles productions from the lakeside nunnery of Kochel, south of Munich towards the border with Austria. If so, the manuscript might have been copied by women. This unexpected relic of a Carolingian Bible now takes the prize as the oldest European manuscript so far recorded in Australasia.

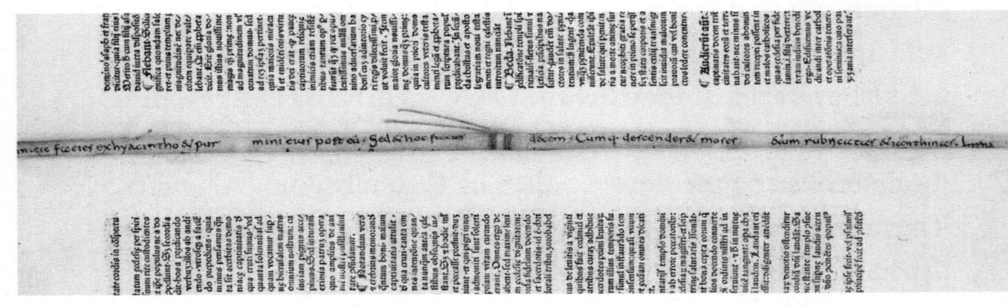

Narrow strips from a ninth-century Bible discovered in 2012 as strengthening in the sewing folds of an incunable of *c*. 1480 in Auckland.

The Auckland incunable belonged to the abbey of Benedikt-beuern, which is about four miles north-east of Kochel. (The library is famous today for having given its name to the Carmina Burana, which it owned.) The incunable's contemporary binding was made at the abbey, and the remains of the ninth-century Bible were probably cut up in Benediktbeuern itself. Again, it may seem unexpected that committed Christians would deliberately destroy a Bible. The motives, however, were very different from those of A. H. Reed wielding his own scissors in the twentieth century. The monks of Benediktbeuern owned an illuminated manuscript Bible dated 1446 and also a new printed Bible of *c.* 1474 (both still survive). They clearly (and understandably) preferred the most up-to-date and accurate copies and had no use for an old and obsolete odd volume, except as a convenient source of parchment. The Bible text might be holy, but the book was not. A similar but later cull lies behind the three ninth-century Gospel leaves in Dunedin, which were pragmatically re-purposed as parchment folders for administrative documents in the late seventeenth century, seemingly in a French cathedral archive, quite possibly where the volume had once been new eight hundred years earlier.

By the time of these dismemberments, old pages from Carolingian manuscripts would hardly have been recognizable as Scriptural at all. The physical Bible, as we know it now, was effectively an invention of around 1200. The story is complex and I have told it elsewhere, but the gist is that by the mid-twelfth century, the old monastic monopoly of learning was being broken by the new foundation of cathedral schools, which taught that the framework of historical narrative in the Bible was an essential prerequisite to subsequent study of allegory and moral interpretation. At the same moment, the number of texts in circulation in Europe became for the first time more numerous than any one person could reasonably read and remember. They faced, as we do in our own time, what is now called information overload.

In an attempt to deal with these two problems, a new kind of Bible was devised. All the components of Scripture were collected up into a new, logical and consecutive historical order, from the Creation to the predicted end of the world in Revelation. Introductory prologues were inserted and standardized throughout. Pages were divided into two columns (as was the custom then), and the script made so compact that the entire Bible could be compressed into a single volume. The texts were then equipped with various twelfth-century devices to allow them to be rapidly searched and cited, including breaking the text into numbered chapters (exactly as they are today but not used until then) and the insertion of the names of each book in the upper margins of every page. The Bible became a single book instead of a set of books, and it was made usable for private study and quick looking up of references.

An early and primitive example of this new biblical format is in the library of the Bible Society in Wellington. It dates from about 1210 and belonged to the Cistercian abbey of Holme Cultram in Cumbria, where the monks had never seen anything quite like it. They have added mnemonic verses on the front flyleaf to help them understand and learn the books in their new sequence. The page layout is clumsy and the chapter numbers are inconsistent. A very much more professional-looking manuscript of about the same date is also among the books given by Henry Shaw to Auckland. This time the volume is elegant and ordered, illuminated with gold, and it was made in northern France, possibly Paris.

This newly devised format for a Bible was then disseminated from Paris in the thirteenth century. It is one of book history's absolute triumphs of design and convenience. The format has never changed, even now; it survived the transition into print and other languages and most Bibles today remain almost unaltered in appearance eight hundred years later. Open almost any new printed Bible today. What we see is an early thirteenth-century book, compactly executed on very thin white pages, like the 'uterine' parchment of the time, with writing in two columns (as books were then and seldom are now), the texts in their modern sequence from Genesis to Revelation, chapter numbers and running headings, as still used, all devices of the late twelfth-century revolution, and even the binding of the modern Bible is quite likely to be in red or blue with gold letters, the three principal colours of thirteenth-century manuscripts. It is no surprise that when A. H. Reed looked at his manuscript, he recognized at once that it was a familiar Bible.

Reed's manuscript has the prologues, chapter numbers and page layout descended unambiguously from the innovations of around 1200, but it is a big book in more than one volume, and in this it still resembles the older Romanesque monastic Bibles for lectern use. It clearly has mixed ancestry, like so many of humankind. The order of its texts is nearly but not entirely of Parisian descent. When complete, it comprised I–II Maccabees, the Gospels, the Catholic Epistles, Revelation, the Epistles of Paul, and Acts, in that order. That oddity alone suggests monastic use and manufacture probably some distance from Paris, as we will see.

The earliest modern description we have of the manuscript is from its sale at Sotheby's in 1923, when it had 139 leaves and was described as being German in origin. Even then, it was seriously incomplete. One can work out the probable structure of the volume at that moment from traces of sequential numbers and catchwords surviving in the lower margins at the end of each gathering, and from gaps in the text, where the extent of what is missing can be measured from a printed text of the Latin Bible. In the palaeographical formula of a manuscript collation, as it is called, it would be expressed as i^4 [of 8, lacking ii–v], ii^6 [of 8, lacking iv–v], iii^8, iv^6, v^6 [of 8, lacking iii and vi], vi^8, vii^4 [of 8, lacking iii–vi], $viii$–xi^8, xii^6, xiii^8, xiv^9 [of 10, lacking vi], xv^8, xvi^2 [of 8, lacking ii–vii], xvii^7 [of 8, lacking viii], $xviii$–xx^3, xxi^1 [of unknown number, lacking all after i]. As a diagram of the volume's twenty-one gatherings in 1923, this would translate as:

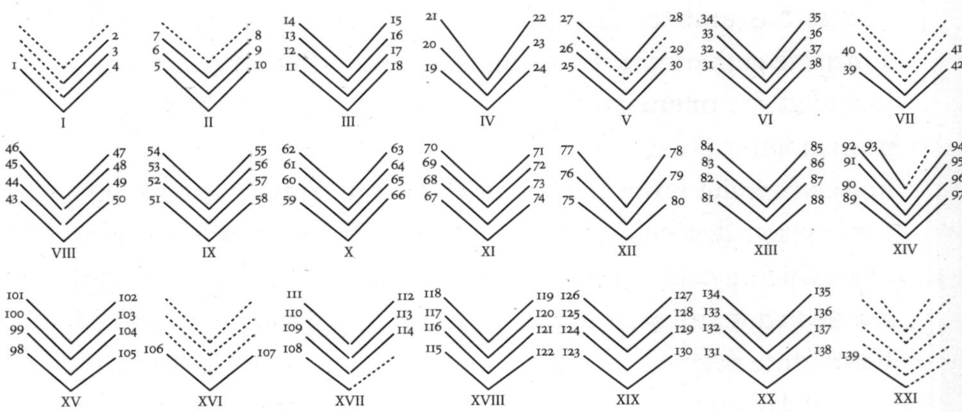

Most gatherings were originally of eight leaves each, which is normal in many medieval manuscripts. Gatherings iv and xii were of six leaves and gathering xiv was originally of ten. The last gathering could also have been of ten, or two sixes: we do not know, but the amount of remaining text might have required it. Such variation is not unusual but is perhaps especially characteristic of manuscripts made locally away from the more formulaic professional workshops of the big cities, where scribes would often buy in prepared parchment neatly folded in advance.

Already by the 1920s, the volume was lacking at least twenty-seven leaves, probably fairly obviously, for there are jagged stubs where pages have been roughly torn out. This may have first persuaded A. H. Reed that there was no harm in dividing it up further to distribute specimens of the manuscript around the country. To sustain the simile of acclimatizing new plants on Kawau Island, this was like Grey offering cuttings of trees and bushes to nurseries across New Zealand, hoping that some would yield fruitful results. Reed began by removing loose gatherings from the end. The minutes of Knox Theological College in Dunedin, the seminary for the Presbyterian Church, record receipt of biblical gifts from Reed on 23 August 1928 and 26 November 1929. He gave them folios 131–139, the last complete gathering and the single leaf from the very end. These included the opening of Acts with big initials for the text and its prologue. These leaves were exhibited (or rather, not exhibited) when the governor general, Lord Bledisloe, visited Knox College in 1934. He was ushered by the master over to the glass case which usually displayed the manuscript, to find that high-spirited students had removed Reed's donation and replaced it with white mice.

The previous gathering but one, folios 115–122 in the diagram above, was given by Reed to the library of the evangelical Bible College of the Church of Christ, in Glen Leith, Dunedin, founded in 1925. In my own time as a resident in Knox College in 1968–72, it was on deposit there together with the Knox portion, and after the closure of Glen Leith in 1971 it became the property of the Hewitson Library at Knox, still situated within the college in Dunedin but administered since 2013 by the Presbyterian Church of New Zealand in Wellington. It is safely there but, by a twist of fate, Knox College's own nine leaves seem to have disappeared again.

The intervening gathering, folios 123–130, is currently unaccounted for. In a letter of 18 December 1950, Reed recalled the recipient of one fragment as the Baptist College in Auckland and another as possibly the Canterbury Museum, 'but I wouldn't be quite sure now.' There is no trace of it now at either the Canterbury Museum in Christchurch or in the library of the Carey Baptist College in Auckland, founded in 1926. It is probable that it is somewhere in New Zealand and if this chapter can flush it out, I would be delighted, for I have sought it for sixty years. It will have the text from I Timothy 3:16 to Hebrews 11:32.

Having detached the end gatherings, Reed then gave folios 1–47 from the beginning, together with the manuscript's binding, to Trinity Methodist College in Auckland. Presentation of this 'manuscript copy of portions of the Holy Scriptures' was announced and a vote of thanks to Mr and Mrs A. H. Reed was given at the Methodist Conference meeting in Dunedin in February 1931. The College dates back to the mid-nineteenth century, originally for training Māori converts to work as teachers and ministers. In the early 1970s, the Methodists joined in partnership with the Anglican seminary of St John's, and the two colleges are now united in Auckland, where this portion of the manuscript is preserved and valued.

This then left sixty-seven leaves in Reed's possession, folios 48–114 of the volume. As the diagram above shows, folios 48–50 would have been loose and unanchored, since the conjoint pairs of the same leaves were by now in Auckland. Sometime in the 1940s, Reed gave folio 48 to Otago University Library, including the opening of Luke's Gospel. Therefore, sixty-six remaining leaves formed part of the bequest to the Dunedin Public Library in 1948. The manuscript is described as being on exhibition in 1949. However, Reed always regarded his donations as still practically his own property – a frustration familiar to many curators of public collections in dealing with benefactors. He continued to give away leaves from each end, or to instruct the Library staff to do so. Folio 103 was presented in 1969 as the Public Library's Centennial Gift to Otago University. I was there at the time and remember the occasion. Folios 49, 112 and 114 were given to individuals at Reed's request, including to his local Baptist minister who, with his wife, helped him greatly in his old age. This leaf (112), with Galatians 2–4, was bought back in April 2012. Thus, there are now sixty-six leaves in the Public Library.

The dispersal of fragments around New Zealand is not unlike the scattering of immigrant families who arrive together in one place and, within a generation or two, are all around the country, some becoming part of society and well-known, others seemingly vanishing from sight. In time, one descendant commonly sets out to re-establish contact and to look into the family history and its earlier ancestry.

The portion of the manuscript given to Trinity College in Auckland is the one which initiates the investigation. The twinned Methodist and Anglican colleges share the beautiful site of St John's on the hillside in Meadowbank, an upmarket suburb of Auckland, founded by the Anglicans in 1845; their wooden chapel of 1847 is still in use. The rare books are in the Kinder Library. Its glassed-off reading-room is called 'Te Aho Mārama' ('the quiet space', I am told), looking out over gardens enclosed by tree ferns and Norfolk pines with a distant glimpse through the foliage of Auckland harbour and the volcanic Rangitoto Island far below. It is very different indeed from the setting of a medieval European monastery but has something of the same sense of calm and spiritual purpose. It transpires that the librarian was at school with my brother Michael's wife; things like that happen in New Zealand.

The manuscript's forty-seven leaves (and a flyleaf) are still contained within the sides of its sixteenth-century binding of wooden boards covered with dark brown leather stamped with roll-tooled borders including Adam and Eve, with the words 'PER ADAM MORS', the Crucifixion, with 'PER CHRIST[UM] VITA', and its Old Testament antetype, the brazen serpent, with a reference to Numbers 21. The binding is north German or central European. It is fitted with metal corner-pieces and edging with protruding bosses, which would support it safely on a lectern. There are traces of old repairs re-using paper scraps of a sixteenth- or possibly seventeenth-century printed liturgical book, which must have been at hand, perhaps in a sacristy. Other bits of the same printing are clinging to the leaves in the Dunedin Public Library and at Knox College.

Inside the front cover is a coloured bookplate of the 'John C. Curtiss Library, Chicago', with a coat of arms, as if this were an institution. He was an individual, however: John Christlieb Curtiss (1874–1923), an executive at Caltex Oil. It was his widow, Harriet Elizabeth, who sent the manuscript for sale at Sotheby's, 11 December 1923, lot 299, when it was bought by the bookseller Thomas Thorp, as is reflected in his private price code in pencil here as 'gg/-/-', for Thorp used the phrase 'go to it, boys', whereby 'g' = 1, 'o' = 2, and so on: the manuscript made £11, confirmed by Sotheby's own copy of the catalogue. Reed recalled paying £15 in 1925. The late owner had been the son of the Reverend Professor Samuel Ives Curtiss (1844–1904), of the Chicago Theological Seminary, an Old Testament scholar and writer on biblical manuscripts. Curtiss senior studied in Leipzig, where his doctorate of 1876 was on the name of the Maccabees, and he had then stayed on in Berlin for two further years. As our manuscript has nineteenth-century notes in German and opens with the books of Maccabees, his own research topic, there can be little doubt it had been acquired by him, perhaps in Leipzig or Berlin.

Towards the centre of the otherwise blank front flyleaf in Auckland is an inscription, in large handwriting, of the first half of the nineteenth century: *Ist im Jahr 1325 von Pater Nicolaus geschrieben im Kloster zu Bischewo, zur Ehre un[sere]r heil-[igen] Jungfrau Maria*, 'It was written in the year 1325 by Father Nicolaus in the monastery of Bischewo, to the honour of our holy Virgin Mary'. This is in modern German and the wording is not medieval: 'Pater' is what a monk might be called in the nineteenth century, not the fourteenth. Could it be based loosely on some medieval Latin colophon once at the end of the volume, among the leaves already lost by 1923? A date in the early fourteenth century is certainly stylistically credible. Now turn to folio 28r of the portion in the Dunedin Public Library (folio 77r of the whole book). A marginal note there says, in slightly odd German, *Dieses Buch ist über 3 Jahre 500 Jahr alt, 1820* – that is, that in 1820 this book was calculated to be more than 503 years old, not quite consistent with 1325, but bringing the estimated year more exactly to 1316.

With this, it falls into place with the most gratifying precision. Byszewo ('Bischewo' in German) was the original name for the Cistercian monastery of Koronowo, dedicated to the Virgin Mary, on the River Brda in northern Poland, about fifteen miles north of the modern city of Bydgoszcz. The new name was being used by at least 1383 in honour of the crown of the Virgin, venerated at the abbey, and so the archaic 'Bischewo' would have been authentic for a colophon from the first half of the century, a detail unlikely to have been known or invented in retrospect. Almost no records survive from the early medieval scriptorium of the abbey, except the commemoration of a single scribe. His name was Nicolaus. The monks remembered that in 1313 he had copied a Missal, begun in the time of Abbot Berthold and finished under Abbot Conrad, and that he afterwards made two more manuscripts, the five books of Moses and – imagine my thrill of triumph in finding this in a few blessed words of Latin in a publication in Polish – a New Testament, written by him at Byszewo in 1316. That must be it. We have it.

Koronowo Abbey was sacked and plundered during the wars with the Teutonic Order in 1409–11 and again by the Swedes in 1655–57 and was occupied by troops in 1703–9, and some of the rough mutilation of the manuscript might have occurred at any time to furnish waste parchment. It makes effective gun wadding (among other uses). The abbey finally closed in 1819. By then, following the Congress of Vienna in 1814–15, the north-eastern Polish province around Koronowo had become part of the kingdom of Prussia, which is why the manuscript was inscribed in German in 1820 and was for sale in or near Berlin when Samuel Curtiss was a student there.

Everything about the manuscript is consistent with Cistercian book production. The parchment has a characteristic home-made quality. The pages are thick and crackle as you turn them. I would guess they are made from the skins of sheep, animals farmed in quantity by medieval Cistercians (and modern New Zealanders). The edges of pages sometimes preserve the arcs of the animals' necks and legs; accidental cuts or flaws are quickly stitched by the parchment-maker and marked off with outlines in red to warn the scribe to write around the holes. A professional workshop would usually have avoided using flawed parchment altogether: Cistercian monks seem almost to have relished it, as if by a lofty and deliberate indifference to the vain trappings of refinement. The same features occur in that early thirteenth-century Bible made by the Cistercians of Holme Cultram. In both manuscripts, the monastic scribes use the *punctus flexus* punctuation, a distinctive mark a bit like a comma over a dot, which was characteristic of Carthusian and Cistercian books.

The large red and blue initials without pictures or gold conform also to the understated preference of the famously austere Cistercian Order.

Since Brother Nicolaus also copied a Pentateuch in 1316, it is very likely these were intended as the first and last volumes of an entire lectern Bible. We do not know whether the text between them was ever made. This opening page in Auckland has a sixteenth-century title, *Machabeorum libri 2° et Novum Testamentum*. If it was always to be a separate volume, the books of Maccabees might have seemed a preliminary to the Gospels, as they describe events in the Holy Land much nearer in date to the life of Christ than most of the Old Testament.

Brother Nicolaus must (obviously) have had access to at least one other Bible to copy from. The medieval Cistercians clearly had highly organized lines of manuscript loans following back along the chains of foundation. The Cistercian Abbey of Pontigny sent manuscripts to a daughter-house as far east as Hungary. Byszewo / Koronowo was established by the monks of Sulejów, in central Poland, founded in turn in the 1170s from Morimond Abbey in eastern France, itself (like Pontigny) an original foundation from Cîteaux. An exemplar might have been lent from somewhere along that trail. There is a large twelfth-century lectern Bible, probably from the library of Morimond itself, now in the municipal library of Chaumont, in France. It too begins with the Pentateuch as a separate volume, and its fifth and last volume comprises the New Testament in the sequence of the Gospels, Acts, Catholic Epistles, Revelation and Epistles of Paul: with only one difference, this is the same as the order in the Byszewo / Koronowo Bible and might reflect a tradition of that monastic family. The exemplar was most decidedly not the little thirteenth-century study Bible also from Koronowo Abbey and now in the library in Kórnik, between

Bydgoszcz and Wrocław. It is almost the only other manuscript known to have been at the abbey. It opens with Tobit and Maccabees and it includes the Gospels, Acts, Catholic Epistles, Revelation, Epistles of Paul, Ruth, Books of Kings and other Old Testament texts, in that sequence, concluding perversely with the Pentateuch. That is all so eccentric it makes Nicolaus's Bible seem positively normal.

The large initials in our manuscript are in bright red and deep blue in which blocks of colour with complex outlines abut neatly up against matching patterns in the contrasting colour, interlocking together like the pieces of jigsaw puzzles. They are then decorated further by elaborate penwork in both colours around the initials and chasing and exploding up and down the margins, bursting regularly into cascades of little buds and curls. This can be drawn very quickly, and I too became very practised in doing it in my childhood copies from the manuscript. I used to add flamboyant penwork like this to my school textbooks. I can still draw it deftly on my notes during tedious meetings or lectures, all learned from Byszewo. Initials and decoration in the style are common throughout northern Europe from the mid- to late thirteenth century onwards, right through to the handmade additions to copies of the Gutenberg Bible in the mid-fifteenth. Early examples seem to occur in an arc extending north-west from the region of Champagne (which might include Morimond) up towards Reims, Cambrai, Tournai and Lille, often in Bibles and service books, commonly but not uniquely Cistercian. A trail of copies of copies has reached Poland by 1316. The migration of pattern is as fascinating and mysterious as the migration of birds.

This was a lectern Bible. It was not for shelving in a library or for consultation on a reader's lap (like the little Bible in Kórnik), but was kept on a lectern or sloping desk, as the metal bosses on the binding indicate, and was intended for reading aloud.

Nicolaus had previously copied a Missal and he here again uses the formal Gothic script of liturgical use. Long Latin words are sometimes marked up with red stress marks in red or black, such as *manifestáta* or *testámur* (in I John 1, for instance), for fluency in enunciating the text. Latin numbers are generally written out in full words rather than as numerals: even a reader familiar with Latin might stumble on suddenly encountering 'MDC' while reading Revelation 14 aloud, for example, but could unhesitatingly enunciate *mille sexcenta* as it is written here. Although Nicolaus was copying entirely in Latin, he betrays traces of the native German or Polish of himself or the audience in his monastery: he spells *ewangelium* and *ewangelista* with a 'w', pronounced as 'v' in Polish, as in 'Byszewo' and 'Koronowo'. That must be how the manuscript sounded aloud. Several sections are marked up in sixteenth- or possibly seventeenth-century hands with dates during the ecclesiastical year, such as passages from Revelation and the Catholic Epistles suggested for the weeks after Easter. These correspond so loosely to the liturgical lections of the printed Cistercian breviary in the sixteenth century that they probably indicate use in the refectory, read out to the monks during meals, when the current and much shorter biblical lessons of the chapel services might commonly be extended to include prologues and full chapters, as marked here. These notes and the new binding show that the manuscript was still being used in the monastery two hundred or more years after it was made.

It takes about five hours today to drive in a rental car from the new Berlin airport to Koronowo, following back along a likely route taken by the manuscript out of Poland after 1819. For a large part of my lifetime, East Germany and Poland were unimaginable and inaccessible behind the Iron Curtain. Now it is all within the seamless European Union and you cross the Polish border with little indication of having done so beyond a change of language in the road signs. Northern Poland is unexpectedly monoglot. Outside the big cities, few people appear to know much English or any German, and if older generations were once taught Russian, they prefer to forget it. The landscape of the countryside, after you have turned north beyond Poznań and are approaching Bydgoszcz, is not unlike that of rural New Zealand, richly agricultural and gently hilly. It is planted mainly with cereal crops – wheat or maize – in fields of such strange shapes, interrupted by random clumps of trees, that one could believe they have not changed much since the Middle Ages. The parchment of our manuscript grew up here. There are few animals visible now (and therefore little need for fences), except for parties of ducks and geese chattering along the village kerbsides and ungainly storks in their messy nests balanced on high telegraph poles.

It is a strange sensation, so many decades after first encountering the word in the manuscript in the library in Auckland, to see a road sign to Byszewo. It is a small cluster of houses, probably not much more extensive than it was in 1253, when a first Cistercian monastery was founded here, beside the lake. Monks were in residence by 1256. The parish church of the Holy Trinity, apparently part of the original monastery, has the date 1253 above its west entrance. Push in through a heavy door and the church is small and dark inside, with a recent icon of the venerated Polish Pope John Paul II. In 1288, as a result of a trade-off of territories with the bishop, the monastic community of Byszewo was moved from here about four miles to the east, up through the woods and across and down into the valley of the River Brda. Initially it kept the name Byszewo, as it was still called when the manuscript was made there, but doubtless confusion with the village of its former site soon helped the adoption of the new name of Koronowo, which is now a substantial market town. Its modern central square, encircled by pastel-coloured gabled houses, has leaping synchronized fountains through which children run in and out, squealing in the summer sunshine, a coincidental echo of the water systems which entranced so many Cistercians in the Middle Ages.

To locate any Cistercian site, look for the river – in Koronowo a few minutes' walk south of the town square. The large abbey church survives intact, mostly built in brick in the late Gothic style with tall round-topped windows, trimmed in white, and tiled roofs almost as intensely red as the colour in the manuscript. It is all on a scale infinitely greater and more extravagant than that of the tiny church in Byszewo. You enter either on the north side through a kind of spacious cathedral close or down the steps from the quite small west door on the street frontage. The first impression of the interior is of a strong smell of incense, for the church is still in use. The nave is very high and long, painted in a pale cream colour with the ceiling details picked out in gold. There is a grey and red stone floor. There are wooden pews with red cushions. The church was refitted in the Baroque period, late in the monastery's life. There are hanging chandeliers and huge paintings high up on either side of the nave showing aspects of the life of the monks here. Preparations for a funeral later that day were going on while I was there.

Following the closure of the abbey, the complex of buildings became a prison; it still is, except for the church, to which (as its website reassures anxious visitors) the prisoners have no access. Our old and obsolete image of Warsaw Pact Europe as encircled by impregnable barriers is vividly re-created in microcosm up against the right-hand edge of the west front and tightly adjoining the exterior of the north-east end of the church, for here are high grey walls topped with barbed wire and watchtowers. As a

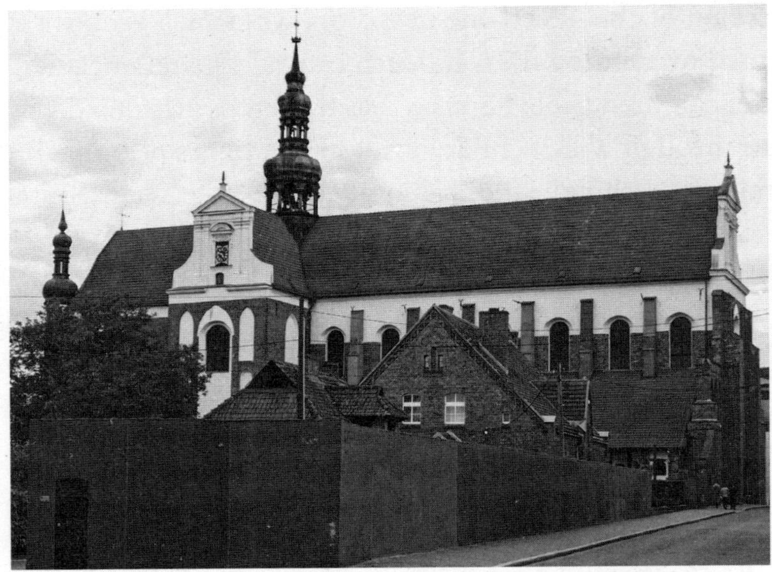

The former abbey in Koronowo, where the Bischewo Bible was made.

result, I could not get into the former monks' quarters. The buildings are post-medieval but presumably built on the original footprint. Aerial photographs show what must have been the cloister, on the southern side of the sanctuary. The doors still there at the end of the south transept probably once led up into the monks' dormitory, for access into the church during the night offices, and into the cloister, where the manuscript may have been made and where, I imagine, prisoners now take their exercise.

I sat outside in the sun in the well-kept gardens on the north side, among flowers by a big apple tree, thinking about monastic life and the freedom of individuals as well as nations, and about the liberation of manuscripts. Swallows darted about overhead, cheeping and swooping, annual migrants to the far south coming back home again every summer to Koronowo, as their ancestors have done for as long as the monastery has been here, to build their nests in its eaves.

Leaf of the manuscript Bible given by A. H. Reed to the author in 1969.

Here I must return for a moment to my late teens. On 16 May 1969, A. H. Reed sent me a letter which included, 'First time you are in the Library, Miss Mercer will have something which it will be a pleasure to pass on to you.' I went in on the 19th. Ngaira Mercer, now promoted to reference librarian, gave me a package. Mr Reed had torn out one final leaf from his lectern Bible, 'a fragment of a MS that I bought as long ago as 1925 . . . Accept it with our good wishes.' My overwhelmed thank-you letter, dated 20 May, is among Reed's papers in the Public Library. The leaf was folio 49 in the diagram of the manuscript above. It has the text from Luke 1:20 to 2:15, including the Annunciation and the birth of Christ, probably the most important of all passages of Scripture for the Cistercians. It has been in my happy possession ever since, now already for much longer than it was ever owned by Reed or the Curtiss family of Chicago. I brought it with me to Koronowo. I was reminded of when you have been on holiday with your dog and are returning home: the dog on the back seat suddenly wakes up and seems to recognize where it is as you get closer. If I ever bequeath my fragment back to Dunedin one day, which I might, imagine the tale it will tell its wide-eyed and envious fellow leaves in the Public Library. In a silent procession of one, I carried it slowly up the length of Koronowo church. I went up the steps of the sanctuary and, moving aside the printed Polish Bible, placed the fragment briefly on the lectern and gazed out down the long nave. For a moment, in one torn-out leaf, the Bible from New Zealand came home.

6

Dunedin

On 29 November 1965, when I was just fifteen, an African guest came to our morning assembly at King's High School in Dunedin, introduced by the rector as Duki Du-bray, from Senegal. His visit was topical, for it was during the crisis in Rhodesia, which had declared unilateral independence from Britain a few weeks earlier. Du-bray, informally representing the Organization for African Unity, had been attending the eleventh conference of the Commonwealth Parliamentary Association, which had just taken place in Wellington. He had horn-rimmed spectacles and spoke to us with a few platitudes about the future of African nations. We had never seen a Black man before, and I am ashamed to report that as a school in general – not me in particular – we behaved rather badly. We thought he looked comic in his strange full-length embroidered kaftan and his brightly coloured kufi hat fitting tightly over his hair. The next morning, the rector reprimanded us, quite rightly, explaining that people of other nations look and dress as they do and that this man was a visitor to our country and we owed him courtesy and respect. I remember those remarks more vividly than what Du-bray had actually said.

Ten days later, on 8 December, the principal front-page headline in the local *Evening Star* newspaper was SCOTTISH ORPHAN HOAXED N. Z. PUBLIC COMPLETELY. It transpired that he was not African at all but a sailor from Glasgow called Kenneth McBride, who had been denied entry into Australia because of a record of theft in Oban and had jumped ship in New Zealand, disguising himself by blacking-up his face and pretending to be the son of the kabaka of Senegal. What probably began as a bit of a lark must have got seriously out of hand when he was unexpectedly swept into the conference in Wellington and had no choice but to maintain the untenable charade. His close-fitting hat might have been to conceal telltale sandy hair. His story and accelerating moral dilemma of how to disentangle himself would make a fascinating novel. The fact that it could happen at all is symptomatic of the distance of New Zealand from the rest of the world in the 1960s. Our rector had probably never seen a Black man either or knew quite what they should look like. We schoolboys felt vindicated, as if we had guessed all along that something was not right, which of course we had not.

The immense isolation of New Zealand, still largely true at that time, may be hard to comprehend now by anyone brought up in these days of instant communication and easy travel. Most New Zealanders then had never been abroad. On the whole, it was a contented and self-contained society. It is a difficult question as to whether internationalism necessarily brings greater happiness. Knowledge of other peoples in my childhood depended mostly on old *National Geographic* magazines, their sun-crisped pages prised open on verandas and in bedrooms of holiday baches (as holiday cottages are called in New Zealand). We used to smile at a line in the National Anthem (1876), 'Men of every creed and race . . .', since it was so patently untrue. In so far as any other country was part of New Zealand consciousness, Britain was the place from which almost all migration had come, and older people, even those who had never travelled, still referred to it as 'home'. For some reason, we once joined in an evening of musical entertainments in the community hall of Macandrew Bay, where a man sang what I now know was Andy Stewart's 'A Scottish Soldier' (1965): the whole room was almost in tears in identifying with his haunting lament of exile: '. . . not highland hills, or the island hills, they're not my land's hills . . . of home.' Many New Zealanders who had been to fight in the War looked back on their experiences with pride and patriotism for Empire and Commonwealth. It was old-fashioned, no doubt, and generally nostalgic. Perhaps I was not as much of an oddity as it might seem now, or, put the other way round, we are all products of place and time.

I still had the stamp collection but now restricted it entirely to British issues, as early as possible, even adding some unstamped letters from before 1840. Inspired by the Reed Collection, I started embellishing the albums with calligraphy and specimen autographs. I wrote to famous people for their signatures, finding addresses in *Who's Who*, the thrilling big red volumes kept downstairs at the Public Library. Most of them, including Harold Wilson and Anthony Eden, replied promptly in October 1965, and, about a year after I had written, Bertrand Russell and, eventually, Henry Moore did so too. The Duke of Windsor and Salvador Dalí did not. I put on a small exhibition in the school library, and most people assumed I had written the autographs myself. We were once assigned an essay in our English class about allegory in the *Lord of the Flies*, our set text for the term, and so I looked up William Golding's address and wrote asking him what to say. His reply was a bit disappointing, but I submitted it anyway.

I began to collect coins too. Until mid-1967, the currency in New Zealand was pounds, shillings and pence, and before 1933 they had simply used British coinage. It was occasionally still possible to find Victorian pennies in circulation; I once received a George III sixpence in my change from the corner shop next to the school. It might have come out to New Zealand in some early settler's pocket. Arranging sets and looking for lateral patterns are the instincts of all collectors: one example of each reign, for instance, or a penny from every date (1933 was the mythical rarity), or all denominations from single years. I cut circles in cardboard and lined the apertures with red velvet. I enjoyed labelling things.

There was no particular tradition of collecting in our family, or at least not since an antiquarian great-grandfather, who died in 1931. My parents allowed it as harmless, as long as my spending power was limited, and relatives in England were evidently relieved that I could be so easily satisfied with being sent presents of little curiosities they owned anyway. On Christmas Day 1965, I unwrapped a half-groat of Henry VI sent by my mother's cousin Ruth Aspinall; a chapbook, *The Illustrious and Renowned History of the Seven Famous Champions of Christendom . . . The Seventeenth Edition, c.* 1800, from one grandmother; and John Taylor's *The Old, Old, Very Old Man, or, The Age and long Life of Thomas Par*, dated 1635, from the other grandmother, whose father had owned it. I have all three still. The latter is especially curious, quaintly printed and utterly beguiling, a credulous poem about a man who is said to have lived to the age of 152. I believed it to be my oldest book, and it gave me inestimable joy in twentieth-century New Zealand to cradle and turn the pages of an actual item 'printed for *Henry Gosson*, at his Shop on *London-Bridge*, neere to the Gate, 1635'. I hardly noticed a line below about having been reprinted for one J. Sturt of 40 High Street, St Giles. Many years later, I began to sense there was something odd about the paper. It gradually dawned on me that the book was not genuine at all but is one of those uncannily realistic early nineteenth-century type facsimiles. It

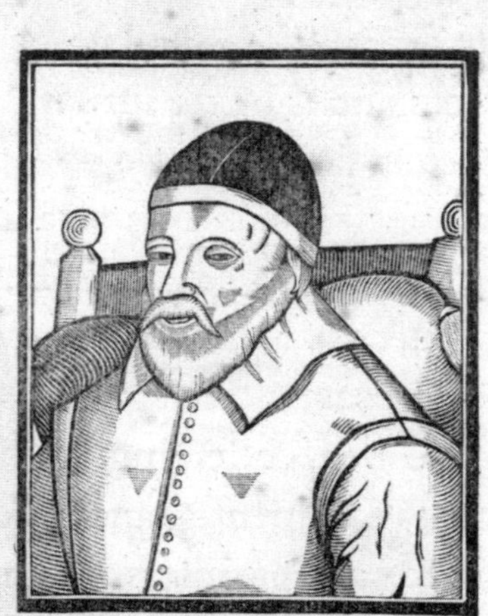

The Old, Old, very Old Man, or Thomas Parr, the
Son of John Parr of Winnington, in the Parish of Alberbury, in the County of Shropshire; who was borne
in the Raigne of King Edward the Fourth, being aged
152. Yeares and odd Monthes, and now lies buried at
Westminster.

The Old, Old,

Very Old Man:

OR,

The Age and long Life of *Thomas Par*, the
Son of *John Parr* of *Winnington* in the Parish
of *Alberbury*; in the County of *Salop*, (or *Shropshire*)
who was borne in the the Raigne of King *Edward*
the fourth, in the yeare 1483.

Hee lived 152 yeares, nine monthes and odd dayes,
and departed this Life at *Westminster* the 15 of *Novem.*
1635, and is now buried in the Abby at *Westminster.*

His Manner of Life and Conversation in so long
a Pilgrimage; his Marriages, and his bringing up to
London, about the end of *September* last. 1635.

Whereunto is Added a Postscript, shewing
the many remarkable Accidents that
hapned in the Life of this *Old Man.*

Written by IOHN TAYLOR.

LONDON,
Printed for *Henry Gosson*, at his Shop on
London-Bridge, neere to the Gate.
1 6 3 5.
Re-printed for J. STURT, No. 40, High-street, St. Giles's,
By J. Barker, 19, Great Russell-street, Covent-Garden.

John Taylor, *The Old, Old, Very Old Man*, with date 1635, given to the
author for Christmas 1965.

is not much comfort to learn now that the rare book libraries of both Harvard and Yale have in the past bought various
Sturt reprints in the erroneous belief these were seventeenth-
century originals. Even today, I feel strangely cheated. All that
emotion and thrill of tangible antiquity was poured into an item
which betrayed me. When the library of Robert S. Pirie was
sold at Sotheby's in New York in 2015, it included a copy of the
real 1635 *Old, Old, Very Old Man*, and, to salvage some of that
wasted passion retrospectively, I left a valiant bid but merely
drove the price up by several thousand dollars in vain. Authenticity mattered to me and still does, and what seems to be historical evidence may be wrong.

I can date another revelation to 1965 because I wrote a
dreadful little poem about it which appeared in the school
magazine that year. I was lying in my bed at home looking out

over the Otago harbour and watching the full moon in the night sky. It struck me with sudden Damascene intensity that I was gazing directly on the very moon worshipped by the druids and ancient priests of Babylon and Nineveh. It was known to Aristotle and Shakespeare. It gave its name to Mondays more than a thousand years ago. Every one of my ancestors saw it, without exception, since the dawn of our species. It may have been upside-down (it is, viewed from New Zealand), but it was not a copy or reproduction or visionary re-creation in any way, but the same actual physical object of such immense significance and familiarity to all human history, literally present for inspection in my immediate eyesight, in Dunedin, now. No museum could equal that. When I tried to explain this over breakfast, they gazed at me pityingly.

By this time it was becoming less clear whether we were temporary sojourners in New Zealand or acknowledged immigrants and settlers. We still spoke with very English accents. The dreaded curse of the consequent stammer never quite vanished and could immobilize me when I least expected it. These days I never think of it, but I learned to open sentences with vowels and often still do. After a slow start, I finally began growing rapidly and jerkily and lost my treble voice, and in time underwent unpredictable forays of teenage acne, a cruel defacement which coincides with a time of life when self-image first matters so intensely. I began to notice girls but had neither the looks nor sporting skill or reliable speech to impress them, and, in any case, I did not know any. I had brothers only, no female relatives in the country (except my mother), and I attended a school exclusively for boys – and indeed continued like that until well into my twenties in Knox College and then Oxford, neither yet co-residential as they are now. I had seen girls in the street, of course, but I am not sure I had ever spoken to one. I knew all about them, however, because I had read Jane Austen and Virginia Woolf.

For a few days in 1966, I amused myself greatly by taking detailed notes on our classes at King's High School, writing down verbatim as fast as I could every single word spoken by the masters, the flow of chatter and inanities as well as the instruction. Stream of consciousness may also have been learned from Virginia Woolf. I recently found the little red notebook in which I had done this, but much is so scribbled at white-hot speed that it is hard to decipher. Here are exact words of our French teacher, Mr Anderson, on Tuesday 25 October:

The idiom in French is '*ouvrir de grands yeux*' and, Mount, you should be getting hold of it by now. It's your fourth year. I assure you, it's worse for me to have you. You see I'm up against infantile minds. I don't know why I'm so patient with you . . . This is the sort of thing which makes me wonder if you ever listen to what I say. I'll take in your proses. You what? . . . You didn't do them: you're still in the cart. Yes, what's your excuse? I can see you're thinking it up . . . McKerrow, what's funny? You're grinning round there with Davidson . . . McKerrow, I don't want to see your teeth any more. Any questions? Thank you. McKerrow, you have anything to ask? But you have! While you're communicating, will you come up here please . . . Haven't I spoken to you about haircuts before? It hasn't been cut at all. At once! I don't care who does it. Did I see you looking up in the dictionary? You see! Why are you sitting doing nothing, Purdie? Now have you got it? You see, you've got to think.

Within a few months, I was actually required to speak some French in Paris for the first time. In late 1966, my parents took a brave decision, which had a huge effect on the direction of my life. They sent me and Michael on our own to Europe for Christmas. I had just turned sixteen and Michael was nearly eighteen. Every detail was meticulously planned, and we had contact addresses for emergencies in every location. I looked forward to it all with a fervour that became almost unbearable. I acquired a first passport of my own, British, of course, issued by the High Commission in Wellington on 22 November. It described me as being six feet tall, but I was still growing and added several more inches within a year. We were to travel by aeroplane the whole way, still a novelty. Tickets were exciting long paper booklets, which copied each hand-written leg of the journey by carbon paper through to the next layer. Time off school was negotiated and agreed. We left on Wednesday, 7 December, from Dunedin to Auckland, refuelled in Honolulu and arrived in Los Angeles the same day by moving backwards through the dateline. The absolute immensity of the Pacific Ocean is really only apparent when one crosses it.

I do not know what most teenage boys on their own for the first time in their lives would do with two unsupervised nights in California in the 1960s. We went out to the Huntington Library to see the Gutenberg Bible and the Ellesmere Chaucer. There had been an American exchange teacher in mathematics from Los Angeles at King's High School, called Mr Ranyard, and I had written to him to say we would be coming. When we met up, he asked what we would like to see, probably expecting Hollywood and Disneyland, and I said, 'Medieval manuscripts, please.' To his credit, he took us to the library of Claremont College, where we were shown the then uncatalogued collection of illuminated manuscripts and incunabula given by Egerton L. Crispin (1877–1963), far more extensive than anything in Dunedin. There was another Gutenberg Bible leaf, as I recall. Some years later, unknown numbers of these books and manuscripts were stolen from Claremont by a temporary library assistant, Peter French, and I was in the unusual position of being one of the few outsiders who had ever seen the collection intact. Alas, I took no notes and my memory a decade or so afterwards proved too imprecise to help the police in recoveries.

Our flights then took us to a day in New York, where I was awed by the great Raphael Madonna at the top of the staircase in the Metropolitan Museum, and across the Atlantic towards London. It was the year of the new Beatles' song 'Yellow Submarine', beginning, 'In the town, where I was born . . .', insistent words, hard to get out of the head. I knelt at a window between cabins to wait for the coast of England to come eventually and slowly into view, and then the outlines of London.

No paragraph can truly describe the following three months of revelation. First of all, I learned that we were normal and spoke like everyone else. That sense of tribal identity and belonging was overwhelming. We stayed with my father's sisters Barbie and Peggy and our Fergusson cousins in Ebbesbourne Wake and Maclaren and Shortt cousins in Britford, near Salisbury, where we spent Christmas itself. We were thrown headlong into the teenage party season of south Wiltshire and Dorset. This was all new to me. Every well-bred household seemed to hold a dance or supper party to which suitably approved young people were invited, while parents hovered just out of sight. Jane Austen was not so wrong. My eldest cousin Nick offered sage advice: 'Approach the tallest girls first,' he told me, looking me up and down; 'most boys are shorter than we are,' he said from his own considerable height and the wisdom of nineteen years of age, 'and you'll have a better chance.' (I might add that I was best man at his wedding eleven years later and his wife is as tall as he was.) At a party in Radnorshire I was kissed by a girl on a sofa, further and more wonderfully towards the perfumed garden than I knew existed. We were taken by Aunt Barbie to Longford Castle, the first time I had knowingly met an earl, and we saw Holbein's *Erasmus* and the Velásquez *Juan de Pareja*, which was bought by the Metropolitan Museum for over $5,500,000 in 1971; and by Aunt Peggy to Cornwall, where our hosts had a prehistoric fogou in their garden. We walked with Albert Morley Hewitt around the excavations of his own Roman villa at Rockbourne in Hampshire. The librarian brought out the Magna Carta for us to hold in Salisbury Cathedral Library. We went to Oxford, which was under snow, as it was when the Empress Matilda escaped in 1142, and we saw the Bodleian and New College, which my father had attended. We stayed too with our grandmother in Ewhurst in Surrey, and in London with the bookbinder Elizabeth Greenhill, a friend of Aunt Mary, my mother's sister, whose little Chelsea flat had no guest room. We watched a Sotheby's sale, a ballet at the Royal Opera House, a trial at the Old Bailey, and sessions of both Houses of Parliament. Harold Wilson and Alec Douglas-Home were speaking in the Commons. We walked through Carnaby Street. We saw the Vinland Map exhibition at the British Museum; and the Codex Sinaiticus. I bought cheap Roman coins from Spink's, a strip of 1841 twopenny blues from Stanley Gibbons, and several incunable leaves from H. M. Fletcher in Cecil Court, off the Tottenham Court Road. On 20–23 January 1967, we went to Paris by plane to Le Bourget airport, with our Ewhurst grandmother and Aunt Mary. We stayed at the Hôtel de la Tamise, still there today between the rue Saint-Honoré and the Tuileries gardens, as my grandmother's family had always done in Paris since before the First World War. Michael was convinced he was propositioned by a girl of the streets (if so, it escaped my understanding). More importantly by far, I bought a partial leaf from a fifteenth-century French manuscript choir book from one of the *bouquiniste* stalls by the Seine, for 5 francs (Plate 13). I designated it as my MS 1 in a collection which, from that moment on, has never ceased, and has run in time to over a thousand items.

We returned to New Zealand through stops in Rome (walking in the forum where Julius Caesar stood was a defining highpoint), Athens (another, standing where King Aegeus could have seen black-sailed ships returning from the minotaur in Crete), Hong Kong, Sydney, Christchurch and – oh, so small an aerodrome! – into Dunedin on 6 March 1967, where our parents were waiting with the car. I knew by then, with absolute clarity, that I would be returning to Britain and an antiquarian life as soon as it could be managed. Michael, on the other hand, perhaps not so quickly, decided it was not for him; he still lives and flourishes in New Zealand.

On the long flight home, we discussed what was the single most impressive thing we had seen on this extraordinary and intense Grand Tour. The choices were very wide. In the end, we both agreed it must be the Alfred Jewel in the Ashmolean Museum, the sublime and supreme masterpiece of the late ninth century, where one looks through a lens of transparent rock crystal into the eyes of the great Anglo-Saxon king himself, proclaiming its own identity in golden capitals around the edge, AELFRED MEC HEHT GEWYRCAN, 'Alfred had me made', the jewel speaking. That direct encounter across 1,100 years in words and art, inches from our noses pressed to the glass case, was (we decided) the most intensely moving experience of all. Years later, when I got to Oxford, I was told that in the 1960s the item on exhibition was usually only a replica, not the original at all. Did we actually see the Alfred Jewel? I do not know. Does it matter? Indeed it does, desperately.

Perhaps an even more heightened sense of authenticity and meeting the past face-to-face came out of that trip to

Europe. I took down from my bedroom wall at home most of those copies and reproductions made by me from items in the Public Library, and I hung up instead my newly framed manuscript fragment from Paris and the early printed leaves bought in London. My room looked out over a garden of hebes and kowhais and cabbage trees, with bellbirds and tuis, but inside I could gaze up in wonder at an actual page of a Bible in German printed by Johann Grüninger in Strasbourg in 1485. It has the opening of II Kings 19, with a hand-painted initial 'E', formed of three quick curving strokes in dark red, which I learned to imitate. It is like Japanese brushwork calligraphy, overlapping black type so deeply impressed into the coarse paper I could almost feel the writing with the tips of my fingers. I could imagine myself like St Jerome in his study in Dürer's woodcut, where he has papers of some kind secured to the wall behind his head, tucked in with a pair of scissors.

The Alfred and Isabel Reed Trust had also been buying specimen fragments of medieval manuscripts and early printing for the Dunedin Public Library, as a way of filling gaps and adding more biblical items after the Reed Collection had been made over to the city in 1948. I found they too had bought a leaf – a rather better one – from the 1485 Grüninger Bible. Several of their manuscript fragments were sourced in 1949 from Erik von Scherling (1907–56), a Swedish dealer in Leiden, including a thirteenth-century Bible leaf priced at £7. Another similar leaf, acquired in 1952, was from a Bible broken up for sale as separate leaves by the Ohio teacher and controversial entrepreneur Otto Ege (1888–1951); it had already reached New Zealand before purchase. Many came from the London dealers Maggs Brothers, who represented the Reed Collection at auctions; from Alan Thomas (1911–92) in Bournemouth and then Chelsea, such as a leaf from a Book of Hours for £4.5s. in 1965; and from Folio Fine Art, an enterprise of the Folio Society in London initiated by Charles Ede (1921–2002), including leaves from a thirteenth-century Bible once at Villeneuve-lès-Avignon for £3.3s. in 1962 and a late fourteenth-century Breviary in 1963 for only £2. The prices may seem modest but that was the market then and Mr Reed was thrifty. He usually asked book-sellers for a discount in the good cause of benefiting the public. Cuttings with illuminated miniatures were more expensive. An early sixteenth-century French Book of Hours leaf with a night scene of the Annunciation to the Shepherds cost a giddy £23.10s. from Sotheby's through Maggs in 1961. Mr Reed issued a press release about its acquisition, printed in the Dunedin *Evening Star* on 3 June 1961:

> It is becoming increasingly difficult to secure material such as this. During the two world wars, many rare books were destroyed and the cost of those that find their way on to the market has risen sensationally . . . In another generation, illu-minated manuscripts will probably have become unavailable or procurable only by millionaires.

The question of manuscripts being good investments is one not normally considered by libraries in Europe but is a recurrent theme of Mr Reed's public announcements, maybe in the hope of making the indifferent citizens of Dunedin more appreciative of his generosity. An interview with Reed about his bequest in the *Otago Daily Times* in July 1966 was headlined, A COLLECTION WORTH THOUSANDS, subtitled, IT HAS TAKEN 50 YEARS. He told the journalist that the Gutenberg Bible leaf alone had cost £175 in 1954, a price which he predicted in 1967 'will probably be doubled in a few years'. Reed's allusion to the destruction of books by warfare suggests safer custody in libraries of New

Zealand than in Europe, which is probably true (although there are earthquakes, and fire is universal).

Another kind of destruction is a much more delicate matter: every one of the fragments just mentioned, and many others in the Reed Collection (and all mine so far), came from books which had survived from the Middle Ages more-or-less intact until dealers in the twentieth century divided them up for sale leaf by leaf. There are immensely complex ethical issues involved in this, which certainly did not trouble A. H. Reed. He would have taken the view expressed by John Ruskin, who (teasingly) suggested, 'There are literally thousands of manuscripts in the libraries of England . . . of which a few leaves, dispersed among parish schools, would do more to educate the children of the poor than all the catechisms that ever tortured them.' The usual justification by booksellers is that a badly defective and routine manuscript such as a Book of Hours or medieval choir book is of no great importance in the study of manuscripts and is not good enough for millionaires, whereas single leaves are affordable by libraries and collectors in remote countries where people would not otherwise have any first-hand access to such things. It is a plausible argument, especially in somewhere like New Zealand, far from old European collections. If encountering and touching illuminated manuscripts matters at all, which I suppose we must believe, then the widest dissemination of this experience to the largest number of people in the world can be achieved principally through accessibility of fragments. The Dunedin Public Library acquired many dispersed leaves, and there are some now also in the Turnbull Library in Wellington and in Auckland University Library.

Breaking up manuscripts after acquisition is a very different matter, however. The Library staff in Dunedin grudgingly tolerated Mr Reed removing occasional loose leaves from the defective Byszewo / Koronowo New Testament as diplomatic gifts. They watched, and even helped in mounting and framing, when Reed bought an unbound portion of a printed Book of Hours of 1544 and distributed leaves in pairs to local schools and others, with accompanying notes. (King's High School received a set and promptly lost it.) The brink of the Rubicon was reached when Reed instructed the Public Library's binder to remove and frame a leaf from the Middle English manuscript Wycliffite Gospel Book that the Reed Trust had bought for the Library at Sotheby's with great drama in 1956, still in its seventeenth-century armorial binding (Plate 10). The matter was brought to Mary Ronnie, City Librarian, who absolutely refused to countenance such action. Mr Reed, unaccustomed to being thwarted, insisted. Miss Ronnie, in her prim Scottish accent (I can just imagine it), said the Library would prefer to return the manuscript to him than to have any part in its dismemberment. By the following morning, the request was never mentioned again.

Even leaves and cuttings can have stories to tell. Three of the fragments in the Dunedin Public Library, by entirely different migrations, are from manuscripts – a Psalter and two Books of Hours – once owned by the Mayfair jeweller John Boykett Jarman (1782–1864). He kept his collection in tin boxes on the ground floor of his house at 84 Grosvenor Street, just around the corner from what became my office at Sotheby's in London many years later. The premises had by our time become an Italian coffee shop and I used to take people there for lunch. The late summer of 1846, shortly before Dunedin was founded, was one of the hottest then on record, and newspapers reported temperatures of 92° Fahrenheit (33° Celsius) in London on Saturday, 1 August. That night a massive thunderstorm occurred: giant hailstones and more than three inches of rain fell overnight, windows broke in many parts of London, and cellars were flooded. The Tyburn river, which still crossed Mayfair, burst the confines of its channel and entirely inundated the collection of Jarman. When he returned three days later, the manuscripts were still under water. Chance plays such a big part in the history of manuscripts. 'I wonder Mr Jarman did not hang himself at once', wrote Sir Frederic Madden of the British Museum in his journal. Instead, Jarman dismantled every book, dried and flattened the pages, and employed a facsimilist, Caleb Wing (1801–75), to restore the damaged illuminations. All three items now in Dunedin can be matched with lots in the catalogue of Jarman's sale at Sotheby's in 1864 and all show damp-staining in their margins. One of them is that cut-out leaf with the Annunciation to the Shepherds bought by the Reed Collection with such jubilation in 1961. No one noticed that its margins had been restored and its lovely painting probably gently refreshed by the hand of Caleb Wing; authentic but maybe after all not entirely authentic.

Another which withheld a detail from me in those days is a leaf from a fourteenth-century Swiss or German choir book, which used to hang on the Library stairs. It has a large red and blue initial 'H' with elaborate penwork decoration, not unlike that in the Byszewo/Koronowo New Testament but incorporating two roundels, which enclose animals (Plate 14). The lower of these is a white creature bending round to bite something between its back legs. In so far as I thought about it, I assumed it was a dog. It is actually a beaver. According to the fancy of medieval Bestiaries – encyclopaedias of animals and their religious significance – the reproductive organs of male beavers had spectacular medicinal virtues and the animals were hunted for this purpose. When the beaver is being chased, it will therefore bend round to bite off its own genitalia, so that the hunter has what he wants and the beaver can escape (a short-lived triumph, for European beavers were reduced almost to extinction). The Bestiary text interprets this supposed habit as a symbol of holy virginity, since the beaver voluntarily renounced its sexual life for a higher cause. The initial in Dunedin opens the chant for the immaculate birth of the Virgin Mary, and therefore the beaver illustrates the text.

As a result of our visit to England, I came to realize that medieval fragments were not merely restricted to public collections and that I too might be an owner. I used dealers' directories and the acquisition files in the Public Library to find addresses of as many antiquarian booksellers as I could and I wrote to them, inquiring about manuscript and early printed fragments for no more than a few pounds. I still have their replies. I do not know how many guessed that I was a schoolboy with a budget limited by weekly pocket money. Some were loftily dismissive, like Frank Hammond of Sutton Coldfield, and Bernard Breslauer, who wrote, 'I rarely do get single leaves . . . as I always try to obtain the most perfect copies in the best possible condition.' Folio Fine Art replied at once in May 1967, offering an illuminated Breviary leaf at £2.15s., which I bought (it became my MS 2), and I joined their catalogue mailing list. Clifford Maggs was endlessly kind and patient, and I knew him well years later and spoke at the memorial service after his death in 1985. He once sent several manuscript leaves to me in Dunedin on approval, more than I could possibly afford and they all had to go back. My early letters to Alan Thomas are in a separate file in his archive now in the British Library. He eventually became probably my closest friend of my parents' generation. From the outset, his replies to Mr de Hamel in Macandrew Bay were long and welcoming, despite the limit I gave him: 'You are certainly correct in believing that manuscript leaves – and even fragments – are difficult to find now for £10 or less.' Nonetheless, every few months another treasured addition arrived by post, mostly from Folio, Maggs and Thomas, and early printed leaves from Charles Traylen and H. M. Fletcher again. I would report acquisitions to Mr Reed: 'I congratulate you', he would say every time. In August 1967, he gave me a tiny piece of a printed Latin Bible, which in turn put me in touch by post with the British Museum, where George Painter identified it for me as Nuremberg, Anton Koberger, 1477. The printer, I discovered, was Albrecht Dürer's godfather, and it went up on my wall too.

One day, my mother suggested I should invite Mr Reed to tea at home, and I wrote him a careful letter. To my surprise and awe, he accepted. We went to collect him in the car from his home in Glenpark Avenue, where he had lived alone for thirty years since the death of his wife. It is a residential road along a crest of the hillside suburb of Mornington, west of central Dunedin. Reed's house, no. 153, was a small mock-Tudor cottage with panoramic views out over the valley. I was sent in to fetch him. He mostly lived upstairs in a large book-lined room, partly divided up by a bookcase with sliding glass doors. There was a low chair by the window with his portable typewriter beside it. He slept up against another window in a sleeping-bag on a wooden bunk, with drawers beneath. It was spartan and startlingly unmodernized, like a hermit's cell. He was a vegetarian and life-long teetotaller. I remember the house's distinctive sour smell of human old age.

Back in our drawing-room in Macandrew Bay, Mr Reed settled himself down in an armchair with a cup of tea and chattered away. He was tall and bony and wore boots and a jacket with a Youth Hostel lapel badge. He had blue eyes, like Sir George Grey. Reed was a practised raconteur and had told his stories many times. He was born in 1875 in Hayes, west of London (near what is now Heathrow airport, although that

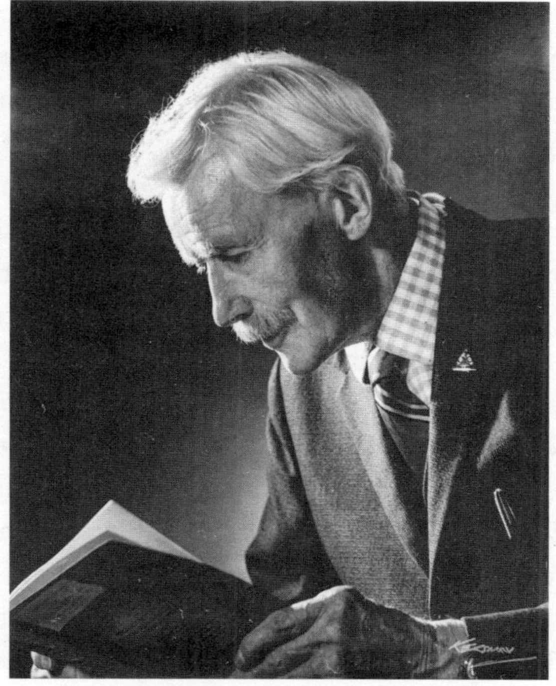

A. H. Reed, photographed in 1966.

came long after his time), and then his family had moved out to Walthamstow, towards Epping Forest, where his father was the manager of a brickworks. Knowing we were also from England, he recounted to us how as a boy during the British General Election of 1885 he and his mischievous friends interrupted local Conservative meetings by shouting 'Vote for Gladstone!' and then they would run into the nearby Liberal headquarters calling 'Vote for Salisbury!' I was entranced; it was a voice from history. He asked my mother, in a conversational opening probably unchanged from the meeting of colonial migrants in the nineteenth century, how it was that we too had happened to come, and outlined his theory that all decisions are right ones, given the information available when they were made.

The market for building material had collapsed in the British slump of the 1880s, as familiar to him as if we all remembered it, and the Reeds arrived penniless in Auckland in 1887. They landed only a month after Grey had opened the Public Library there and they could have met him (but did not). Although his schooling was curtailed at the age of twelve by osteomyelitis, a disease I myself had at almost the same age (there was penicillin by then), young Alfred Reed broke free of poverty by teaching himself shorthand and then typing, a new invention. They were a Christian and literate family, both useful assets in adversity. A. H. Reed came down to Dunedin in 1897 as the local branch manager of the New Zealand Typewriter Company. He lodged initially with a Mrs Hamel, and he wondered if we were distantly related, which is not impossible. Reed recounted how one of his elderly fellow lodgers had as a young man once met a very old Māori chief who had been present as a boy when Captain Cook first landed in New Zealand in 1769. He loved those kinds of connections leaping across time.

The typewriter business had evolved into stationery and Sunday School supplies, and finally into publishing. The firm of A. H. and A. W. Reed (A. W. being his nephew) were throughout my childhood probably the best-known publishers of books in and about New Zealand. The emblem on their imprint was a reed plant. The company still survives, after various changes of ownership, as Raupo Publishing, now part of the Penguin Group ('raupo' being a Māori reed). In his old age, Mr Reed became famous for his immense intercity walks, over mountains and along country roads, often in a jacket and tie and carrying a battered little suitcase, as far as land stretched in every direction across New Zealand and once, in his ninetieth year, from Sydney to Melbourne, in long loping strides. These journeys he wrote up as popular travel books, in a chatty fireside style, like his conversation. The list of his publications was extensive, often on historical or religious subjects, or both, not deeply researched but very readable. He was easily recognized in the streets of New Zealand and expected to be. There was no small element of self-promotion of his own image, but he used this to public benefit, visiting hospitals every week, always with a pocketful of sweets for children and distributing cards with his signature and photograph, talking to everyone he met as equally worthy of attention, asking and remembering their names, writing letters to newspapers, maintaining correspondences, promoting Bibles and medieval manuscripts, and campaigning for good causes. He received a knighthood in his hundredth year. One could probably sum him up best by calling him a Christian Fabian. He had cards printed with his personal credo:

> I believe in the Gospel of work, of laughter, and of goodwill to men; in the power of choice between good and evil, and of reaping what we sow; in life beyond, and the imperishability of character and thought; in the evolution of the soul; in God, the all-good, all-wise, and ever-present; and in Jesus Christ who revealed Him to us. With supreme confidence I believe in the reunion of loving hearts in the Hereafter.

A very different view of belief was being expressed in Dunedin at this period by the Reverend Professor Lloyd Geering, principal of Knox Theological College 1963–71. From late 1965 onwards he had been writing articles for *Outlook*, the Presbyterian weekly, articulating unusually liberal views of Christianity, including denial of the Resurrection as a historical event and questioning the existence of human souls surviving into an afterlife. Because of his high-profile position as a senior clergyman and instructor of ordinands, this caused enormous controversy in New Zealand, dividing public opinion immoderately. A. H. Reed wrote to Geering at Easter 1967, saying that his own unshakable certainty that he would be reunited with his late wife in heaven was the anchor of his life on earth. I was both fascinated and upset to hear fundamental tenets of Christian faith being challenged by people of intelligence. My father, who used to leave more and more deliberate gaps in his recitation of the Creed in church as he grew older, thought it was wonderful, and it became awkward at home. My mother, who knew Geering's wife, Elaine, arranged for me to talk to the professor himself at Knox College, my first visit to the college's Senior Common Room. Geering was both charming and courteous. I began by asking how anyone could doubt the evidence of multiple Gospels. 'You are a historian,' he said (I was flattered and beguiled): 'What would you say if you found four different accounts saying exactly the same?' 'That they must be accurate,' I replied triumphantly, sensing I was falling into a trap. 'No, you wouldn't,' he told me. 'You would say they were all copied from the same source.' It was an eye-opening moment, both in the use of the Bible as historical material and in understanding a rather more nuanced relationship with religion, for Geering was transparently a wise and spiritual man. Soon afterwards he was charged with 'doctrinal error' and brought to tribunal at the General Assembly of the Presbyterian Church of New Zealand, convened in Christchurch on Friday to Monday, 3–6 November 1967. The local and international press gathered for what was described as the last heresy trial in Western Christianity. After immense debate, Geering was finally acquitted and came back to Knox College. Many years later he officiated at my youngest brother's wedding.

That year, 1967, was my class's final year at King's High. By then our legs had grown too long and hairy for dignity in our shrinking but still compulsory dark blue school shorts. I began to explain that my name wasn't really Clive and no one believed me. I was mostly forgiven when I hid in the stationery cupboard from school sport and pretended it was revision for the university scholarship exams, which were the final hurdle. I came sixty-eighth from bottom out of 409 passes in the entire country, but it was enough to get me through. My classmate Ross Jenner and I would talk endlessly about Renaissance art and civilization, which he really did seem to know about while I pretended and wrote excruciatingly bad poems in free verse on the meaning of existence and dead seagulls. Perhaps Ross was bluffing too: I do not know (he eventually became a professor of architecture). It is not an easy age, being sixteen or seventeen, fancying oneself as intellectual on not the slightest evidence, and I would not like to be it again. I have elsewhere told the story of our Latin master playing recordings of the Carmina Burana, which made me realize that this was the language of medieval manuscripts and that some parts of the school curriculum perhaps finally had a practical use.

I was sitting upstairs in the Public Library one day with one of the Reed Collection's two Books of Hours, adapted for use in the English Midlands in the second half of the fifteenth century. I puzzled over a long Latin prayer which included the words, *Deprecor te domine . . . per illam pacem quam confirmasti inter angelos et homines fac pacem inter me Margeriam Fitzherbert et omnes inimicos meos . . .*, and so on, and I remember piecing it together word by word with my little black school Latin dictionary: 'I beseech you, Lord' – that is easy – 'by that peace which . . .', and then there was a word which looked like *confinasti*, which I was unable to find until I noticed a tiny zig-zag mark over it which must be the 'ir' or 'ur' abbreviation over an 'm' (not 'in') and suddenly there was 'that peace which you confirmed

Part of a Latin prayer in a Book of Hours in Dunedin,
naming the user as Margery Fitzherbert.

between angels and men, make, make, make . . .' – *pace*, it
seemed to be, but a horizontal line above the last letter turns it
to *pacem* – and so, 'make peace . . .' (oh! this was the resonant
catchphrase of our Vietnam generation) 'make peace between
me . . .' – look! – 'Margery Fitzherbert and all my enemies . . .',

a real name leaping out of the page, almost certainly until that moment unnoticed in the manuscript and unread by any single person since the Wars of the Roses, into which, as I soon discovered from the encyclopaedias next to the copies of *Who's Who* downstairs, the Fitzherbert family of Derbyshire became actively involved as Yorkists. I learned that day that manuscripts can talk.

7

Norbury

The manuscript containing the name of Margery Fitzherbert
was always the poor Cinderella of the two Books of Hours in the
Reed Collection. The much-vaunted favourite had been bought
from a bookseller in Exeter in March 1949 for £250 and was reproduced on numerous greetings and Christmas cards in the 1960s
and 70s, and on the front cover of Mr Reed's guidebook to the
collection (1968). It was illuminated in northern France, probably
Rouen, around 1490, and was almost always out on exhibition
(Plate 9). When I look at it now, it seems to me nice enough,
but small, blousy and unexceptional. The unloved Fitzherbert
Book of Hours, however, which was seldom put on display, is
damaged by damp, incomplete and bound badly out of order,
and it is an ill-matched confection of three different fifteenth-
century components. It was acquired by Dunedin from a bookseller in Darlington in November 1954 for only £50. It is actually
by far the more interesting manuscript (Plates 15–18).

The new Dunedin Public Library was opened in 1981, further
round Moray Place clockwise from the old Carnegie building,
on the upper northern arc of that same road encircling the
Octagon. You approach the gleaming white building either up
brick steps with chrome banisters off the street, or through
a municipal complex leading off the Octagon. As in the new
Auckland building of the same year, the 'Heritage' collections

are on the Library's top floor. Here is everything Mr Reed wished and campaigned for over many decades, including an impressive rare book reading room and offices for full-time staff and facilities for specialized exhibitions and seminars (I taught one here in 2005), and, out of sight through doors behind the invigilators' desk, secure and controlled storage facilities where the manuscripts and books are safe for ever. It is magnificent, but formal and somewhat forbidding, quite hard to find up the stairs. I was reminded of the story of Sir Alexander Fleming, discoverer of penicillin, showing a visitor round his expensive new laboratory late in life. 'Dr Fleming,' the guest is reported to have said admiringly, 'if you could have had facilities like this when you were young, what things you could have discovered!' Fleming, remembering his dirty and unmodernized hospital in 1928, replied, 'Not penicillin.' In 1963, I would never have dared venture into a room like this or known what to ask for. There are no children in here now. I loved the creaky old Reed gallery off the staircase where anyone could stop for a moment and see the Book of Hours and the Gutenberg leaf, the autograph of the day and the tantalizing ancient bindings packed tightly into the glass-fronted cupboards below. Now Margery Fitzherbert's Book of Hours is carried out from an invisible safe and laid before you. The broken and useless old eighteenth-century binding has gone, and the manuscript is in a neat grey card conservation box lettered, DISBOUND, VERY FRAGILE.

When possible after school or in the holidays, I would sit with this manuscript at a table in the ordinary reference section of the old library, turning pages back and forth. Whole afternoons vanished in a moment. Although the leaves are entirely disordered, there seemed to be three distinct constituents. The core of the manuscript is a Book of Hours of the Use of Sarum (which effectively means for use in Britain) made in a professional workshop around the early 1470s. This was supplemented with extra prayers on added leaves, including those naming Margery Fitzherbert, for whom the volume was personalized and adapted shortly afterwards. In addition, the manuscript now incorporates a calendar and a few other leaves extracted from a very different Book of Hours, which looked to me much earlier and in better condition.

It was through trying to disentangle the original order of the pages of this jumbled manuscript that I really came to understand for the first time what is contained in a medieval Book of Hours. I copied out more-or-less every page and tried to match up text at the bottom of a verso with its continuation at the top of a following recto, which was very often misplaced somewhere quite different in the volume. I still have those transcriptions rearranged in a green ring folder, which I later kept behind my desk at Sotheby's and used for decades as my principal source for identifying the text of fragments from other Books of Hours. Put into order, the original corpus of the manuscript in Dunedin – 94 leaves (out of 126 here altogether) – comprised the following sections: the Fifteen 'O's on the Passion of Christ and prayers to Saints Christopher and Thomas Becket; the Hours of the Virgin [Use of Sarum], with further short prayers, including the Verses of St Bernard; the seven Penitential Psalms and the fifteen Psalms of Degree, followed by a litany; the Office of the Dead, with the Commendation of Souls; and the Psalms of the Passion. There would once have been a calendar of saints' days at the front, now missing (or at least replaced with one from another manuscript).

A Book of Hours is a layperson's prayerbook, mostly (but not always) used by women; it is not part of a communal church service but is for reading and meditating on in private. A very large part of its text is made up from selections of psalms and a few other biblical readings, mostly from the Old Testament. The reason for this is that a medieval woman was encouraged to envisage herself as being as much as possible like the Virgin Mary at the Annunciation, the most spiritual experience for any woman in human history, who found such ultimate favour with God that she was chosen to be the mother of the Saviour. In medieval art and tradition, the Virgin was at that moment kneeling in her house in Nazareth quietly reading either the psalms or the prophecies of Isaiah. By choosing to recite what might be identical Old Testament passages that the Virgin could have been using, the medieval owner of a Book of Hours could aspire to recapturing thoughts and utter commitment to the will of God similar to those of the Virgin Mary herself at that most holy instant.

A Book of Hours takes its name from the eight canonical 'hours' which divided up the medieval day – Matins, Lauds, Prime, Terce, Sext, None, Vespers and Compline. The central component of the volume, with prayers and short readings for each of these hours, was the Office of the Virgin, adapted from its first use in monasteries in the eleventh to twelfth centuries. In most European Books of Hours, these hours were illustrated with incidents from the life of the Virgin Mary which she had originally experienced at that particular time of day: the Annunciation, which occurred at the hour of Matins before dawn, the Visitation at break of day, the birth of Jesus at the hour of Prime, the arrival of the shepherds in Bethlehem at Terce, and so on, through to the Flight into Egypt in the evening sunset of Vespers, and the Virgin's eventual coronation as Queen of Heaven in the late night sky at the hour of Compline. This is what we find in the French Book of Hours in the Reed Collection. In that manuscript (and in countless others), the Office of the Virgin is followed by other separate and much shorter cycles of hours from Matins to Compline again, on themes of the Passion of Christ, known as the Hours of the Cross, and the working of the Holy Spirit, or Hours of the Holy Ghost.

In England it was rather different. Perhaps as a result of the popularity of the *Speculum Ecclesiae* of St Edmund of Abingdon (d. 1240), which recommended that meditation at each of the hours of the day should be on Christ's Passion, the main Office of the Virgin in English Books of Hours is usually mixed together with the Hours of the Cross, and even overwhelmed by them. In England, the pictures in this text too are most likely to be from the Passion: in Margery Fitzherbert's manuscript, the surviving full-page miniatures in the Hours of the Virgin are the Agony in the Garden (Lauds), Christ before Pilate (Prime), and the Flagellation (Terce). The subjects are harrowing and not as suitable for modern Christmas cards as the equivalent happier images from Christ's birth and infancy in the Library's other Book of Hours from France. The purpose was still emulation of the Virgin Mary, but now the reader was to envisage herself sharing the thoughts of the Virgin and her agonizing experience as she followed and witnessed the last hours of her son's life on earth.

Another characteristic feature of the Hours of the Virgin in manuscripts for English use was the insertion of illustrated prayers to saints at the end of Lauds, and the emphasis given to Prime – as if the night offices of Matins and Lauds were mere preliminaries before the true opening of the day at Prime. The Middle English word for a Book of Hours was 'Primer', probably (although the evidence is finely balanced) named from the hour of Prime. It was apparently pronounced to rhyme with 'glimmer', a counterintuitive oddity shared with the word for the most junior classes in New Zealand schools in my childhood, spelled 'primer', pronounced 'primmer'.

Further distinctively English components of this Book of Hours include the prayer to St Thomas Becket (martyred in Canterbury in 1170) and a litany invoking names of English saints, the Office of the Dead with antiphons appropriate to the Use of Sarum, and the Commendation of Souls, which was a recitation from the long Psalm 118 (119 in modern numbering) to be recited between the death of a person and his or her funeral. At this point I should explain that the 'Use' of a Book of Hours referred to small variants distinctive of local diocesan custom: Sarum's was originally that of the diocese of Salisbury (for which Sarum is the Latin name), but it was adopted by the metropolitan province of Canterbury and became universal by the late Middle Ages for all southern and central England. The manuscript has texts too which were not unique to English manuscripts but were certainly characteristic of them, such as the Fifteen 'O's ascribed (no doubt spuriously) to St Bridget, each a meditation on the Passion opening with the interjection 'O', and the Verses of St Bernard. These are supernaturally efficacious sentences from the psalms for use by people in a hurry, and their origin is explained in a preface in red ink on folio 64, which translates:

> It is found in a book of Saint Bernard that the Devil said to him that he knew eight verses of the Psalter which would give salvation to whoever said them every day; and when he was asked by Saint Bernard what they were, he refused to reveal them to him. Saint Bernard replied to him and said that he would say the entire Psalter. Hearing this, the Devil, afraid that too much good would be achieved, revealed to him the eight verses here.

All this seeming evidence, then, suggests that the manuscript was made in England, as it was believed to have been when the

Dunedin Public Library bought it in 1954 and when I knew it first. It was not. It is a remarkable fact that most Books of Hours for English use (which this certainly is) were written and illuminated abroad, in Flanders in the southern Netherlands, principally in Bruges. There survive nearly eight hundred manuscript Books of Hours used in medieval Britain; of those datable to after about 1430, as many as three-quarters of those eight hundred were made in Flanders for export and sale across the Channel. It is a manuscript trade route which goes back to the late thirteenth century, when cheap Psalters were being written in Bruges for markets in England and elsewhere, and it continued into the age of print; William Caxton set up his first shop to mass-produce books for the English (in 1473) not in England, but in Bruges. A Book of Hours of English use, now in Durham, has a colophon explicitly recording its completion in January 1409, in Bruges. In 1446, William Revetour of York bequeathed to his goddaughter Isabella Bolton a 'large primer with pictures in it, in the style of Flanders'. That was the norm.

There are, as far as I know, fifteen manuscript Books of Hours currently in New Zealand. Of these, four are of the Use of Sarum and were owned in fifteenth-century Britain; three of those four were made in Flanders. One of these is the large and grander Book of Hours that was among the manuscripts sent out on approval by the bookseller Boone to Sir George Grey on Kawau in 1863. It was probably in use in Scotland by the late 1460s for its calendar includes added obits of the Colquhoun family of Luss and the dedication of their chapel of St Mary of Rossdhu beside Loch Lomond in 1469. Another, acquired by the Dunedin Public Library in 1987, has texts added in Middle English after its arrival in Britain.

The Fitzherbert Book of Hours has nine remaining full-page pictures on single leaves inserted into various texts of the book, all 'in the style of Flanders'. They are not of high quality but have undoubted charm. To pretend that these vigorous little dressing-up-box tableaux are remotely like the work of the great contemporaneous Flemish painters such as Jan Van Eyck (d. 1441) or Rogier van der Weyden (d. 1464) would be absurd, but there is an element here of those early southern Netherlandish panel paintings in which biblical and saintly scenes are re-created in domestic settings, with homely tiled floors and Gothic architecture peopled by angels on earth. The picture of Christ being brought to Pilate is shown partly inside a Flemish manor with red tiles, tall lattice windows and crenelated turrets on the roof, like the Town Hall of Bruges (1421), all in the foreground of a flat Netherlandish landscape with a river like the Reie meandering slowly between meadows with little round bushes (Plate 15). St Barbara is attended by a small red angel with a portable organ, not at all like the stately brocaded angels with their majestic organ in the Van Eycks' great Ghent Altarpiece, but maybe it is a trickle-down echo, as similar as a musical night in the Macandrew Bay hall is to the Royal Opera House (Plate 16). St Barbara stands here with her Book of Hours on a lawn before a wall topped by a trellis of roses; it is a pantomime stage set compared with the petal-perfect arbours of the Virgin and Child as painted by Hans Memling and the Master of Flémalle (Robert Campin), but it comes from the same world.

The manuscript belongs in a group of works by the artist known today as the Mildmay Master, named from a Flemish Book of Hours of the Use of Sarum once owned by the Mildmay family of Chelmsford in Essex (and now in Chicago). Apart from the exaggeration of using the term 'master' for any illuminator of such modest skill, this was not necessarily an individual artist but probably represents a prolific production line or collaborative enterprise in Bruges, specializing perhaps exclusively in Books of Hours of the Use of Sarum, or 'Use of England' as their scribes often called it in manuscripts (including in the Mildmay Hours itself), *secundum usum Anglie*. Unlike manuscripts made in England, which were probably always commissioned by clients in advance, these standard Sarum Books of Hours from Flanders were speculative creations, produced in confident anticipation of subsequent sale, as printed books were to be later. The litany here mixes invocations of local continental saints (Vedast, Bavo and others) with names expected by English buyers, including Saints George, Edward the Martyr, Oswald, Dunstan, Sexburga, Milburga and Osyth; but look closely – the Flemish scribes of this workshop, unfamiliar with Anglo-Saxon archbishops, commonly misread the fourth of these names as Dinistan.

The identities of the numerous manuscript illuminators operating in Bruges in the fifteenth century are generally unknown. However, most would have belonged to the guild of St John the Evangelist, a professional fraternity of those involved in every aspect of book production, including writing, illuminating and binding, and eventually printing, bookselling and even school-teaching (considered to be a bookish profession). There are very good surviving records of the guild, including its handwritten register which listed the payment of annual subscriptions. I have looked at the manuscript itself in the city archives in Bruges. For the years 1474–75, for example, which is the approximate date of the Fitzherbert manuscript in Dunedin, we have the names of about a hundred members. These must surely include the Mildmay Master and his various assistants and collaborators, but we do not yet know which they are. Some are very familiar names, such as the manuscript artists Loyset Liédet (*fl.* 1454–84) and Willem Vrelant (*fl.* 1449–*c.* 1482), the bookbinder Antonius van Gavere, and the enigmatic early printer Colard Mansion. There are a reasonable number of women, including widows and daughters of members, who might well also have been involved in book production. There are foreigners too, working in Bruges in 1474–75, such as Antonio of Florence and Rombaut of Utrecht, and several with English-sounding names, which approximate as Gabriel Cooper, Victor Hughes and Hubert of Newcastle ('van den niewen Casteele'); one of these might be the Mildmay Master, working abroad exclusively for the English market.

It need be no surprise that book production was so important in Bruges. It was the most international mercantile city of northern Europe, especially for luxury goods, traded there by merchants from the Mediterranean and Britain and from the Baltic and the Hanseatic towns of Germany. Commodities and raw materials were imported, such as wool from England, timber and skins from the far north, oriental silks and precious stones brought through Venice, and copper and silver from the mountains of south-eastern Europe. Each country had its commercial headquarters and hostels in Bruges with storage cellars and trading floors, under the supervision of resident governors. The English merchants were based in Engelsestraat, which runs at right angles directly off the main canal. At the end of this street, even now, is an iron gate with steps down to a landing-stage where boats would have been loaded. The governor or 'meester van der Ingelscher nacien' in Bruges in the 1460s was none other than William Caxton. Deals were facilitated and ships returned home from Bruges with cargos of freshly manufactured Flemish textiles, lace, leather goods, brass utensils, paintings and, probably not least, boxes of manuscript Books of Hours to sell.

One of the great difficulties of all industry in the Middle Ages was distribution, and the cheapest transport was usually by water. Bruges was still a seaport with access for large ships up the Zwin channel, a tidal inlet which eventually silted up in the sixteenth century. In good weather, the coast of Kent was no more than a few hours from Flanders. It was incomparably easier and faster than sending goods out overland from most English towns, when many country roads were inadequate. Ships could sail from Bruges across to the Thames or up the eastern coast of England to the ports of King's Lynn in Norfolk and Grimsby with access to Yorkshire and the north, at no cost beyond the price of wind. Maybe the Rossdhu Book of Hours was imported through Berwick on Tweed, on the border with Scotland, or even Newhaven on the Firth of Forth by Edinburgh. The more expensive Books of Hours might be ordered by book-shops in London, Oxford or York. Cheaper examples were probably bought up by traders who could offer them for sale at provincial fairs and in market towns, with other small luxuries like decorative trinkets and Flemish textiles. A. H. Reed's book-plate, designed by himself, shows a medieval woman behind a trestle counter in an open-air stall displaying a selection of tempting manuscripts to a customer standing in the street, a fictitious fantasy but not unimaginable. Books of Hours from Flanders were the first ready-made books, sure of a market, ancestors of the modern publishing trade in which Reed made his money.

This particular Book of Hours then has twenty-four addi-tional leaves, supplementing and personalizing the manuscript soon after its arrival and sale in England. This is the portion which includes the name of the manuscript's owner as Margery Fitzherbert. The three pieces of evidence which will help us identify her are the use of her full name six times in prayers; a marginal vignette of a kneeling woman and a man, presum-ably representing the owner and her husband; and a sixteenth-century ownership inscription in English at the end, which

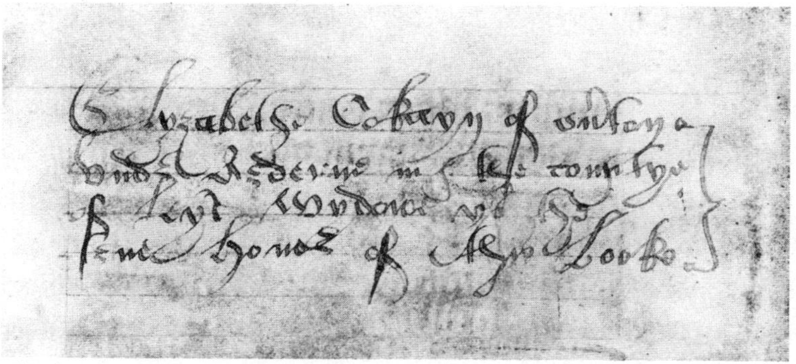

The sixteenth-century ownership inscription of Elizabeth Cokayne
in the Book of Hours of Margery Fitzherbert.

reads, 'Elyzabethe Cokayn of overton under Ardenne in the
countye of Leyc' wydowe ys the true honor [= *owner*] of this
booke.' The overwhelmingly probable identifications of those
two women are Margery (or Margaret), née Babington, wife of
John Fitzherbert of Etwall, Derbyshire, and Elizabeth, widow
of Margery's grandson Thomas Cokayne, evidently in Orton-
on-the-Hill, in Leicestershire.

The additions to the manuscript made in England are specifically for use by a woman, more obvious in Latin than English,
since the user prays to the Virgin as *famula tua*, 'your servant'
(female), and to all saints as *ego miserrima peccatrix*, 'I, miserable sinner' (female). Margery Fitzherbert is named in prayers
for use on a journey and for peace with her enemies. There
is a long rubric in red recounting that St Thomas the Martyr,
archbishop of Canterbury, used to recite the temporal joys of
the Virgin devoutly every day but that the Virgin herself once
appeared to him and asked why he commemorated events of
long ago, when he might now invoke the celestial joys she currently receives as Queen of Heaven, the text that follows. There
is also a Mass of the Holy Name, preceded by a rubric explaining
that Pope Boniface IV [608–15] granted three thousand years'

indulgence to whoever says this Mass or hears it or has it said, and that Robert Hallam, bishop of Salisbury [1407–17], in his castle in Sherborne on 29 July 1411 granted forty days' indulgence for each time the Mass is said.

The Mass of the Holy Name opens with a large initial and the full illuminated border which encloses the little portraits of the owner and her husband (Plate 17). It is entirely English in style. Its central frame sprouting into coloured acanthus leaves and the surrounding decoration including little green prickly trefoils all have close parallels in a page of the Luton Guild Book datable to 1475, probably painted in London. The marginal vignette of the kneeling couple has some background details copied from the earlier Flemish miniatures already in the manuscript: the tiled floor, the hanging green textile behind, and the exaggerated perspective of the roof beams all occur, for example, in the miniature of a funeral service now bound as the volume's frontispiece. The woman in the vignette is wearing a red dress with white collar and cuffs. On her head is a double or cleft hennin draped with a hanging white veil. By the 1470s, this headdress would already have seemed out-of-date, for the style was in vogue in the mid-century: an almost identical cleft hennin, for example, is in the portrait by Petrus Christus of a goldsmith and his wife painted in 1449. An event in any family life (even now) when a young woman commonly wears something old-fashioned is a wedding, and it could easily be that this is a marriage portrait. This is consistent with the unusual inclusion of Margery's surname. Normally, when an owner's name occurs in the prayers of a Book of Hours, only the first (or Christian) name appears. It is imaginable, however, that a wedding present might celebrate the union into a notable family by emphasis on the bride's new surname.

The Fitzherberts and Cokaynes were both wealthy families of old-established gentry in south Derbyshire in the English

Midlands. The Fitzherberts lived at Norbury, about halfway between Derby and Stoke-on-Trent; the seat of the Cokaynes was Ashbourne, a market town about four miles to the north-east. A few seconds of online searching brings up multiple sites constructed for modern family historians and seekers of ancestors, supplying conveniently detailed trees for both families, including John and Margery Fitzherbert, often with unsupported and even contradictory dates and connections where none are likely to be knowable with such assured precision. This over-confidence is not so different from the credulous genealogies in the fifteenth-century Maude (or Canterbury) Roll in Christchurch. We recall Professor Geering's reminder that texts which seem to buttress one another may mean no more than that they were all uncritically copied and pasted from common sources, not necessarily historical in the first place. However, the basic facts are clear, and we can check some by visiting Norbury.

Today there is a small and unlikely turning off the B5033, easy to miss, looking like the gateway into a private drive. At the end are two medieval houses, the fourteenth-century hall ('Old Manor') and its adjacent 'Norbury Hall', built in the 1440s for John's father, Nicholas Fitzherbert (d. 1473), eleventh lord of Norbury. Behind Old Manor and to the right, almost touching it, is Norbury Church, all three spectacular buildings standing together and alone in the countryside. The elaborate alabaster tomb of Nicholas is in the chancel on the south side in front of the altar, showing a knight lying with his head resting on his helmet and his feet on a lion. In niches around the edges are his seventeen children, from two wives. Most can be identified by attributes, including Nicholas's heir, Ralph Fitzherbert, twelfth lord of Norbury, first on the north side. Many are clerics or women. The south side of the tomb begins with a man standing

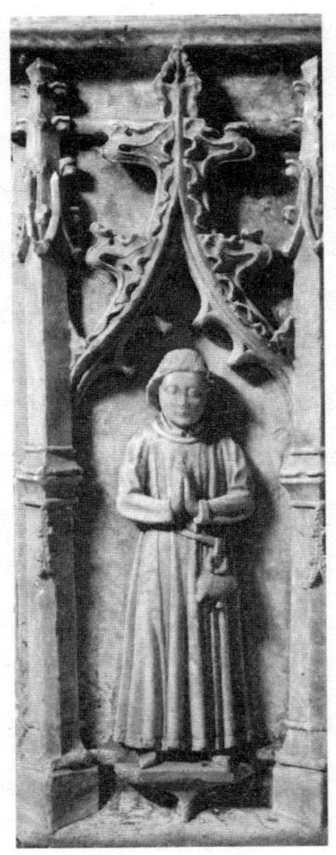

Detail from the tomb of Nicholas Fitzherbert, Norbury Church, *c.* 1473 or soon after, showing one of his sons, probably John, husband of Margery Fitzherbert.

with his hands together in prayer and with a purse dangling from his waist. This may well be John Fitzherbert (*c.* 1447–*c.* 1502, as online genealogies tell us), who was Remembrancer of the Exchequer in London, which involved the supervision of royal tax collection, perhaps explaining the money bag. He looks exactly like the portrait of the husband in the Book of Hours in Dunedin, in a robe with high collar and his straight hair cut neatly in short pageboy style around the head.

His wife, Margery (or Margaret, both names are used), was the daughter of Robert Babington, of Lower Kidding-ton, Oxfordshire, and his wife Maud d'Arches. The date of the Fitzherbert wedding is not securely known, but their children appear to have been born from about the mid-1470s onwards, which would make marriage around 1475 possible. The Flemish Book of Hours might even have been bought new and then immediately personalized to commemorate the wedding. The bridegroom doubtless often travelled professionally to London and could have transacted the deal there, consistent with the metropolitan illumination in the additions for Margery and the reference to a bishop of Salisbury in Sherborne, far nearer to London than to Derbyshire. The added Fitzherbert texts include a prayer to say before departing on a journey, 'so you will not fear danger or be captured by enemies', a reality during the Wars of the Roses. The Fitzherberts were Yorkists; London was largely Lancastrian.

When at home, John and Margery Fitzherbert lived principally at Etwall, about thirteen miles south-east of Norbury. The manor house has gone, and a modern school is on its site. Across a small green by the bus shelter and up on the spur of the hillside immediately opposite is Etwall Church, much of it late medieval. I was taken round by the vicar, the Reverend Stella Greenwood. There are no surviving monuments of the Fitzherbert family, but the building would have been familiar to them. The beamed roof above the chancel, although a replacement, resembles that in their portrait in the manuscript, and they doubtless sometimes knelt here. Books of Hours were not texts for public liturgy, but they were often brought to church: their owners contemplated the sacred pictures and read simple prayers in private while the priest was saying Mass, which the laity would not necessarily follow. A reference to this practice is in the *Book of Margery Kempe* (*c.* 1438) in which the woman, who was hardly literate if at all, was kneeling in church looking at Matins in her Book of Hours one day when a piece of masonry fell from the roof and knocked the manuscript from her hand.

The Fitzherberts' daughter was Barbara. There is a miniature of St Barbara in the Book of Hours, together with one of St Margaret, patron saint of childbirth. Barbara Fitzherbert probably learned to read from this manuscript, as was the domestic custom, mingling both meanings of the word 'primer'. We know exactly what she looked like, for she married Sir Thomas Cokayne (d. 1537), who was knighted at the Siege of Tournai and was present at the Field of Cloth of Gold in 1520. Their joint tomb is in the corner of the Boothby Chapel in the church of Ashbourne. Engraved on a marble slab is Sir Thomas, with substantial beard and handlebar moustache, and Barbara, with a small mouth, a lace collar and a tight-fitting cap with hanging lappets. They were the parents of Thomas Cokayne (d. 1546), of Overton Ardsley (or Overton Ardsey). Here we need a leap of faith, for if Overton Ardsley of the genealogical websites is the same as Overton-under-Arden, then we have it, for his wife was Elizabeth, née Ferrers, who would therefore be the Elizabeth Cokayne who wrote her name in the Book of Hours there as a widow.

The small village of Overton was close to the northern extremity of the Forest of Arden, known to Shakespeare, reaching up from Warwickshire. The name was compressed in speech from O'erton to Orton, and is now Orton-on-the-Hill, to distinguish it from the nearby Little Orton. It is on high ground rather than a true hill, sloping down on the east towards the site of the Battle of Bosworth, where the English Middle Ages finally ended in 1485, almost within earshot. Orton is mostly modern, well-kept with neatly mown verges, and is still suitable for widows, if my fellow lunchers in the Unicorn Inn were typical. The church, slightly out of the village, has white painted walls and box pews, its medieval glass and early monuments all gone, now made as Puritan as possible.

If already a widow, Elizabeth Cokayne must have been inscribing her Book of Hours after her husband's death in 1546, more than a decade into the turmoil of the English Reformation. Books of Hours were never illegal in England, but they had to be pruned of all excesses of Roman Catholicism. First of all, any acknowledgement of the papacy became treasonable when Henry VIII broke with Rome by the Act of Supremacy (1534) to enable his marriage to Anne Boleyn. By royal proclamation in June 1535, all references to the bishop of Rome were required to be 'eradicated and erased out' from every book. In November 1538, images of St Thomas Becket were ordered to be destroyed and his name in prayers 'erased and put out of all books'. It is remarkable how thoroughly these two injunctions were carried out, right down to domestic and parish level across the country, for almost every extant liturgical or devotional manuscript which transited through this fateful time in England was dutifully expurgated. Elizabeth Cokayne conformed only to the most minor extent. Two of the three uses of the single word 'pope' in the indulgences attributed to Boniface IV here are very lightly crossed through, and the two-page prayer to Thomas Becket is cancelled with a thin pale vertical line which in no way affects its legibility and use. The long rubric about Becket and the celestial joys is left entirely untouched. To judge from these, Elizabeth may have been a closet recusant, still adhering – as many did – to the old faith. Her use of 'widow', hardly essential in an ownership inscription, is perhaps a diversionary tactic, for widows were generally left alone by the royal commissioners. Her self-description as 'true' owner is ambiguous: she was indeed the rightful owner but was also true – faithful – to Catholicism.

Here we may regret the loss of the original calendar from the front of the Book of Hours, for such texts were commonly used for noting family anniversaries and events, especially in the sixteenth century, and the manuscript might have included names which would help us trace where it went after Elizabeth's death. Instead, it now has a calendar and two other illuminated leaves transferred from a quite different and much earlier manuscript. This had been made in London around 1410 by an artist now known in other notable Books of Hours, including the Neville Hours at Berkeley Castle. I used to hope that this cuckoo's egg substitution of a few pages might have happened early in our manuscript's history, and that this calendar might already have been grafted in here by the time of Margery Fitzherbert and Elizabeth Cokayne. However, this is not possible. Close the manuscript up tightly and you can see that the outside edges of the pages were decoratively mottled with red dots, a common feature of books in the seventeenth century, except on the eight inserted leaves, which are uncoloured. Therefore, these leaves were added to the volume only in time for its eighteenth-century rebinding. Furthermore, the eight additional leaves were from a slightly larger manuscript, trimmed to make them fit neatly, which necessitated cropping the extremities of some additions in the margins not made until the later sixteenth century, long after Elizabeth Cokayne could have owned it. They are not as drained out by damp.

The added calendar is from a manuscript which certainly belonged to Catholic recusants in the reign of Queen Elizabeth. The word 'pope' beside the names of saints who held the papacy has sometimes (but not always) been discreetly smudged, perhaps with a wet finger. The two feasts of Thomas Becket were rubbed out and then almost at once re-written. There are added anniversaries of the deaths of Roger Bolbet (1572) and what are presumably his parents, William (1552) and Margaret (1544): he was a Jesuit priest, a native of Staffordshire, who died in exile ministering to victims of the plague in Douai. There are obituaries too for the Catholic Queen Mary (1558) and David Pole (1568), Catholic bishop of Peterborough until his ejection by Elizabeth in 1559 for refusing to take the Oath of Supremacy. Several festivals of saints have been added, such as that of the Translation of St Osmund, the last English saint canonized before the Reformation, which is marked here as being a solemn feast in the diocese of Li[. . .], cropped at the edge of the page, which must be Lichfield, which included Derby, Norbury and Etwall within its eastern boundaries. David Pole had been a canon of Lichfield and archdeacon of Derby. Most striking of all is St Barloc, abbot, added on 10 September, in the same sixteenth-century hand as reinserted the feast of the Translation of St Thomas Becket. If St Antidius, the flying bishop of Besançon, is obscure, St Barloc must be one of the rarest names in the entirety of sainthood. There is no biography. As far as is known, only one church in Christendom has ever been dedicated to him, and possibly only a side chapel rather than a whole church. This was at Norbury, the family church of the Fitzherberts. He is still there, in the fifteenth-century stained-glass windows of the Lady Chapel off the south nave of Norbury Church, standing between Saints John the Baptist and Anthony, a tonsured cleric in a dark burgundy cloak, holding a book and crozier and named on a scroll in Gothic script as 's[an]ctus barlok abbas'. His inclusion in the calendar inserted into the Book of Hours of Margery Fitzherbert can only mean one thing: that manuscript too must have belonged to the Fitzherbert family, or to someone extremely intimate in their household. The Fitzherberts were committed recusants.

There is evidence of a lost Book of Hours which might have been the volume from which the eight leaves came. Elizabeth Fitzherbert was the wife of Ralph Fitzherbert (d. 1484), twelfth lord of Norbury. She was the sister-in-law of John and Margery Fitzherbert of Etwall, and she is buried beside her husband in another beautiful carved alabaster tomb in Norbury Church, parallel to that of her father-in-law, Nicholas Fitzherbert. In her will, dated from Norbury on 20 October 1490, she asked for her body to be buried 'in the Church of Saint Barloke before

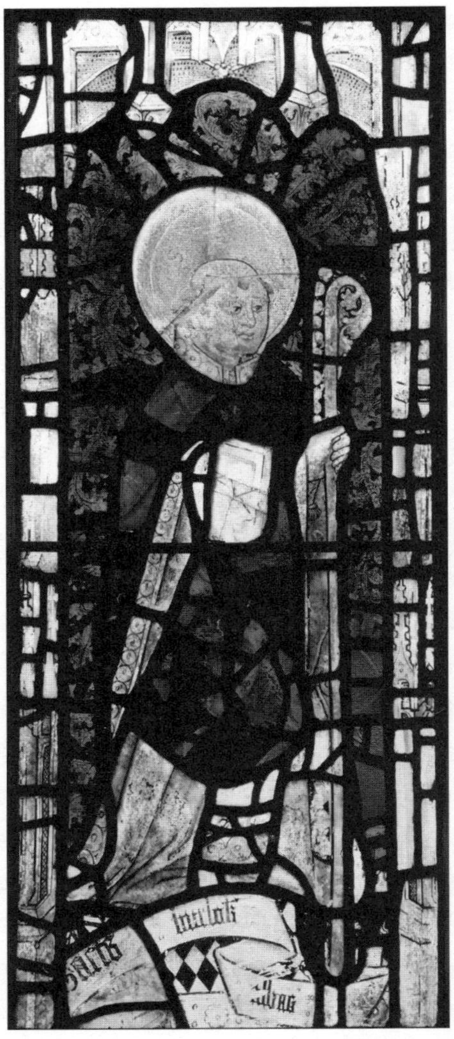

Saint Barloc, shown in the medieval stained glass of Norbury Church.

the image of Saint Nicholas beside the body of Ralph Fitzherbert late my husband', and she bequeathed 'my best prymer',
a Book of Hours, to her daughter Edith, who had married Sir
Thomas Babington. The eight leaves here include, in addition
to a calendar, the opening of Matins in the Office of the Virgin.
Almost uniquely in Books of Hours, this is illustrated with a
miniature of St Anne teaching the child Virgin Mary to read
(Plate 18). It is a reminder of the mother–daughter relationship
in Books of Hours and literacy, as in Margery to Barbara and
Elizabeth to Edith. The fifteenth-century stained glass in the
east window in Norbury Church includes a panel of this same
subject so uncannily close in composition, even to the pink of
St Anne's dress, that it might almost have been copied from the
manuscript. More than that (and knowing none of this), when
Dunedin lent this early fifteenth-century miniature for exhibition at the State Library of Victoria in Melbourne in 2008, I
suggested in the catalogue entry that the unexpected promin-
ence given to St Anne on the manuscript's opening page might
indicate that it had originally been made for a woman of that
name. Elizabeth Fitzherbert's mother's grandmother was Anne,
husband of Sir William Marshall (d. 1438), son of the earl of
Pembroke. It is just possible this was her book.

The Babingtons, like the Fitzherberts, became a high-profile
recusant family of Derbyshire in the sixteenth century. Edith
Babington's great-great-grandson was the Catholic conspirator
Anthony Babington, hanged, drawn and quartered in 1586 for
his part in the Babington Plot to assassinate Queen Elizabeth
to put Mary Queen of Scots on the throne. The Fitzherberts
maintained Norbury as a secluded outpost of recusancy and
preserved the medieval church with its wooden choir screen
and its almost entire complement of medieval stained glass. Sir
Thomas Fitzherbert, son of the fourteenth lord of Norbury,

died in the Tower of London for recusancy in 1591. His brother John was betrayed by his own son Thomas following the Babington Plot and died in the Fleet Prison in 1590. John's son Nicholas was an exile and secretary to Cardinal William Allen, founder of the English college in Douai, and died in Italy in 1612. Nicholas's cousin Thomas Fitzherbert was a Jesuit, rector of the English College in Rome, where he died in 1640.

By the eighteenth century, Catholicism in England, although still illegal, had lost the extreme stigma of treason, and it came to resemble some surreptitious and even romantic, often aristocratic, private fraternity, like the Jacobites or the Freemasons. Priests' hiding holes and concealed cavities were unbricked. Relics and trinkets of covert Catholicism were brought out and carefully admired and preserved. We can never know, but we might imagine that many damaged and damp-stained leaves from two different recusant Books of Hours were found hidden together somewhere in Derbyshire, maybe still at Norbury, and were gathered up and bound without regard to use, to make one manuscript, unusable for prayer but nostalgic of the persecuted past. The Flemish miniature of a funeral service, suitably Catholic in appearance since it shows three priests and a church service, was placed as a frontispiece. By coincidence, its illuminated border includes a cockerel, the heraldic device of the Cokayne family, who had owned most of the book two hundred years earlier.

The only explicit evidence of later ownership of the manuscript is the armorial bookplate of William Ridley Richardson (1856–1935). His middle name, that of the Protestant martyr of 1555, does not suggest Catholicism. I once bought on eBay a photograph of Richardson and his wife seated on the veranda of their house, Ravensfell, in Bromley, Kent, looking out over an elegant and spacious lawn with flowering shrubs and tall trees. The house, built for his father in 1858 in ornate brick in the Tudor style, appears as a quintessential evocation of unchangeable English late Victorian prosperity and comfort, and I set out to find it. It is now built over in the outer suburbs of south-east London. From Bromley South station you walk uphill until the High Street becomes a modern pedestrian shopping precinct, paved right across what was once the Richardsons' lawn. Close along the frontage on the street where their veranda stood is a row of commercial premises called Ravensfell Parade, keeping the name. Beside this and rising above a temporary-looking gambling shop, offering slot machines and online betting, is the main brick gable and one chimney of Ravensfell House itself, shorn of its wings, as lonely as Ozymandias. I walked backwards, holding the photograph, until I stood precisely where the picture had been taken in another age, with my back to a coffee shop. Flanking the betting shop are dealers in second-hand computer equipment and cut-price office supplies, all overlooked from the right by the concrete Churchill Theatre. To experience the past as it once was, it may be better to look at the Book of Hours in Dunedin. The Richardson family came originally from Lascelles Hall in Yorkshire, about eighty miles north of Norbury, but their Book of Hours was doubtless bought as an antiquarian collectible, not as a relic or for prayer, for they owned other medieval manuscripts. William Ridley Richardson died in Torquay. His last surviving son lived until 1982 and may have been the consignor of this book to Sotheby's, 29 November 1952, lot 8, where it was catalogued in five lines.

8

Wellington and Auckland

There were two things any teenage enthusiast for manuscripts needed in New Zealand in the late 1960s: a sleeping bag and a copy of David M. Taylor's *The Oldest Manuscripts in New Zealand* (1955). There was a tradition there then, which must derive from necessity in early colonial experience and probably still exists, that friends of friends would always allow a fellow traveller to bed down for the night, sometimes on the floor or in an outhouse. Everyone owned a sleeping bag and a parka, a kind of short waxy raincoat essential in Dunedin and in the tropically wet New Zealand bush. A. H. Reed used his sleeping bag even at home. Mine was orange and neither it nor the parka were ever quite long enough as I grew older, and I do not recall what eventually happened to them back in England. I still have the copy of Taylor, however, all the more precious to me for its battered state, faded pale-blue cloth binding, and pages annotated and thumbed throughout like an old cookery book. A damp rucksack, or 'backpack' as it is called there, probably contributed to its dilapidation.

The Reverend David Mortimer Taylor (1910–95) was born in England, and emigrated with his family to Christchurch in 1913, a little younger than I did. His father and later both his brothers were Anglican clergymen, and he too was ordained in 1934 after a degree in classics at Canterbury University. From 1964 until his retirement a decade later, he was general secretary of the

National Council of Churches. He and his father were out-spoken pacifists, rare then, and he became a campaigner for nuclear disarmament, in which all New Zealand now shares a powerful international voice. In the 1940s he was amazed to encounter a display of medieval manuscripts at Bible House in Wellington, the national headquarters of what was then called the British and Foreign Bible Society. 'Indeed, I may say it was the sight of these treasures that started me on the investigations which have resulted in the present book,' he wrote.

> Never having seen any hand-made volumes, and knowing that the vast majority of New Zealanders were equally unfortunate, I was thrilled to find, tucked away in an office on the third floor, such a delightful collection. It made me wonder whether these were the oldest pieces of writing in New Zealand, or not.

The result, which took him nine years to write and was mostly finished by about 1950, is almost a travel book, in which Mr Taylor works his way north through the provinces of Otago, Canterbury, Wellington and Auckland, in that order, listing and describing whatever medieval manuscripts he was able to find, a total of seventy-seven altogether, often with specimen Latin transcriptions and translations. In spirit, it is not unlike some of those discursive itineraries around European manuscript librar-ies by pioneer antiquaries such as Bernard de Montfaucon OSB (1655–1741) or Johann Georg Keyssler (1693–1743), often clerical too, and, like them, Mr Taylor could sometimes be credulous and too trusting of old descriptions. His engaging *Oldest Man-uscripts in New Zealand* has a conversational style, easy to read, and one shares the author's wonder and excitement of first trying to comprehend and record what he was looking at. There are no great discoveries: its most important is that medieval books were living quietly and unnoticed in New Zealand all this time, like the kakapo in the bush in the South Island. He takes us to meet Sir George Grey's Besançon Missal, without attempting to identify its patron, and some parts of the fourteenth-century lectern Bible broken up by A. H. Reed, with whom he discussed its dispersal. The Hours of Margery Fitzherbert reached New Zealand too late for inclusion, but the French Book of Hours in the Dunedin Public Library is here; indeed, Mr Reed paid for its reproduction as a coloured frontispiece, subtly promoting his own manuscript.

I loved the book, and once knew every sentence. In 1969, I wrote admiringly to Mr Taylor, who replied, 'People who show such appreciation of my book have not been too plentiful.' Eventually I met him, spending an evening with him at Knox College in the same Common Room where I had once sat with Lloyd Geering. He told me no one had really taken any notice of his research on medieval manuscripts at all and that sales of the book were negligible. A long time later, in 1985, he recognized my name in some Sotheby's press release about a manuscript auction and wrote to me in London: 'The fact that I kept that letter illustrates the fact that it meant a lot to me . . . To the best of my knowledge, you are the ONLY person who has studied MSS and my book as deeply as you did.' When I replied to that, reiterating how precious and formative his tutorial journey into the manuscripts of New Zealand had been to me, he was so proud he sent my letter off for publication in the *University of Canterbury Chronicle*, September 1985: GRADUATE'S BOOK WINS HIGH PRAISE FROM SOTHEBY'S EXPERT.

At first, I scoured Mr Taylor's travelogue for Books of Hours, since they were my current obsession in the Reed Collection. Eleven were listed there as being in New Zealand, of which three were in private possession. Two of these were owned in Auckland by Dr (Klaus) Volker Heine (1900–1985), who had moved out to

New Zealand from Germany in 1947 after his wife and children had already become established there. I wrote to him in 1969 too. He replied, 'Unfortunately, I had to sell the books about the time Mr Taylor's work appeared in print in order to raise the money for bringing a relative of ours from Germany to N. Z. All my attempts at that time to sell them to libraries in N. Z. were without success, and I had to send them to England.' We will encounter this theme again, the manuscript migrants which did not manage to settle and had to come back reluctantly to Europe to continue their lives. The Books of Hours were sold by Dr Heine at Sotheby's in London, 29 January 1951, lots 2 and 3.

The third Book of Hours then privately owned in New Zealand has a more poignant history after its publication by Mr Taylor, who calls it 'a magnificent specimen of French work' and illustrates as his Plates XI–XII. It had belonged to Percy Watts Rule (1889–1953), an architect in Timaru, a small city south of Christchurch, and it was inherited by his daughter, Hazel, wife of the Reverend H. G. Norris. The manuscript's illuminated borders of gold leaves and trefoils on delicate swirls of black penwork, probably Parisian work of about 1430, were very like those on a bifolium in the Reed Collection acquired by the Dunedin Public Library from Folio Fine Art in London in 1966. In January 1969, I too bought from Folio a very similar leaf from that same manuscript; it cost £9.10s. and became my MS 9. When I inquired from Mrs Norris about seeing their Book of Hours for comparison, she wrote back to say it had, regrettably, also had to be sold. The dreadful conclusion took me far too long to reach. The Watts Rule manuscript was Sotheby's, 7 December 1964, lot 160, bought by Folio Fine Art, who cut it up and then coincidentally sold two leaves back to buyers in New Zealand, the Reed Collection and me. The intact manuscript made £190 at Sotheby's. It had four miniatures, which Folio mounted and

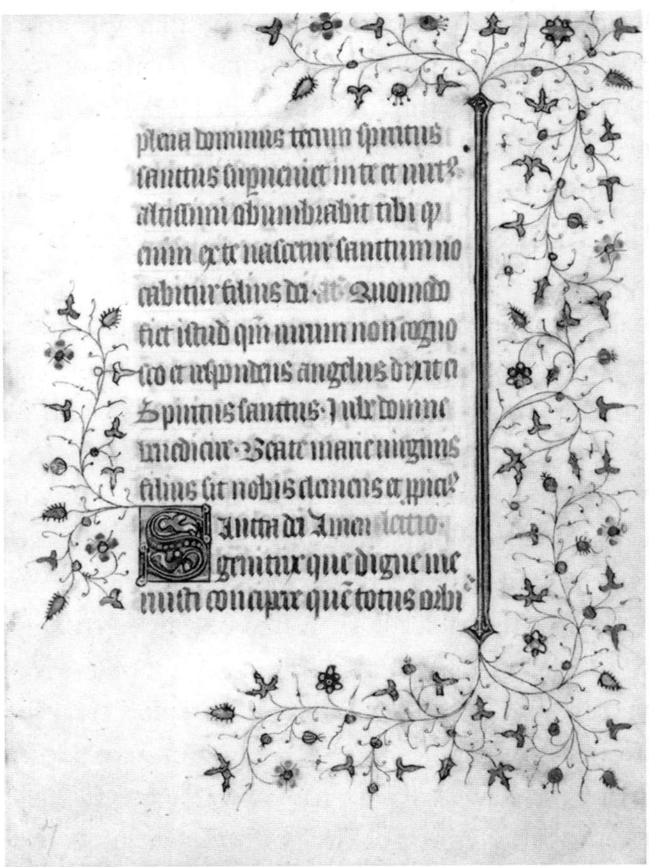

Single leaf from the Book of Hours once owned by Percy Watts Rule, bought by the author in 1969 from Folio Fine Art, who had acquired and dismembered it.

priced at £65 each, and 157 text leaves. If these were all sold for what I paid for mine (which was not necessarily the case), 4 × 65 + 157 × 9½ = £1,751.10s, almost ten times the price at which the manuscript had left New Zealand. These interesting sums may contribute to the reasons in Chapter 7 why manuscripts are sometimes dismembered for sale.

The first migration of the manuscript might go back further. A principal source of the earliest books owned by Percy Watts Rule was the library of his old friend and near neighbour

Benjamin Hibbard (1834–1912), a shopkeeper in the goldfields and later in Timaru, who had arrived with his wife as settlers on the barque *William and Jane* in Port Chalmers in the Otago Harbour in February 1857. There is an early photograph of him in military uniform with a sword, a short man with a thick black beard. After his death, Hibbard's library was sorted for his family by Watts Rule, who acquired four incunabula from the collection and perhaps also the Book of Hours. Hibbard had been educated in France. If he brought the manuscript with him in 1857, five years even before Grey came to Kawau Island, it was the first in the South Island and among the earliest to reach New Zealand.

As we find so often after a few minutes' conversation, everyone in New Zealand seems to have some connection with everyone else. In November 1924, Hibbard's grandson and co-heir, Raymond Walter Hibbard, married Irene Clemas. She was the eldest daughter of Albert Clemas (1880–1956), who was the collector of the manuscripts and early printed editions at the British and Foreign Bible Society in Wellington that inspired David Taylor to begin writing his book. At least one of his incunabula came from Hibbard. Very little has been published on Clemas, and he merits a short digression.

Albert Edward Thomas Baker Clemas was born in the seaport of Teignmouth in Devon in England. He became a pantry boy – a junior galley assistant – on several tall-masted sailing ships operating between Australia and New Zealand. He was on board the *Beacon Rock*, which left Port Pirie in South Australia on 4 October 1900 bound for Wellington with a cargo of wool and tallow. It ran into a great storm, which brought down all three masts. The ship, which was assumed by its owners to have sunk, drifted three months later, fully manned, onto the coast of South America. The crew rigged up a temporary sail and managed to get the ship round the Horn, and let it follow the current eastwards, across the Atlantic and south of Africa. It was eventually brought into Lyttleton harbour, more than nine months after leaving Australia. Clemas worked on several more trans-Tasman runs on the *Mokoia* before settling, initially in Wellington, and marrying Muriel Lewis in 1902. There were two events which brought unwelcome press attention. In 1910, when they were overdue on weekly rent of 16 shillings on their house in Dawson Street, they were violently set upon one night by the landlord's son, Robert Russell. In 1913, after unwise investment in a stationer's shop in Willis Street the previous year, Muriel Clemas was formally declared bankrupt. They then moved out to Masterton, a town about fifty miles north-east of Wellington. He became financial officer of Donald & Sons, importers of agricultural and light industrial machinery, and they prospered gently. Albert Clemas was a keen chess player and participant in community events.

Clemas was an acquisitor from childhood. He gave regular talks to the Optimists Club in Masterton and other local groups on collecting stamps, old maps, oriental china, rare books and early Bibles, even medieval manuscripts (1932, 'a fair attendance', faint praise), usually passing round examples he owned himself. In 1939, he spoke on hobbies in general: ' "All of us are collectors of one kind of another," said Mr Clemas', as reported in *The Wairarapa Age* on 23 September; ' "If we are not collecting things, we collect impressions." ' He lived at 14 Cole Street (now the site of a car park), and a visitor to the house in 1928 described Clemas in slippers and a haze of tobacco smoke taking him through into an Aladdin's cave of 'relics of vanished civilizations . . . Albert Clemas sends out feelers beyond New Zealand for treasures further to grace his room of wonders.'

Early Bibles and illuminated manuscripts became an especial interest. In 1932 he claimed that some were ancestral treasures of his family, 'bought by my people & handed on' or, like his

Book of Hours, had been 'bought many years ago by private treaty'. At least in regard to his five medieval manuscripts, this was entirely untrue, a wishful make-believe of an uprooted first-generation immigrant with no tangible forebears. All were recently bought. His thirteenth-century Bible was probably the first. He said it had cost him £150 'and was considered a bargain', and in September 1926 he wrote to Johannes Andersen at the Turnbull Library saying that his sister had sent it out to him, presumably dispatching a purchase newly transacted in England, and he wondered if it was now the oldest book in New Zealand. Andersen replied that their Boethius *De musica* was a century earlier and that he understood there were twelfth-century books in the Grey Collection. Undaunted, Clemas exhibited his Bible in October 1926 to the Boys' Division of the YMCA and in November to the Methodist Synod. Three more man-uscripts had transited through Sotheby's, not necessarily directly to Clemas: a Psalter (July 1925, £75), the Book of Hours (April 1929, not remotely 'many years ago', £80) and a twelfth-century glossed Gospel of Matthew (November 1929, £15). As soon as his acquisitions reached New Zealand, Clemas generally showed them off. In June 1929, the Book of Hours was exhibited in the shop window of the jeweller L. S. Nicol, next to Woolworth's in Queen Street, Masterton. The press reported, 'The volume had been sent out from England for display at the recent Art Exhib-ition, but unfortunately arrived a mail too late.'

Within a year, the Great Depression had hit New Zealand, exports fell by 40 per cent, wages were cut and unemployment rose. There were modest riots in Wellington in 1932. Albert Clemas, doubtless never forgetting the bankruptcy of 1913, wrote on 23 August 1932, at the suggestion of Johannes Andersen, to the national branch of the British and Foreign Bible Society, explaining that because of the financial crisis he was forced to raise cash. He had offered the manuscripts and earliest printed Bibles first to the town of Masterton for a reported £150 but the Borough Council declined the purchase. Clemas told the Bible Society he had paid £500 altogether but would accept £250. On 3 March 1933, the Society confirmed their agreement to proceed, organizing a public subscription. The manuscripts were placed on display in Wellington and 188 people contributed sums from one shilling up to £25. By the end of February 1934, all the money had been raised, and the governor general came to admire the purchase. CLEMAS COLLECTION SOLD TO OUTSIDE BUYER, bewailed the Masterton newspaper: ASSET TO TOWN LOST, as if this were betrayal across the world, not fifty miles down the road.

The books were then exhibited at agricultural shows around New Zealand, accompanied by the Reverend David Calder from the Society, including displays in three locations in or around Christchurch in September 1934 and at the Market Reserve Building in Napier on the east coast of the North Island in October 1935. This unusual outreach coincides with a similar initiative of the American Federation of Arts, which sponsored travelling exhibitions of illuminated manuscripts round the provincial United States in 1931–37. Nothing like that ever happened in Europe.

In the summer holidays of 1969–70, by which time I was at university, I went to see the Clemas manuscripts in Wellington, accompanied by my copy of Taylor. It seemed quite normal and safe for a nineteen-year-old to travel alone, hitchhiking and sleeping on floors or in the open air. I went first to Christchurch, where I spent a night in the garden shed of my former English teacher at King's High, Reg Graham, by then a school inspector but away at the time. I saw the Maude Roll the next day and took the overnight ferry from Lyttleton to Wellington, sharing a cheap inside cabin with three other men at random. The boat berthed at the Queen's Wharf terminal near Wellington railway station early in the morning of Thursday 8 January 1970 and as soon as I reasonably could I presented myself at Bible House, in Willis Street, the same street where Muriel Clemas's ill-fated stationery shop had closed in 1913, easy walking distance up from the harbour. I was welcomed by the general secretary, the Reverend Edward Moody, who had been a missionary in northern China. I recall his desk with trays for incoming and outgoing post, labelled 'Genesis' and 'Exodus'. The Clemas manuscripts and earliest printed Bibles were all propped up in rows and tied open as a wall display filling most of one side of the office, as they must have been when David Taylor first saw them. There are old photographs of the Grey Collection in Auckland similarly exhibited in the 1950s. I was encouraged to take down anything I wanted to look at.

I asked first for the Book of Hours. Taylor's description begins, 'As a work of art, this is much superior' to one he had seen in the Turnbull Library, but maybe in world terms it is not exceptional. It has twelve large miniatures but lacks others, by two artists working in the Parisian style. After the occupation of Paris by the English in 1420, however, many manuscript illuminators had dispersed to the provinces, and this Book of Hours, datable towards the mid-century, was probably executed in eastern France, maybe even in Besançon, like the Missal in Auckland. The flyleaf has offsets from pilgrim badges once attached, a feature of Books of Hours which is quite common and still very little studied. The manuscript was formerly in the library of Lord Brownlow at Belton House in Lincolnshire, the source also of one of the thirteenth-century Bibles in the Reed Collection in Dunedin.

Much more important is the manuscript Psalter bought by Clemas in or after 1925, 'quite different from anything we have examined yet', according to Taylor. I looked at this too. Private

Psalters for lay use had generally been replaced by Books of Hours by the late Middle Ages, except in Germany and occasionally elsewhere. This is high-quality English work of the early fifteenth century, with glittering gold (Plate 19). As was already known when Clemas acquired it, the manuscript has a long and almost contemporary inscription in Middle English in which one Beterice Carneburgh presented it to Dame Grace Centurio of the Franciscan nunnery just outside the city wall at Aldgate in London, to be used by her and then by other nuns of the convent after Grace's death to pray for the souls of those named in the manuscript. This is precious information, for books from female communities in medieval England are not common. Some years later, after the Bible Society manuscripts had been placed on long-term loan at the Turnbull Library, where they are now, I tried using ultra-violet light to read the erased names added in the calendar, for whom the nuns were asked to pray. I deciphered what seemed to be, '*Obitus henrici de Shrel*[. . .] *patris mei*', the death of the unknown original owner's father Henry (16 January), and the anniversaries of the deaths also of his mother Johanna (10 September), his brother William (21 June), his wife Elizabeth (29 August), and his eldest son Richard (17 November).

This was first picked up from my catalogue entry in a truly brilliant observation by Margaret Connolly, now of the University of St Andrews, who noted how all these facts, except my hesitant reading of the surname, seemed to fit the known biography of John Shirley (d. 1456), the famous London scribe, man of letters, translator, and probable seller and publisher of Middle English manuscripts, including works of Chaucer, Hoccleve and Lydgate. He was a gentleman bookman, working in a well-connected courtly circle, like publishers' editors today and, a bit later in the fifteenth century, like William Caxton in Westminster. In 2023, therefore, I brought the ultra-violet back to the manuscript. Professor Connolly is absolutely right. The compressed Gothic letters 're' and 'ir' look very similar, but I am now convinced: the entry with the surname reads, '*Obitus henrici de Shirl*[. . .]', cropped, leaving a trace of the left-hand stoke of an 'e'. It is the name we want, and this must have been written by John Shirley.

In his will of November 1452, Shirley asked to be buried in the chapel at St Bartholomew's Hospital beside his mother and his late wife Elizabeth and his children already deceased. He also made provision for an annual commemoration of the dead on the anniversary of his mother's death in September 'for the soulis of my fader, of my moder, of my wiff Elizabeth passid to God, of my childer . . .', all listed in this Psalter, mostly our only record of their names. Furthermore, the family entries appear to be in the same calligraphic liturgical hand as the script of the calendar itself, and I could believe that the whole text was copied for his own possession by Shirley, who wrote an accomplished Gothic hand, often used in signing his name. John Stowe's *Survey of London* (1598) prints the wording of Shirley's eventual tombstone in St Bartholomew's, giving his age as ninety. If this is not some implausible exaggeration, as it may be (like the reported age of the *Old, Old, Very Old Man* Thomas Par in 1635), Shirley would almost certainly have known Geoffrey Chaucer, who died around 1400 and whose manuscripts he copied. This is important because the evidence for Chaucer's own scribe being called Adam, the subject of much debate, hangs entirely on the testimony of John Shirley, who cites or invents a verse saying so. Shirley's second wife, after the death of Elizabeth (recorded in 1420–21), was Margaret Lynne. Her sister was called Beatrice, and Shirley wrote both their names in an anthology of Middle English literature, now in the Huntington Library in California. This Beatrice married Avery Cornburgh (d. 1487), London ironmonger, Member of Parliament and Under-Treasurer of England. She lived until 1501 and was evidently her sister's heir. She is therefore the 'Beterice Carneburgh', who inherited the Shirley Psalter and gave it to the Franciscan nunnery. It all makes good sense. At the very end of the manuscript is a list of psalms and a note apparently saying that on 23 September 1486, 'I bygan ye C pater nosters in good tyme', which may be Sister Grace's record of starting the obligated prayers for the Shirley family departed.

After a morning in the Bible Society in January 1970, I went across to the Alexander Turnbull Library, in Bowen Street. We will leave the account of this collection to Chapter 9. However, to keep together two English manuscripts of the fifteenth century and my own misreading of names in their calendars, let us look quickly at one item, enough for an afternoon.

There is a Missal of the first half of the fifteenth century given to the Turnbull Library in 1958 – again too late for inclusion in Taylor's book – by Sir John Ilott (1884–1973), advertising magnate, art collector and philanthropist. It is of the Use of Sarum. Unlike Books of Hours for English owners, manuscripts for the Sarum liturgy (and Psalters) were almost always made locally and to order in England itself, not imported ready-made from Flanders. English Missals were once extremely common in that every religious house and church in the country owned at least one, often many. They were systematically discarded and destroyed at the Reformation, when their use became illegal in England. This copy is a wreck of a once stately and graceful book. All references to popes and Thomas Becket were thoroughly removed in the sixteenth century, and many illuminated leaves are missing. What remained was salvaged, flattened, repaired and beautifully bound in 1900 by Douglas

Cockerell (1870–1945), brother of Sydney Cockerell, director of the Fitzwilliam Museum, for the library of the Arts and Crafts connoisseur Michael Tomkinson (1841–1921), in whose sale at Sotheby's in July 1922 John Ilott bought three manuscripts. This is one of the few instances in New Zealand of manuscripts being selected not for their texts or antiquity but simply as examples of elegant design and fine book production. Ilott was in England at the time (I know this from the immigration record of his return in November 1922), and his purchases must be practically the only medieval manuscripts in New Zealand which were viewed and bought from first-hand judgement in advance, rather than being ordered from afar and relying on descriptions by other people.

There is an added entry beside 19 October in the calendar, which I read long ago as '*Obitus Will[elm]i Abyngton' sen[ior] Armigeri A[nn]° M° CCCC° xlvi°*', the death of William Abyngton the elder, esquire, in the year 1446. I was never able to identify who this might be. Looking at it now, all these decades later, I realize the name is Alyngton. One letter changes everything. It is now easy. William Alington was Speaker in the House of Commons and High Sheriff of Cambridgeshire, and died, exactly as noted here, on 19 October 1446. He was buried with a monumental brass recording this fact in Horseheath Church, ten miles south-east of Cambridge. It is a late medieval flint and stone church with brick crenellations (but locked when I visited), and the Missal may well have been commissioned by the family for use there. William Alington was succeeded as squire of Horseheath by his son of the same name, who died in 1459. The manuscript may have been made in London, where the elder Alington worked, or locally in Cambridge. About 140 manuscript Missals for the Use of Sarum survive. Of these, only about a quarter can be even tentatively associated with any specific parish churches in Britain, of which there were around 13,000 in medieval England alone. It is hard to grasp the immensity of what was lost.

That evening, I took the overnight train up to Auckland, from the huge pale-yellow classical railway station where I had left my luggage during the day, near the Wellington ferry terminal. This saved a night's accommodation. The Main Trunk railway, as it was called, had been finished in 1908. I slept for most of the journey but I remember being aware of the train's descent round and round the Raurimu Spiral, an engineering solution devised in 1898 to connect two very different land levels, before a stop in the dark about half way at Taumarunui, where passengers stretched and bought hot meat pies, such a rite of passage for New Zealanders that it became a 1950s folk song, 'Taumarunui on the Main Trunk Line'. We pulled into Auckland early in the morning. This time I stayed for just over a week near the harbour bridge on the sofa of a student flat, where occupants included the brother of someone from my class at school. They played loudly and incessantly the late 1960s Peter, Paul and Mary pop song 'I'm in Love with a Big Blue Frog', about racial discrimination, an unfamiliar American topic just beginning to reach New Zealand.

I spent my days that hot January in the old Auckland Central Library in Wellesley Street, opened by Sir George Grey in 1887. I looked at the Besançon Missal for the first time and made drawings of its erased coats-of-arms, and I turned the pages of Grey's Rossdhu Book of Hours, so much grander than its little cousin in Dunedin, adapted for Margery Fitzherbert. I had the benefit not only of Taylor's book but also a little booklet in dark green and gilt buckram boards published by Auckland City Council in 1908, *A Guide to the Principal Manuscripts, Early Printed Books, Autograph Letters, etc., contained in the Auckland Free Public Library*, by Henry Shaw (1850–1928). Taylor opens his Chapter 6 by explaining,

Mr Henry Shaw served the people of New Zealand not only by cataloguing the Sir George Grey Collection (which includes the twenty-eight MSS described in our last chapter) but also by presenting in 1913 sixteen more MSS which he had collected himself. These, together with the Sir George Grey Collection, are all housed, and well displayed, at the Central Library, Auckland.

Shaw's preface to his catalogue says that it is based on the British Museum guidebooks. It is impressive in its range, for it covers not only rare European books but also specimens of Ethiopian and Persian and Javanese manuscripts, for example, and even one in an Aboriginal language of New South Wales, dated 1857 and 'tastefully illuminated in gold and colours'. Connoisseurs of improbable reaches of the Gothic Revival would do well to look at that manuscript. The entries by Shaw are short, in the style of nineteenth-century booksellers' catalogues, from which as many as possible were probably directly copied. Of the Rossdhu Hours, for example, Shaw notes, 'Books of hours written by English scribes for English use are extremely rare in good condition. This specimen is in perfect condition.' It is actually, as we now know, by a Flemish scribe for Scottish use (even rarer), and is missing leaves in several places. To be fair, it was probably the only Book of Hours Shaw had ever seen.

I wish I could find more to like in Henry Shaw. He sounds tedious and self-important, but perhaps he was shy. He was certainly a generous public benefactor and a considerable collector of books from medieval manuscripts and incunabula right through to contemporary literature and private press books. He was born in Birmingham and migrated with his parents to New Zealand in 1859. His father was a jeweller. He worked for various local firms in Auckland, including land agents and a drapery,

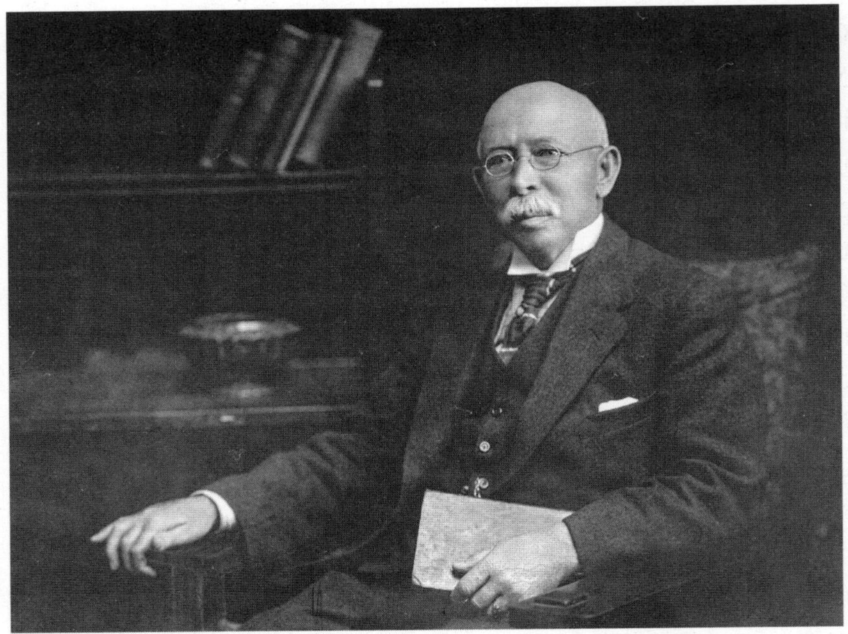

Henry Shaw, Auckland accountant and book collector.

but the same economic depression of the 1880s which had brought the Reed family to the brink of penury also rendered Shaw unemployed. He opened a small bookshop, partly to sell his own library. His customers included Sir George Grey, who bought numerous items, including incunabula. Once back on his feet and able to collect again, Shaw joined the American Tobacco Company, and by 1902 had opened his own accountancy business. He served as an Auckland City Councillor and managed their finances. By middle age he was bald with a white moustache and wire glasses, like a solemn oriental mandarin; he never married and lived with his brother, also a book collector, in Vermont Street in the west Auckland suburb of Ponsonby.

Henry Shaw evidently idolized the philanthropy of Sir George Grey, even slightly muddling their two libraries. In

1904 Shaw gave 150 early books to supplement Grey's in the Central Library, including a seventeenth-century manuscript of Matthew Paris, *Historia minor*, which he described in the catalogue of 1908. In late 1912, after a period of very serious illness in hospital, which must have focused his mind on mortality, he presented the rest of his collection, with sixteen medieval manuscripts. In 1913–15 Shaw acted as honorary curator of the Grey Collection, working two afternoons a week. The press noted the financial worth of his donation and Shaw, the city's accountant, doubtless supplied the figures. The headline in the *New Zealand Herald* on 13 December 1912 was LIBRARY VALUED AT £2500, going on to say that his gift included a manuscript of the *Consolation* of Boethius in French (this is wrong: the *Consolation* belonged to Grey and had been shown to Froude on Kawau in 1885). When the Shaw books were unpacked, the proclaimed value went up, suggesting a satisfyingly rising investment. SHAW LIBRARY WORTH £4000, announced the *Herald* the following October. This is very unlike the public response to manuscripts acquired by institutions in Britain: it is unimaginable that a gift to a national collection, then or now, would be trumpeted primarily as a financial asset. A. H. Reed was still using the criteria of investment and rising value in his press releases in Dunedin in 1966–67.

I asked for a number of Shaw's manuscripts in January 1970. They are generally rather dull and hard to love, minor texts, usually liturgical or theological, bought from England for very small prices from the mass of manuscripts on the market around 1900. I doubt he spent as much as a hundred pounds or so on the entirety of them. Three were from early sales in 1898–99 of the truly immense collection of Sir Thomas Phillipps (1792–1872), so vast that when I was first employed by Sotheby's in 1975 it was still being catalogued and dispersed. Shaw's best medieval manuscript is perhaps the Latin Bible of around 1210 mentioned in Chapter 5, from that earliest generation of one-volume portable Bibles. There was discussion in 1912 whether this might be the oldest manuscript of the Scriptures in New Zealand, perhaps even in Australasia. By 1913, patriotism had set in: it was definitively declared the oldest biblical text in Australasia, overlooking at least one twelfth-century Greek Gospel Book in Grey's own library and unaware that fragments of an early ninth-century Latin Bible, almost four hundred years earlier, would be found in 2012 in the binding of one of Shaw's own printed books, as recounted above.

Shaw gave a collection of Māori artefacts to the Auckland Museum in 1913 and Japanese antiquities in 1924. The City Council presented him with an illuminated address in 1922 in recognition of his many benefactions. He had by then retired and moved first to Hawkes Bay and then to Wellington, where he died in 1928, not uncelebrated but perhaps not greatly regretted. Obituaries, like that in the *New Zealand Herald*, quite rightly emphasized his gifts of books and manuscripts, 'which would be valued highly in any part of the world, [and] which are almost beyond valuation in a country so far from the centres of ancient culture where such things are naturally found.'

It is interesting to watch the assimilation of manuscripts into New Zealand, and even a pride in their being better or older than anything in Australia. When either manuscripts or people have migrated and settled, there comes a point when they are accepted into their new nation and become part of it. Any departure again somehow seems shameful or an admission of failure to integrate. Dr Heine and Mrs Norris tried first to sell their Books of Hours within New Zealand and apologized for sending them away; Clemas offered his manuscripts first to Masterton, and their loss even to Wellington seemed local disloyalty. The

Auckland *Sun* in 1929 reflected on the Grey and Shaw bequests, noting the patriotism of their owners in not selling the books abroad, 'put into exile for profit'. These are unexpected words. They beg the question that every medieval manuscript in the country had already been quite recently expatriated from where it came from, usually via commerce, but to the journalist in 1929 the immigrant manuscripts now seemed redefined as resident New Zealanders. One Auckland rare book even made its contribution to the First World War. In 1915, after the catastrophic destruction of the university library of Louvain in August 1914 in the first days of fighting, an international appeal was sent out for replacement books. Henry Shaw proposed to the City Council that the Library in Auckland should deaccession one of the two copies he had given them of the four-volume incunable edition of the glossed Bible printed probably by Arnold Rusch, *c.* 1480. This was duly forwarded to Louvain, through the collecting point at the Rylands Library in Manchester. The duplicate copy fortuitously remaining behind in Auckland was the one in which the fragments of the early ninth-century Bible were found in 2012.

The New Zealanders' huge and voluntary part in both World Wars was legendary and a source of great pride to many of the older generation in my childhood. ANZAC Day on 25 April was a major national event, on a level with Waitangi Day. New Zealand had sent troops to Korea in 1950 and to Malaya in 1956. We had compulsory cadets at school, and we used to note sardonically that the targets for shooting practice all resembled hunched-up Orientals. In May 1965 New Zealand committed its first units to the war in Vietnam. Each year, all boys reaching eighteen had their birthdays drawn out at random to decide who would be called up for military service. My brother Michael was selected and declared himself a conscientious objector, a young age at which to have any informed position, and he was eventually let off, with some ill grace. My birth date was not chosen, saved by merest chance, like the duplicate incunable in Auckland not sent to Belgium. William's birthday was picked, but just before training began there was a new government and national service was abolished.

The change in public opinion, a vindication of David Taylor, was largely brought about by Vietnam. Younger people began looking more to trends in America than in the old British Empire. Like the new awareness of racial issues, the anti-war protests in the United States were made vivid through the arrival of television. Peace was the new watchword. We had posters which said, 'What if they held a war and no one came?' On Thursday, 15 January 1970, the week I was in Auckland looking at medieval manuscripts, all youth was summoned, as by the pied piper, to join an unprecedentedly high-publicity march through Albert Park, near the Library, over to the Hotel Intercontinental where the American Vice-President Spiro Agnew was staying on the last stage of a tour of the Pacific. We gathered in huge numbers that afternoon and were briefed by Che Guevara lookalikes on how to respond to police aggression, including predicted attacks by trained dogs, quite unnecessary in that mild and good-natured country. We all surged in thrilling solidarity across the park, past the statue of Sir George Grey, and stood outside the hotel, feeling very grown-up, shouting slogans into the air and hoping for martyrdom. Nothing dreadful happened, but the protest that day is now cited as one turning point in New Zealand's move to pacifism and non-nuclear participation. The next morning, I returned to the Central Library and the collections of Grey and Shaw. I later travelled on up to Whangarei, north of Auckland, to see a manuscript once owned by Frank Reed, brother of A. H., 'if you feel it is worthwhile hitch-hiking up here', as the librarian had written (referring to what I had evidently told her in my letter), and then on up to Kerikeri and Waitangi, where European history in New Zealand had most notably begun in 1840.

It was perhaps unusual that I had made time to travel around the country at all, because most summers were spent in holiday jobs, easy to get in those days and providing a very small income which could be used towards buying manuscript fragments from England. One summer I picked apricots in Central Otago. The next, I worked in Dunedin at Don Distributors, a small car-parts firm which specialized in reconditioning old brake shoes. These were cleaned and stripped, and then new small rect-angles of asbestos were glued and baked on, to provide the fire-proof friction which stopped the wheels of a car. My job was to press the finished brake shoes tightly up against the electric sander, first one side and then the other, tidily grinding off the rough edges of the asbestos in a noisy and dramatic cloud of fine grey powder. One day I found an old French marble clock under a counter there. One of my workmates told me it was his (I cannot think why I believed him) and that I could have it for $5, about half my weekly wage. It is still in my drawing room in London. It has a note inside the mechanism recording its repair in Dunedin in 1868, another early migrant which has come back to Europe. However, it was clear my future did not lie in motor parts. After the trip round the manuscript libraries in 1970, I wrote later that year to each of them, asking if they would employ me during the following holidays. There was a long and rambling letter from Auckland, regretting the impos-sibility. The Turnbull Library sent a telegram, strips of capitals on white paper ribbons pasted to a yellow form, 'ROUTINE VACATION WORK AVAILABLE INDICATE IMMEDIATELY WHEN ABLE TO START'.

9

Canterbury

You will know about elephants from stories of Hannibal and in I Maccabees in the Bible, but if you wonder what they actually look like, I refer you to the twelfth-century manuscript of Boethius in the Alexander Turnbull Library in Wellington. For about 350 years, no one in Europe had seen an elephant, not since the death of Charlemagne's pet Abul-Abbas in 810. The animal in the Wellington manuscript has spindly legs with cloven feet, a spotted body and a small head with vertical ears, a tiny, curled trunk and one small tusk facing uselessly downwards. On its back is a turreted castle manned by four knights in helmets, resembling soldiers in the Bayeux Tapestry (Plate 20). I have always been fond of elephants. As a small child I had a stuffed toy elephant, who still lives out his old age on a miniature chair beside the fireplace at home. I took him once to the Getty Museum when giving a public lecture on manuscript bestiaries. In my schooldays, when the circus visited Dunedin each year, there used to be an elephant race down George Street. The winner was given an ice-cream and much applause. Now that circuses no longer exhibit exotic animals and even London Zoo has moved its remaining elephants out to a safari park, perhaps no one will see a real elephant again and the Boethius manuscript will come back into use as evidence.

It was the one medieval manuscript bought and retained by Alexander Horsburgh Turnbull (1868–1918). (He once also

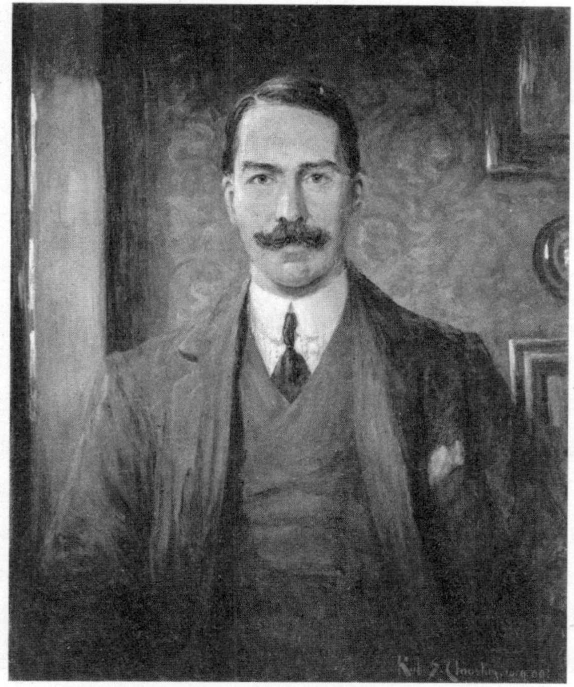

Alexander Turnbull, portrait by R. S. Clouston, 1909, formerly in the
entrance hall of his house in Bowen Street, Wellington.

owned a Book of Hours, resold in England in 1933.) Turnbull
is almost the only major figure in this book who was actually
born in New Zealand, the sixth child of a Scottish importer of
commodities and general wholesale merchant in Wellington,
and even Alexander was sent back to England for schooling at
Dulwich College in south London in 1881–84. Grey, Hibbard,
Reed, Taylor, Clemas and Shaw were all born in England and
arrived, mostly as children, with their ancestral identities interrupted. With that difference, Alexander Turnbull was a collector
of the history of his native New Zealand and became the most
voracious and obsessive acquisitor of them all. His vast library
aspired not merely to great books but total comprehensiveness
in its field. He eventually bequeathed 'to His Majesty the King all

my Library, comprising my printed books, pamphlets, engravings, charts, manuscripts, sketches, maps, photographs, plans and pictures as and to constitute a Reference Library in the City of Wellington', all initially kept in the house where the bachelor collector himself had lived at the end of his life and where I reported for my holiday job towards the end of 1970.

Wellington must be one of the hilliest capital cities in the world, except for a flat commercial area along the waterfront reclaimed by the early settlers from the sea. Turnbull House is towards the foot of Bowen Street as it runs down the hill beside the Parliament buildings in the direction of the harbour. An arc of the small low-walled front lawn has been pared away to allow the road (and now a bicycle lane) to curve round to the right as Bowen Street descends into the central city. The house was finished in 1916, a substantial three-storey brick building with stone mullioned windows reminiscent of those at William Morris's Kelmscott Manor, perhaps intentionally. In 1970 one entered up the main steps of the pillared portico at the front. Straight ahead in the entrance hall was the original framed Treaty of Waitangi (1840),

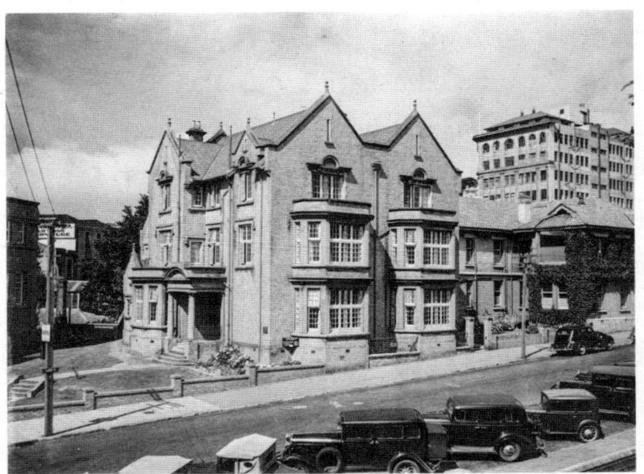

Alexander Turnbull's house in Bowen Street, c. 1930–40,
where his library was housed until 1973.

signed or marked with symbols by numerous Māori chiefs, either the foundation document of a great modern nation or an imperialist manoeuvre to secure land and sovereignty by sleight of hand from unsuspecting inhabitants. There were pictures in the hall too, including R. S. Clouston's portrait of Turnbull himself in 1909, a dapper and good-looking man in a three-piece suit, handkerchief in top pocket, with neatly brushed brown hair and a large, slightly upturned moustache. He looked a bit like the mysteriously late Lord Lucan. Through on the right was the Exhibition Room, Turnbull's own reception room, facing the street and lined with elegantly bound volumes in furniture made from native woods, all smelling agreeably of leather and colonial prosperity. The broad staircase on the left led up past a tall glass-fronted bookcase on the half-landing which contained the Boethius and a few other medieval manuscripts acquired since Turnbull's time, such as Sir John Ilott's Sarum Missal, with the Library's small representative collection of incunabula and early European printing. The Manuscript Room, where I was shown to a small table which was to be mine, was on the top floor in a former bedroom at the back of the building, filled with tall shelves boxing in the tiny desks. It all gave the feeling of working in a family house crammed with treasures, and I revelled in it.

Morning coffee was held in the old kitchen area downstairs. The staff would prop up newly acquired early pictures of unidentified New Zealand scenery, and someone in the room usually recognized the view, and locations were duly and gratefully recorded for cataloguing. The head of manuscripts was Margaret Scott, the only person in the world who could read Katherine Mansfield's handwriting, helped by June Starke, the enthusiastic and kind-hearted mother everyone would have wanted, and young Dorothy Reid, her long dark hair tied behind. The chief librarians were Graham Bagnall, admired by all, and his deputy Ray Grover, a gentle and thoughtful man and writer of historical novels. There too were Margery Walton, Sheila Williams, descendant of one of the oldest missionary families in New Zealand, Phil Barton, Janet Horncy, Tony Murray-Oliver, who had worked in the Library since 1938, especially on topographical art, and who became a loyal friend, and Janet Paul, whose lovely art-filled house I visited several times, the trendy conservator Jeavons Baillie, who dressed like a Beatle, and others, all faces still vivid in my memory. My official tasks were helping to sort New Zealand archives and photocopying and marking up manuscripts for binding, but it was soon realized that my delight was in the early European books and I was allowed a key to the bookcase on the stairs and spent more and more time attempting a typescript catalogue of the medieval manuscripts. The staff petted and indulged me tolerantly. If any are still alive, let me record how much I owe to two happy summers spent sharing their world.

Alexander Turnbull was a man of considerable wealth, both from the family business (sold in 1916) and from his father's property investments, especially in reclaimed land in central Wellington. He appears at first as an urbane and sophisticated man-about-town, yachtsman and boulevardier, moving through dark hints of private vices into depression, cocaine and whisky and a relatively early death. I am sorry, for he was a passionate and perceptive bibliophile. In addition to the New Zealand and Pacific material, Turnbull maintained smaller but distinct collections of fine printing and of Scottish and English literature, especially Milton. In June 1900, Alfred Quaritch, son of the great Victorian bookseller Bernard Quaritch, wrote to Turnbull from London:

> Dear Sir, I do not know whether you are aware or not of
> the fact that illuminated MSS. executed in England . . . are

amongst the rarest things of their kind, and consequently the most sought after and expensive. The late William Morris and others have helped to increase this rarity.

He enclosed a list of medieval manuscripts, varying in price from £18 up to £540. The subtle Morris allusion may have clinched the decision. Turnbull chose the oldest, described as 'a volume containing Boethius de Musica, and the Micrologus of Guido (de Arezzo) written in England in a minute and beautiful semi-Gothic about A. D. 1150'. The firm of Quaritch had bought it at Sotheby's on 22 November 1897, lot 699, for £100, and described it in their catalogue 176, January 1898, no. 198, and catalogue 185, January 1899, no. 509, at £150, which is the figure Turnbull paid.

David Taylor was evidently perplexed by this book in his *Oldest Manuscripts in New Zealand*. Understandably, he did not recognize the animal diagram used to illustrate musical intervals as an elephant. He received courteous but inconclusive advice on the manuscript's date and nationality from A. J. Collins at the British Museum, to whom he sent photostats in 1948, and from J. A. W. Bennett, a New Zealander at Magdalen College, Oxford, who, on a visit back to Wellington, transcribed for him a sixteenth-century song added at the end in the English language. Taylor did, however, print the wording of the nearly contemporary titles on the manuscript's flyleaf, *'Musica boetii'* and *'Musica Guidonis inperfecta'*.

This led to a breakthrough. Bennett, then editor of the journal *Medium Ævum*, commissioned a review of Taylor's book from a fellow tutor at Magdalen, Neil Ker, whose knowledge of British medieval libraries was incomparable. Ker remembered seeing these words in the medieval library catalogue of Christ Church Cathedral Priory in Canterbury, published by M. R. James in 1903, and he wrote to the Turnbull Library in May 1956 to ask

The contemporary title on the flyleaf of the Boethius manuscript in Wellington, which allowed it to be matched with the medieval inventory of the Cathedral Priory in Canterbury.

whether by chance the manuscript had a strange symbol in the outer corner of its first leaf of text. It did indeed. It resembles a widely spaced 'H' with its vertical strokes curling outwards, rather like two 'C's back-to-back (Plate 21). There are two medieval inventories of the manuscripts of Canterbury Cathedral. The first is a partial twelfth-century title-list of teaching books kept in the cloister probably in the 1170s, many in duplicate copies, each volume individually distinguished one from another by use of unique symbols recorded beside the titles in the list and in the manuscripts themselves. The inventory includes 'Musica bo[etii] in as[seribus]', the Musica of Boethius bound in boards, identified by exactly this mark. That, then, is our manuscript. The second Canterbury catalogue dates from the early fourteenth century, in the time of Prior Eastry (d. 1331). No. 438 there, in the modern numbering of M. R. James, is 'Musica Boecii prima. In hoc vol[umine] cont[inetur] Musica Guidonis inperfecta', the priory's first (and maybe best) copy of the Musica of Boethius bound with an imperfect text of Guido d'Arezzo's Musica, using the precise wording of the Turnbull flyleaf. It is this book again.

I asked for assistance from Jeavons Baillie, who secured an ultra-violet lamp from the Health Department in Wellington, and we peered at the book together. Two erased late medieval inscriptions came into view, seen for the first time since the Reformation. The first clearly said, '*De Claustro Cantuarie*', from the cloister of Canterbury, and the second, '*Alexander Staple monachus huius ecclesie*', and it took a few minutes to find two monks of the house with that name; this may be the second, who was tonsured in 1488 and was novice master in 1516–17 and so might well have required use of the book for teaching. Canterbury Cathedral meant a lot to me. I had seen the film *Becket* (1964), starring Peter O'Toole and Richard Burton. Who could not be moved, sitting by the war memorial opposite the Turnbull Library and gazing out over modern New Zealand, realizing that this manuscript was probably present in the cloister in Canterbury when St Thomas Becket strode round it and in through the side door into the north transept of the cathedral, followed by the four royal knights with swords, moments before his martyrdom on 29 December 1170?

The medieval manuscripts of Canterbury have come to play a big part in my life. The Reader in Palaeography in Oxford when I got there was William Urry (1913–81), former cathedral archivist, who would transfix his students in his old-fashioned cut-glass accent, 'Are you Canterbury-minded?' He could conjure up the topography and inhabitants of twelfth-century Canterbury as if he knew them personally. A chapter of my thesis was on the glossed manuscripts bequeathed by Thomas Becket and Herbert of Bosham to the cathedral priory. Many decades later I had custody in Cambridge of the library of Matthew Parker (1504–75), archbishop of Canterbury, who had arbitrarily subsumed into his own possession many of the oldest books from Canterbury, such as the seventh-century uncial manuscript *Juvencus in Romana scriptura* listed in the cathedral cloister with the Turnbull Boethius, and the sixth-century Gospel Book from St Augustine's Abbey. That manuscript brought me to participate in several major events in Canterbury, including two enthronements of archbishops.

There were probably three principal places where books were kept in Canterbury Cathedral in the Middle Ages. Liturgical books of all kinds would have been in the church or its associated sacristies. Very few survive. By the twelfth century there was a teaching collection in the cloister, including the Turnbull Boethius. The principal library of nearly two thousand manuscripts was for several centuries stored in the slype, a long narrow enclosed space (which still exists) leading off the cloister between the chapter house and the door into the north transept. The catalogue refers loosely to two *demonstrationes*, presumably each side of the slype. Many of the surviving Canterbury manuscripts preserve their medieval classification marks, which located their places in the store. A twelfth-century Eusebius in the Parker Library, for example, has 'D. vi^a, g^a. xiii, Demonstr. i^a' on its flyleaf, which is in the sixth *distinctio* (some kind of rack or cupboard) and on the thirteenth *gradus*, a shelf, on the first side of the slype. These books were all moved in the fifteenth century, with their same shelf marks, into a new and specially built library room above the prior's chapel, east of the main cloister. Construction had begun by 1432 and was completed around 1442–43. At about that time, someone, perhaps the librarian, went through hundreds of volumes marking the margins with symbols to draw readers' attention to important passages, sometimes with exaggeratedly pointing fingers, often with vertical rows of dots, singly or in clusters of four, and, most recognizably now, with a mark which resembles a sideways ice-cream cone. At the Reformation the library was scattered (we will come back to this later) and some discarded books were torn up for reuse as parchment flyleaves or other purposes by bookbinders in Canterbury or Oxford, where

A fragment from a late thirteenth-century manuscript of Thomas Aquinas,
with marginal marks at the upper left and lower right, distinctive of the
Cathedral Priory in Canterbury.

many books were sent. Those characteristic marks in the margins
are worth looking out for, since they are unique to Canterbury.
On a visit back to New Zealand, some years after my student
holiday job there, I found another, in a folder of salvaged binding
fragments in the Turnbull Library in the papers of Percy Watts
Rule, the architect from Timaru who once owned that sadly dispersed Book of Hours. It is a single leaf re-used at the Reformation from a late thirteenth-century manuscript of the *De malo* of
Thomas Aquinas, with a chapter on gluttony, duly marked up as
a useful passage by the fifteenth-century Canterbury annotator.
It may originally have been among the many books by Aquinas
brought to Canterbury by Robert Winchelsey, archbishop of

Canterbury from 1293 to 1313, who knew the author personally and had attended his lectures in Paris. That two manuscripts from medieval Canterbury should be in New Zealand is unexpected, but both being now in the same library is a very happy coincidence.

In addition to the main collection, it is likely that the everyday books for teaching remained available in the cloisters in Canterbury throughout the Middle Ages, probably including our Boethius, which has all its medieval flyleaves intact and no numbered shelf mark; instead, like other books from that twelfth-century list, it has a late medieval inscription naming the cloister. These cloister books were all texts usable for instruction of new monks in basic Latin grammar, arithmetic, simple science and classical verse and history. Many were in multiple copies, for they could doubtless be borrowed, unlike manuscripts in the main library, which were chained. This is how the monk Alexander Staple could write his name in a textbook on music.

The *De musica* is the late classical explanation of musical theory by Boethius (*c.* 480–524). It survives in about 140 manuscripts, including, by chance, an eleventh-century Italian copy in Melbourne, which is the Turnbull manuscript's opposite number in Australia as the earliest complete European book in that country. The author's more famous *De consolatione philosophiae* is represented in New Zealand by a fourteenth-century Latin manuscript among those bought by John Ilott at the Tomkinson sale at Sotheby's in 1922, now in the Turnbull, and Auckland's early fifteenth-century copy of the French translation shown by Grey to Froude on Kawau in 1885. Boethius was both a Roman senator and a Christian at the moment when classical civilization seemed to be disintegrating into barbarism. His many writings attempt to recast learning necessary for Christians into the framework of Platonic and Aristotelian philosophy. There is an imagined portrait of him in the Turnbull *De consolatione* as a bearded teacher holding out and commenting on an open manuscript. The *De musica* is on harmony, on how the different musical sounds work together as part of the perfectly balanced mathematical geometry that underlies all of nature, including both the proportions of the human body and the relationships of the spheres orbiting silently in the universe. The text had little practical value to a monk learning to sing, but it came into use when music was defined among the four liberal arts in the medieval *quadrivium*, the second of the two courses in classical learning (with the *trivium*) taught by various monasteries and cathedral schools of late Carolingian France, and then by the earliest universities. This ordered classification of knowledge would have been known in Canterbury through Lanfranc and Anselm, successive archbishops from 1070 to 1109, who had both followed the *quadrivium* at Bec Abbey in Normandy, and through Theobald, archbishop 1139–61, who had been a monk at Bec and was doubtless familiar with it there.

The treatise of Boethius on music is a seriously complex and intellectual text. There is even a passage in Greek, written in red capitals here both by a scribe and for readers who probably had no knowledge of the language. As in most manuscripts of the *De musica*, there are tabulated diagrams, to illustrate the relationships of harmonies and discords. In this manuscript they are of unprecedented luxury and visual imagination. Many are worked up into elaborate multi-coloured patterns and even pictures, some resembling the arcades of overlapping arches in Romanesque buildings, others as elaborate as architects' ground plans of great buildings or cities. There is a diagram of the solar system, with the earth in the centre, within radiating orbits of the moon, the sun (as the scribe first wrote before crossing it out and inserting Mercury), Venus, the sun (in its right place), and so on, out to Saturn in the outermost ring. Some include fish and lions, and one incorporates a horse's tail. There are two bearded blacksmiths, one bare-chested, striking an anvil simultaneously (Plate 22), resulting in tones sometimes in consonance with one another, sometimes not, depending on the weights of the hammers (as supposedly discovered by Pythagoras). Other illustrations include a man plucking a tightly adjusted string across a sound box, and a woman tuning a harp.

One of the functions of art in medieval manuscripts was as an aid to memory. It is much easier to fix a concept or a text in the mind if it is associated with a distinctive and unforgettable image. This is why some of the most amusing or bizarre drolleries occur in Psalters and poetical romances, for these were texts to be memorized for recitation. It may partly explain the extraordinary elephant here, for, according to medieval bestiaries and popular belief today, the animal was an exemplar of great memory. There were two bestiaries in the library at Canterbury in the Middle Ages and this attribute would have been familiar to the monks. Bestiaries also tell us that elephants make music like trumpets, and that the Indian word for elephant is *barro* (whence 'baritone', it suggests), and that elephants are symbols of Christ. The creature in the Turnbull Boethius is carrying arches of a double octave and the lesser intervals, bringing musical theory of ancient Platonism into the service of Christianity, like the armed soldiers riding on its back who fight for the Church militant. A reader would relate to this during the Crusades in the twelfth century. The text could be impressed on the memory by recollection of the extraordinary elephant.

The second text in the manuscript here is shorter and not at all as complicated or as academic. The *Micrologus* (literally 'little word') of Guido d'Arezzo is a practical textbook on singing. The author (*c.* 990–1050) was a Benedictine monk and this is a guide to the monastic music of plainchant and hymnology. Guido is probably most famous today for his invention of the musical stave and for naming the notes, now only slightly adapted as *do, re, mi, fa, so, la* and *ti* from the opening letters of successive lines of a Latin hymn to St John. David Taylor's description of the Turnbull manuscript cites Guido d'Arezzo himself as saying that this text can teach you in five months what might otherwise take ten years to learn. The *Micrologus* here has several diagrams but with little colour and no embellishment, none as elaborate or as consciously made memorable as in the Boethius.

Note the medieval librarian's unexpected description of this copy of Guido as *'inperfectus'*, incomplete. It is a word he used six times altogether for books in the cloister list of the twelfth century and it occurs about ten times in the fourteenth-century Canterbury catalogue, in one place changed to *'non totus'*, not all of it. It must usually mean manuscripts missing leaves. It may have been an indication to potential scribes, even in other monasteries, that this was not a copy to use as an exemplar. The odd thing is that the text of Guido in the Wellington manuscript is not incomplete. Apart from the omission of an optional prologue addressed to Bishop Teudaldus of Arezzo, the *Micrologus* is all present. The only incompleteness is that the opening initial has been left blank and a three-quarter-page diagram was never added on folio 95r, even though it is explicitly referred to in the text. That was evidently enough: to the cataloguer, trying to distinguish the two copies at Canterbury, this was the one with its illumination unfinished, therefore *inperfectus* if only slightly.

The ill-fitting combination of the intellectual Boethius *De musica* with the easy-to-understand *Micrologus* is practically unparalleled. These two texts exist together in only a couple of other manuscripts. The earliest of these is a volume at Trinity

College in Cambridge, written at Christ Church, Canterbury, around 1120. Since ours was made later that century and was owned by Christ Church, the obvious conclusion is that it was copied in the priory from the earlier paired manuscript. This is what is commonly suggested and was my own reasonable assumption too in the typescript description from those holiday jobs of 1970–71. However, this cannot be the case. I have now seen the Cambridge volume and it was irrefutably not the exemplar. There are countless differences, infinite small variations in word order and use of headings, different prefatory matter, chapters opening at different points, and diagrams which do not remotely correspond. The Trinity College manuscript is beautiful, but it is monastic and domestically made, untidy, and utterly English through and through. The book in the Turnbull Library is expensive and professional, polished and urbane, and it is French.

Here I am going out on a limb. I would never have dared do this in 1970, or even 1984 when I described it in the catalogue of the medieval manuscripts in New Zealand. All logic and all previous descriptions point to the book being made in England, but this cannot be right. Even the ambiguous option of being either from England or France is too cowardly. 'You must come to a *decision*', Anthony Hobson used to drawl wearily when I wrote yet another hesitant attribution for Sotheby's in the 1970s. The distinction between southern England and Normandy in the century following the Conquest is admittedly a hazy one, both art-historically and politically. However, I am sure. The script is not English. It looks to me the work of a highly trained probably non-monastic French scribe of early in the second half of the twelfth century, perhaps around the beginning of the 1160s. The illumination is continental, perhaps from Normandy or Maine, south-east of Normandy: Le Mans has been credibly suggested as a possibility on the basis of style. The figures with big staring eyes above long noses turning sharply left into loops like a rounded 'w' occurs in a lectionary of the mid-twelfth century in the Bibliothèque nationale in Paris and this could even be the same artist. The lectionary is insecurely localized to somewhere in western France, although it has been stylistically associated both with Le Mans and centres slightly to the south, such as Tours.

We still have the problem of the combination in one volume of Boethius and Guido d'Arezzo being, at this date anyway, exclusive to Canterbury. It would be too much of a coincidence that a continental workshop would simultaneously invent a pairing not found anywhere else in Europe. Therefore, let us look back very carefully at the six musical manuscripts listed in the cloister at Canterbury in the later twelfth century. With the modern numbering of M. R. James and the distinctive symbols used to distinguish one copy from another, they are:

39.   Musica boethii in asseribus.

40.   Musica boethii in asseribus.

41.   Musica Osberni in pargameno.

42.   Micrologus Guidonis inperfectus.

43.   Musica Guidonis in pargameno.

44.   Musica Hogerii.

No. 39 is the manuscript in Trinity College Library in Cambridge, proven by the symbol like a tall 'EE' still at the front. '*In asseribus*' means in boards, probably a temporary and uncovered binding. No. 40 is the first text of the Turnbull manuscript, also still retaining its unambiguous matching symbol. Osbern and Hogerius were donors, not authors. Osbern was the cantor at Christ Church around the year 1110, and thus involved with music; if his no. 41

was also a text of Boethius, as the context suggests, it may have been the early twelfth-century copy from Canterbury now in Cambridge University Library. No. 44 is a tenth-century musical anthology in the Parker Library, inscribed *Musica Hogeri* (although here with just one 'i') with the mark resembling 'TT'. This then leaves two copies of Guido d'Arezzo, one with the designation specifically assigned to our manuscript, '*inperfectus*', with no mention of a binding at all, and another, bound loosely in parchment. The simplest explanation is that between the late twelfth century and the early fourteenth, no. 42 was arbitrarily bound up with no. 40, and no. 43 with 39. In both manuscripts the two texts are on entirely distinct gatherings and are slightly different in decoration. By the fourteenth-century catalogue, then, these have become:

438. *Musica Boecii, prima. In hoc volumine continentur Musica Guidonis inperfecta.*

439. *Musica Boecii, secunda.*

440. *Musica Guidonis et musica Boecii, tercia.*

If this is right, the first copy, no. 438, is the Turnbull composite, recognizable by the word '*inperfecta*'. The second, no. 439, may be the Cambridge University Library manuscript, and no. 440, the third, is the newly twinned text at Trinity College. This eliminates the necessity for our manuscript to have been copied from a double exemplar in Canterbury.

We need to summarize so far, for we are about to reach a breathtaking suggestion of the manuscript's first owner. There were earlier and much-thumbed copies of both these texts already in Canterbury, used in the cloister by several generations of novice monks. This new manuscript was made in two parts in France, perhaps in the early 1160s, possibly in or around Le Mans. These are both instructional texts, but they are luxurious and doubtless very expensive productions. The academic complexity of Boethius is made easier to follow and memorize by a series of graphic diagrams and pictures, which are entirely without precedent and were presumably prepared for a reason. The second part is the quick guide to mastering monastic music in a few months, rather than the usual ten years. There must have been someone in Canterbury at this moment with considerable wealth, a taste for luxury, good advisers, connections with France, and a need to learn and memorize in a hurry.

A possible patron must be Thomas Becket himself, archdeacon of Canterbury from 1154, chancellor of England and then unexpected royal appointee as archbishop in May 1162. He immediately set about rapid cramming of religious and monastic knowledge. Already in 1162, according to Herbert of Bosham, he had recruited a private faculty of 'eruditi' as his teachers, including the classicist and philosopher John of Salisbury and Herbert himself, both trained in the *quadrivium* in France. After singing in the church each morning, Herbert recounts, the new archbishop met his masters for instruction in religious books. The quaint old cathedral copies of Boethius and Guido would be deemed insufficient and inappropriate for an archbishop. A luxury set could have been brought or ordered from France. Herbert of Bosham describes travelling during April 1163 with Becket and his academic entourage over to Flanders and slowly down through Normandy and Maine, stopping in the principal towns, to a meeting with Pope Alexander III at the Council of Tours on 19 May. Perhaps the book was commissioned in Le Mans, capital of Maine, on their way south, with a view to collecting it on the journey home. They returned to England in June, 'cito', 'quickly', as Herbert says, which might be why the illumination of the Guido was still slightly unfinished, *inperfectus*, if they came back through Le Mans sooner than expected. I cannot prove this, but it fits all the available facts. A book of

102 leaves could easily be made in four weeks or so, especially if your client was the archbishop of Canterbury.

Thomas Becket is also the generally accepted patron by default of the Canterbury or 'Eadwine' Psalter, an immensely luxurious but glossed tutorial text made in the cathedral priory in the late 1150s or early 60s, left behind in Canterbury when Becket's conflict with Henry II forced his flight into exile back to France at the end of 1164. It too, unlike most academic books, has pictures to make it memorable. That manuscript was demonstrably still being kept in the cloister in the later Middle Ages. When Becket eventually and fatefully re-crossed the Channel shortly before his martyrdom in December 1170, bringing a new continental library which was incorporated in his own name into the main collection in the slype, his former instructional books remained apart and undesignated, among texts kept for classes in the cloister. Becket was canonized by Alexander III in 1173, and the shrine of St Thomas of Canterbury became one of the most visited pilgrim sites in Europe.

The Benedictine cathedral priory of Christ Church, Canterbury, was closed in 1540 and reconstituted as a cathedral chapter with a dean and twelve prebendaries, some of them former monks. Much of the principal upstairs library (including at least one of Becket's books) had by then already been sent up to Canterbury College in Oxford for use by the priory's students there. This college was disbanded too at the Reformation and most of its manuscripts were disposed of locally as waste scrap. It is likely that the Aquinas leaf among the Watts Rule papers in Wellington comes from a volume suitable for study, transferred first to Canterbury College and from there into re-use as a pastedown in a sixteenth-century Oxford bookbinding. It is a small aside, but when a new college was founded in Oxford in 1546 overlapping onto the same site, it was called after the former priory as 'Christ

Church', and in 1848 this college name was adopted in turn for a cathedral city in the province of Canterbury, appropriately, being established by the English settlers in New Zealand.

We can now go back to Wellington to look at the Boethius one more time, and to see whether anything more can be learned of its own migration. Like most manuscripts in New Zealand, it has changed its habitat since I knew it. Alexander Turnbull had built his house of brick and stone to make it fireproof, rather than the normal wood of most local construction, but soon after my holiday jobs there it was decided that this beguiling domestic home for his library could be vulnerable to earthquake. In 1973 everything was moved out into a startlingly pink office building in The Terrace, and in 1987 into part of the ugly new National Library of New Zealand. Come out from Turnbull's house, cross the road by the war memorial and continue along Lampton Quay, past the 'Beehive' and Parliament on your left and into Molesworth Street on the far side, up quite steeply past the Court of Appeal, and there is the National Library on the right, opposite the peach-coloured cathedral of St Paul. It has several layers of what look like big concrete teeth hanging down the front. The once atmospheric Turnbull collection is swallowed up and seems to have lost its identity. Back stairs take you up to a rare book glass fish tank for readers on Floor 2, where the Boethius, in a new grey card case, is wheeled over to the table on a trolley, like beef in a carvery. This is very unlike the days when I unlocked the bookcase on the half-landing myself and brought the manuscript up to my desk in Alexander Turnbull's spare bedroom.

It is indeed a beautiful volume, compact and hefty to hold, written on high quality parchment with wide untrimmed margins. The script is smaller than I remembered it, more like that of earliest scholastic texts than was commonly used by Romanesque monks. The gold is bright and the images are hauntingly unforgettable. The book is in unusually fresh condition for its age: this does not seem like a text handled daily by monks for 350 years. Alexander Turnbull chose well.

Inside the front cover is Turnbull's bookplate, with his coat of arms including three bulls' heads. On the verso of the flyleaf are the two twelfth-century titles, quoted by Taylor and recognized by Ker. Immediately below is a short, unsigned Latin inscription of around 1700 in which the writer says he has collated the text against the *De musica* printed among the collected works of Boethius, Basle, 1570. This looks very like the hand of the antiquary Ralph Thoresby (1658–1725), but the book is not in his own manuscript library listed in 1715, or in his sale catalogue of 1764. He was a tireless visitor to English private collections and may have checked the text on behalf of another owner, by which time the manuscript had probably long left Canterbury.

We gain some impression of its passage into private hands from scribbles at the end. Medieval books from the priory of Christ Church were still lying around the cathedral premises, uncared for and unguarded, for much of the sixteenth century. Initially, no one would have been quite sure whether preservation of items from the papist past might be deemed disloyal or treasonable, and so, to be on the safe side, someone added 'god Save the kynge, Amen' on the manuscript's end leaf (datable to not later than 1553, when Edward VI died). Groups of manuscripts were removed privately from the building by successive bookish archbishops, including Thomas Cranmer, 1533–55, who helped himself to eleven, Matthew Parker, 1559–75, my old opportunistic employer, and eventually John Whitgift, 1583–1604, who, with Thomas Neville, dean 1597–1615, finally cleared the shelves and gave most of the residue to Trinity College, Cambridge. Other manuscripts trickled out as gifts or curiosities over

bant falsum testimonium contra ihm. ut eum morti trade
rent. & non inuenerunt cum multi falsi testes accessissent;
Nouissime aut uenerunt duo falsi testes. & dixerunt;
Hic dixit; Possum destruere templum di. & post tridu
um edificare illud; Et surgens princeps sacerdotum.
ait illi; Nichil respondes ad ea que isti aduersum te tes
tificantur? Ihc aut tacebat; Et princeps sacerdotum
ait illi; Adiuro te per dm uiuum. ut dicas nobis si tu es
xpc filius di; Dicit illi ihc; Tu dixisti;
Verumtamen dico uobis. amodo uidebitis filium homi
nis sedentem a dextris uirtutis. & uenientem in nubib: celi;
Tunc princeps sacerdotum scidit uestimenta sua. dicens;
Blasphemauit; Quid adhuc egemus testabus?
Ecce nunc audistis blasphemiam; Quid uobis uidetur?
At illi respondentes. dixerunt; Reus est mortis;
Tunc exspuerunt in faciem eius. & colaphis eum cici
derunt; Alii aut palmas in faciem ei dederunt; dicen
tes; Prophetiza nobis xpe. quis est qui te percussit;
Petrus uero sedebat foris in atrio; Et accessit ad eum
una ancilla. dicens; Et tu cum ihu galileo eras; At ille
negauit coram omnibus. dicens; Nescio quid dicis;
Exeunte aut illo ianuam. uidit eum alia ancilla & ait
his qui erant ibi; Et hic erat cum ihu nazareno; Et
iterum negauit cum iuramento. quia non noui hominem;
Et post pusillum accesserunt qui stabant. & dixerunt
petro; Vere & tu ex illis es; Nam & loquela tua mani
festum te facit; Tunc coepit detestari & iurare; quia
non nouisset hominem; Et continuo gallus cantauit;
Et recordatus est petrus uerbi ihu quod dixerat. prius
quam gallus cantet ter me negabis; Et egressus foras;

12. One of three leaves in a fragment of a Gospel Book, northern France, late ninth century,
bought by the Dunedin Public Library in August 1957.

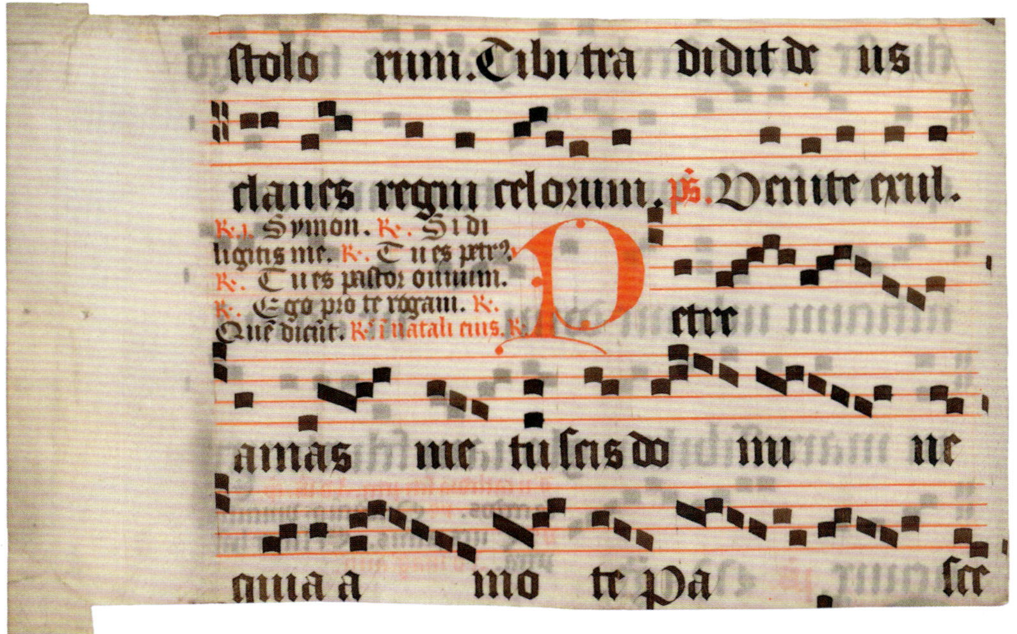

13. Part leaf of an Antiphoner, France, late fifteenth century, bought by Christopher de Hamel in Paris in January 1967.

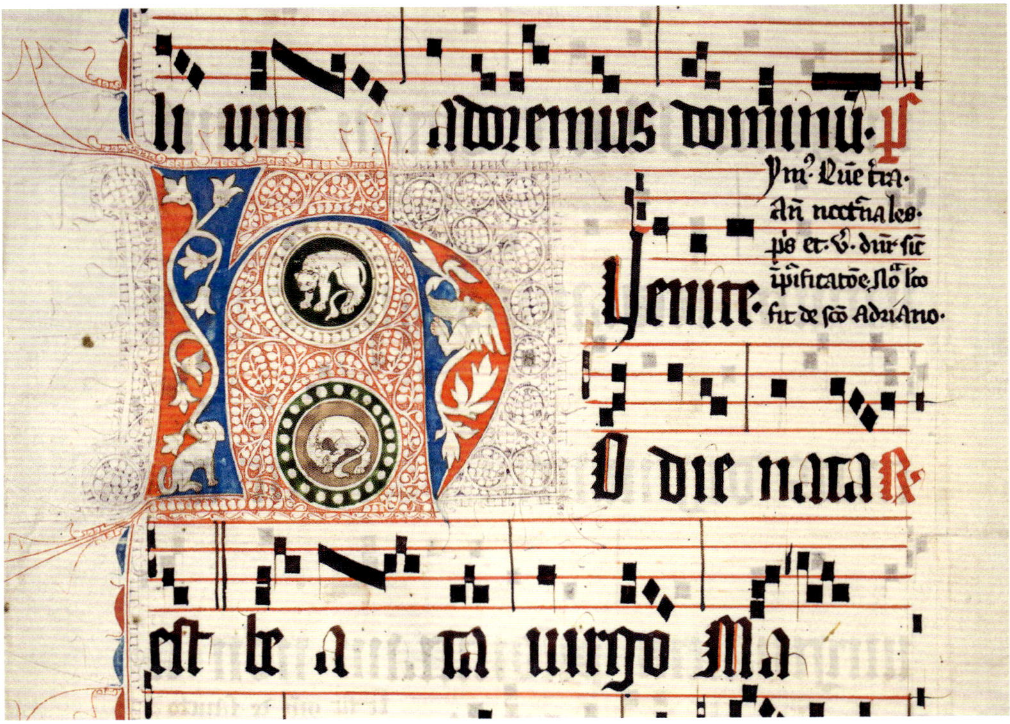

14. Leaf from an Antiphoner, Germany or Switzerland, early to mid-fourteenth century, with initial including a beaver; bought by the Dunedin Public Library in April 1957.

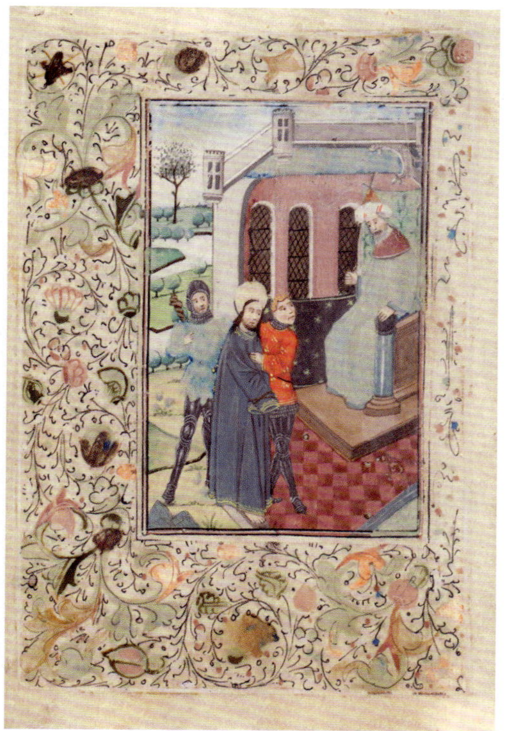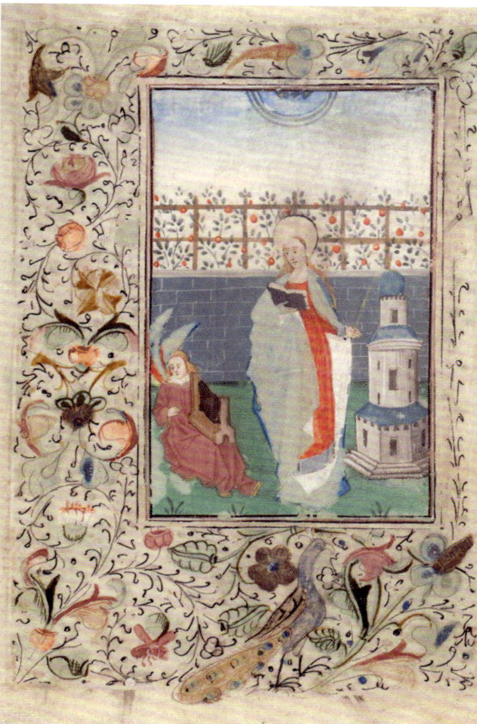

15–16. Christ before Pilate and Saint Barbara with an angel, full-page miniatures in the original portion of the Fitzherbert Book of Hours, southern Netherlands (Bruges), *c.*1470.

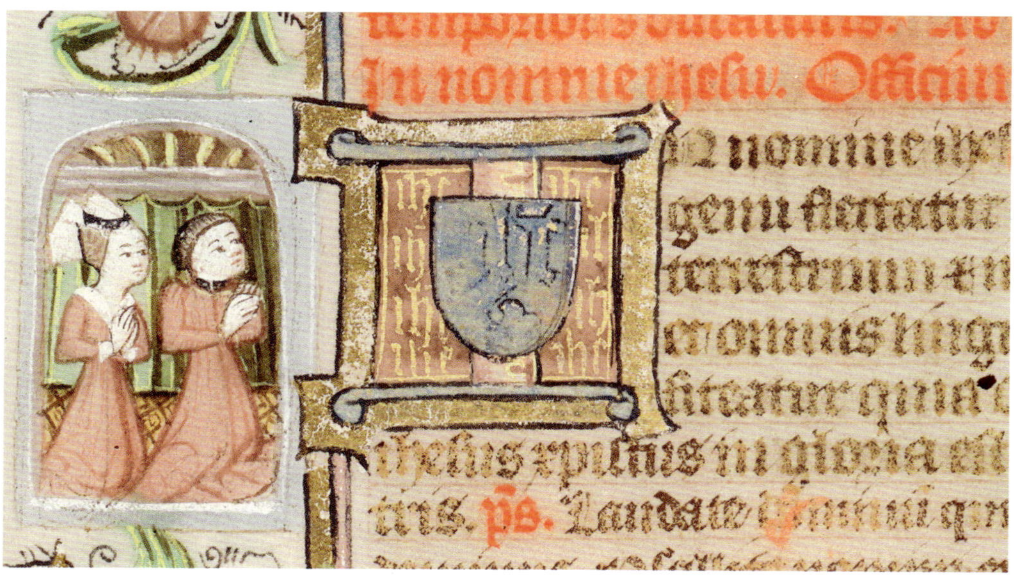

17. Margery Fitzherbert with her husband, marginal vignette in the additions to the Fitzherbert Book of Hours, England (perhaps London), *c.*1475.

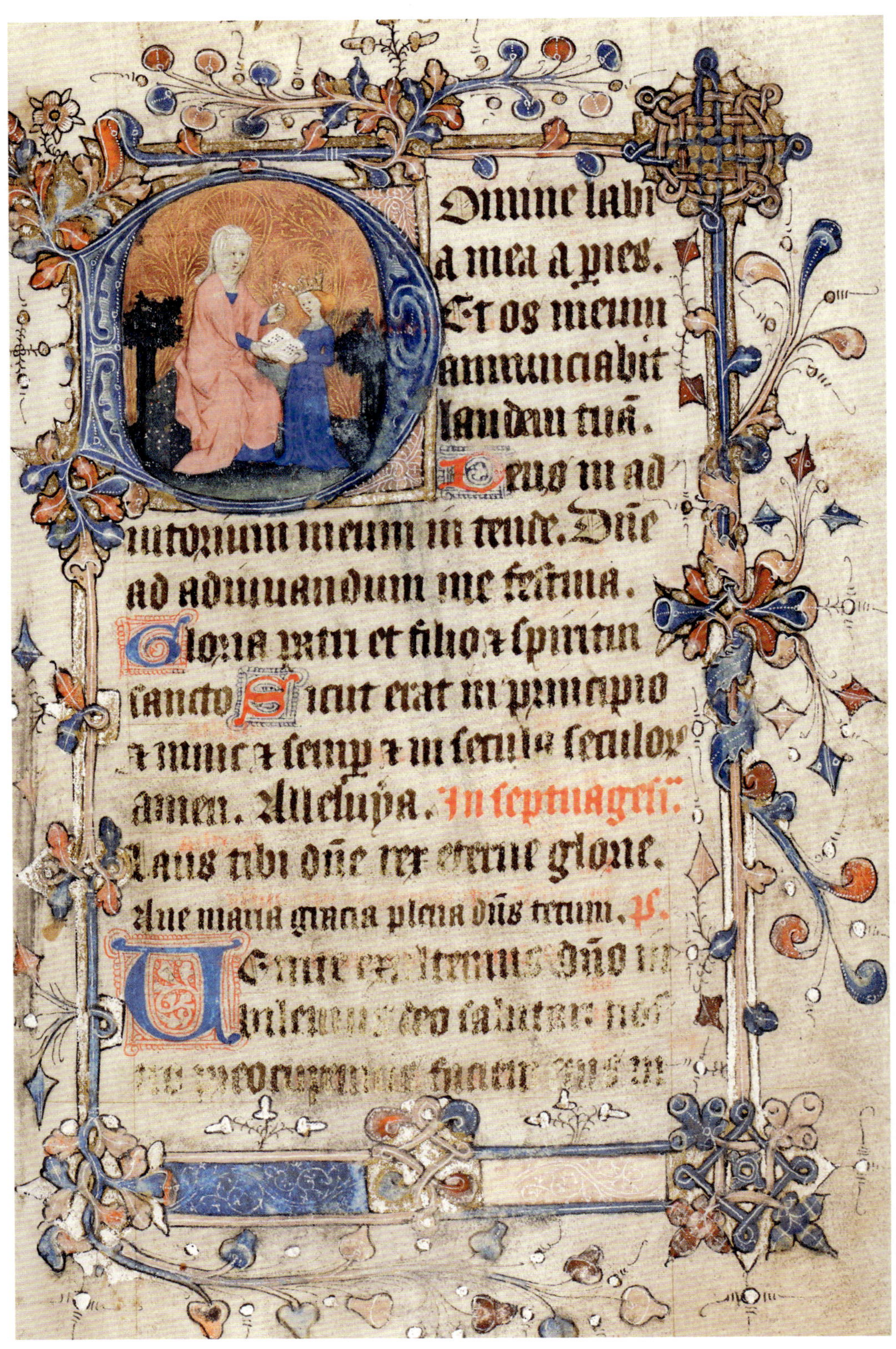

18. Saint Anne teaching the Virgin to read, historiated initial on one of several leaves bound later into the Fitzherbert Book of Hours. England (probably London), *c.*1410.

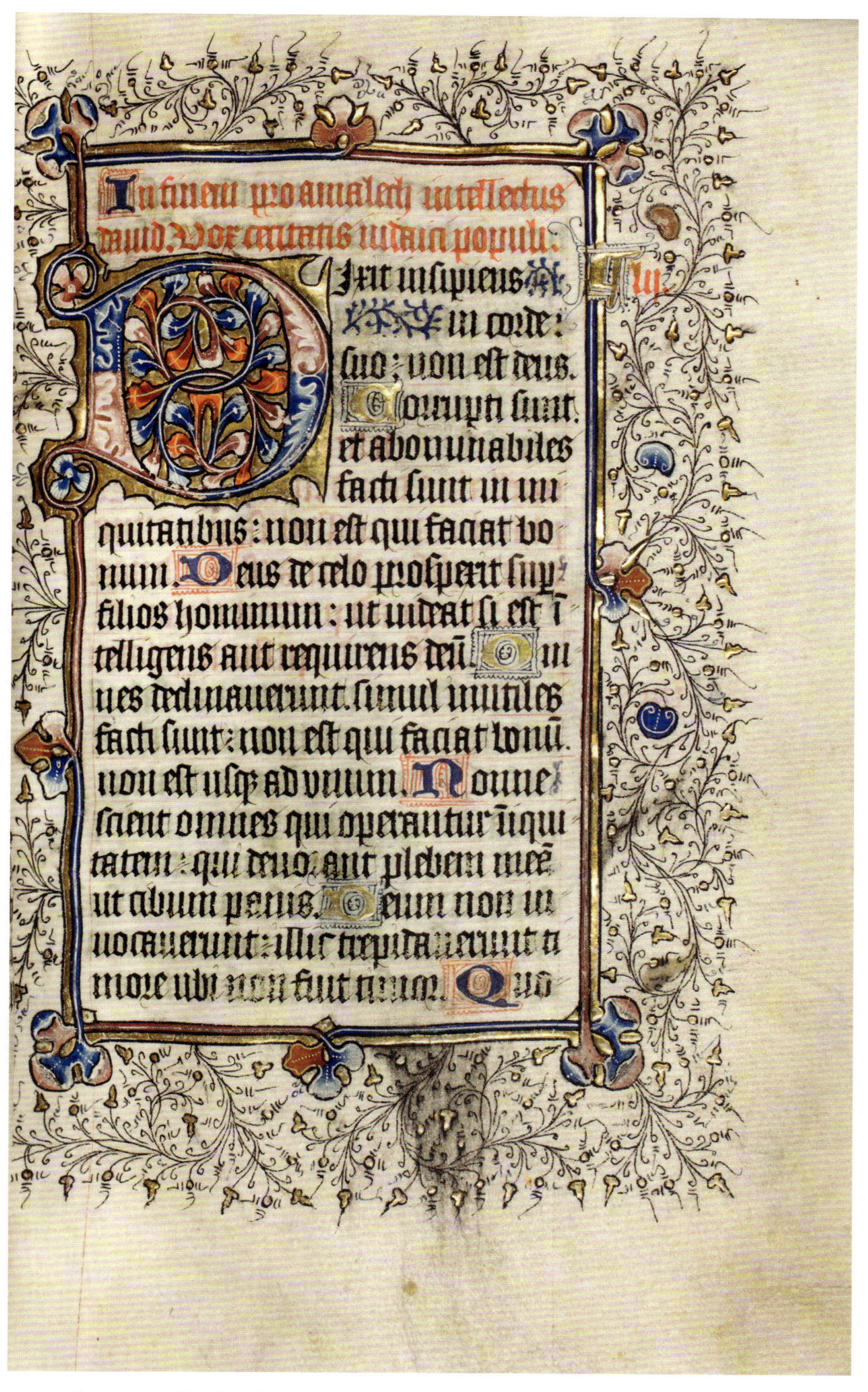

19. Psalter made for the Shirley family, England (London), first quarter of the fifteenth century, brought to New Zealand by Albert Clemas in the mid 1920s.

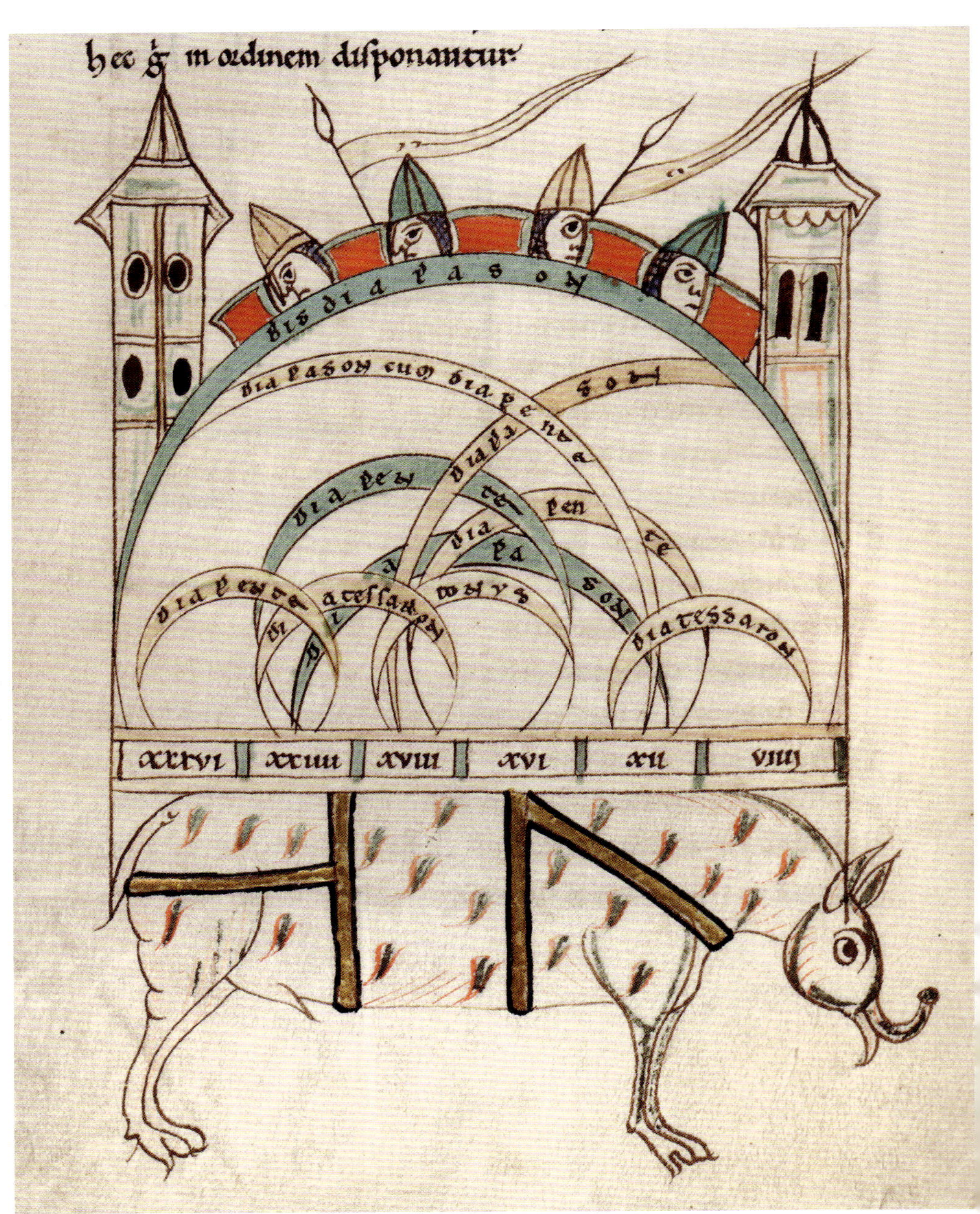

20. An elephant, a diagram showing the interrelation of musical notes and intervals in the Boethius *De musica*, western France (perhaps Le Mans), *c*.1163, bought by Alexander Turnbull in 1900.

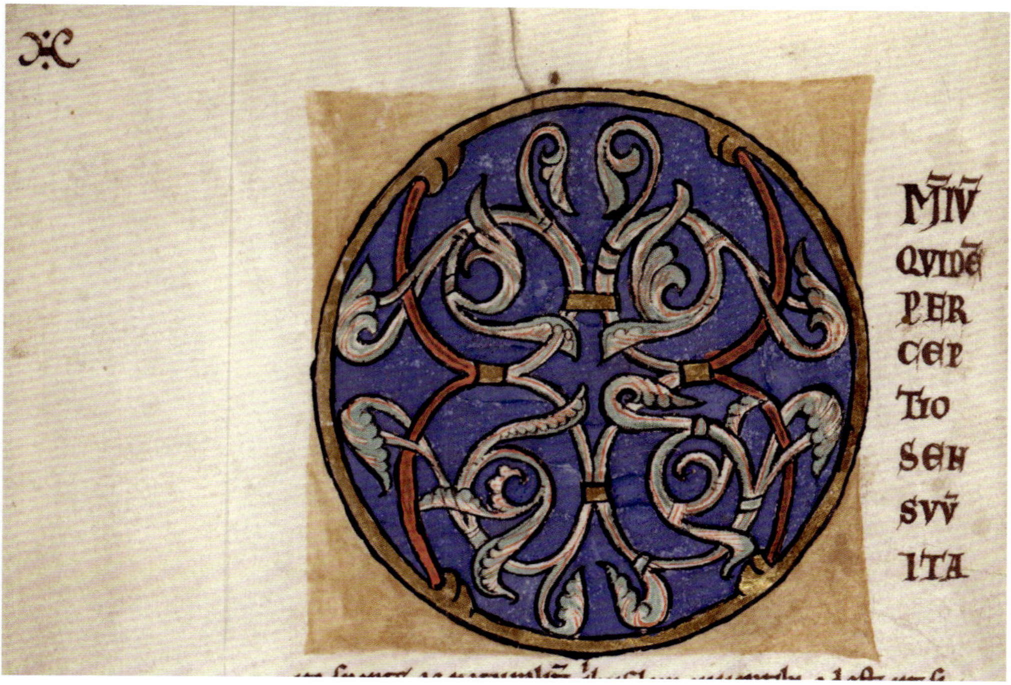

21. The opening initial of the Boethius *De musica*, with the twelfth-century librarian's symbol at the upper left identifying it as from Christ Church Cathedral Priory, Canterbury.

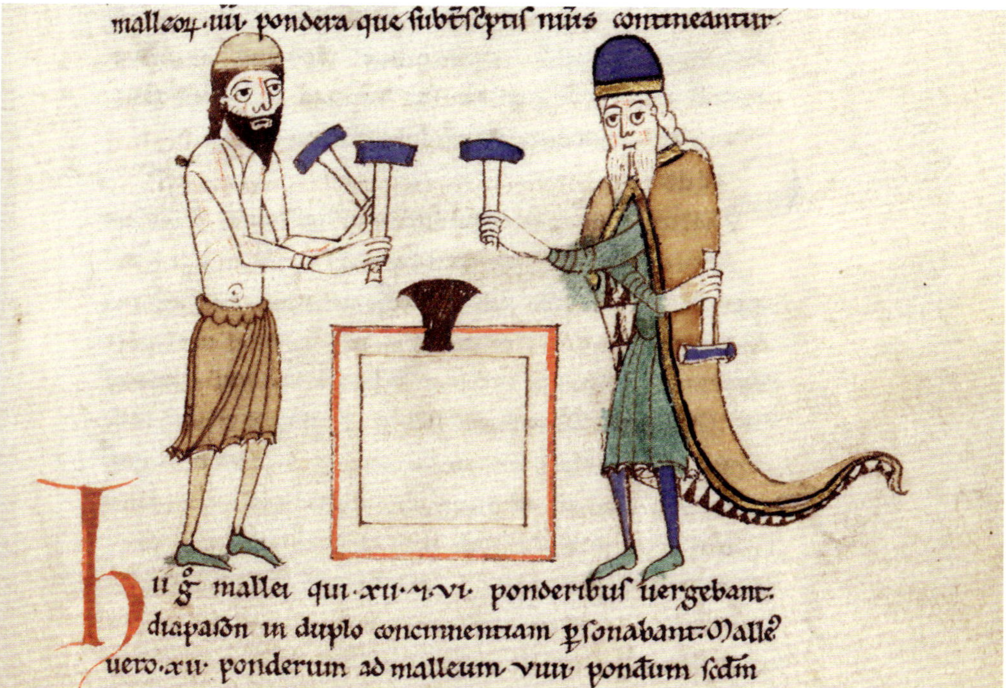

22. Blacksmiths striking an anvil with hammers of various sizes to illustrate the consonance of differing sounds, illustration in the Boethius *De musica*.

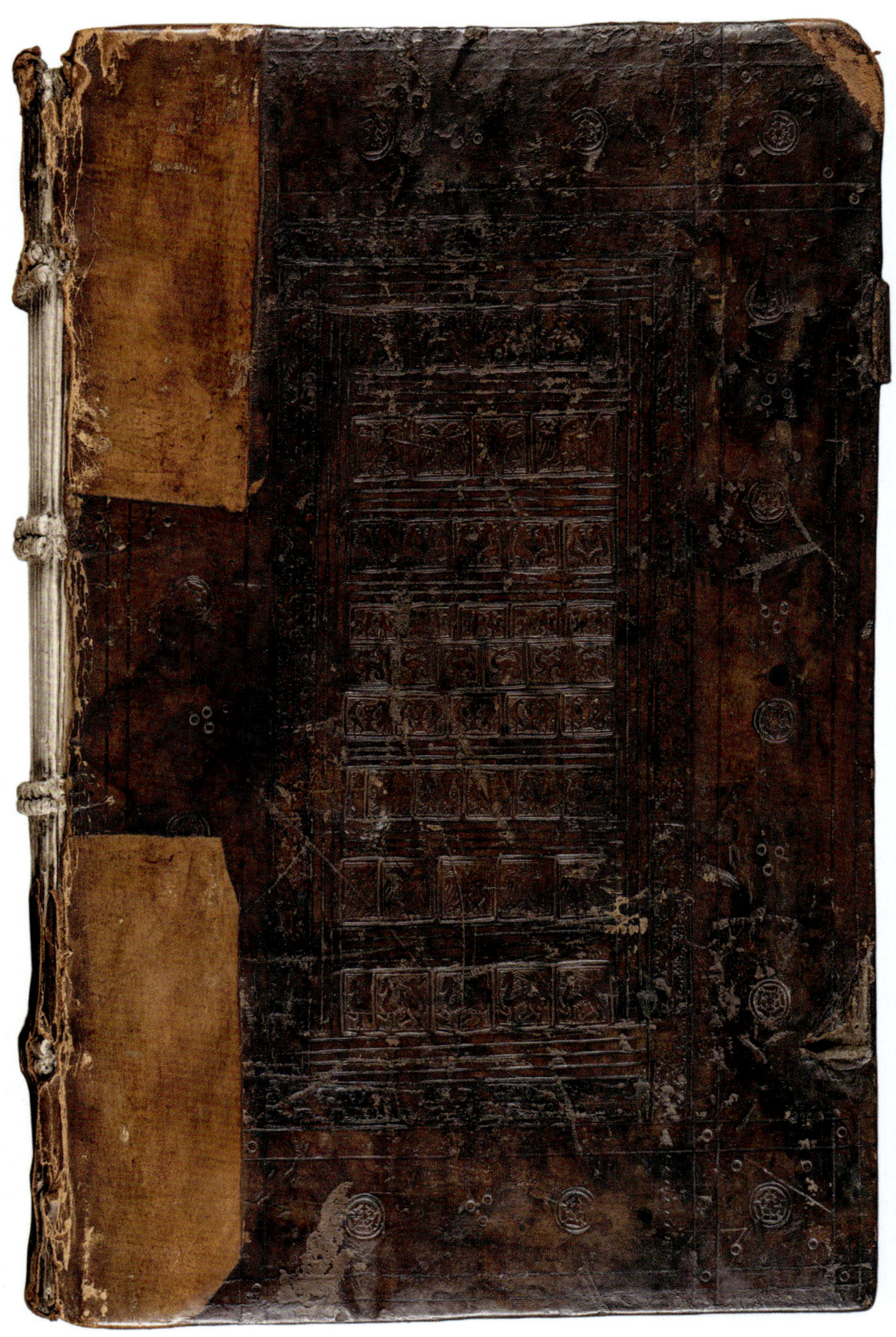

23. The upper cover of the binding made in Oxford by the Rood and Hunt Binder for *Biblia Latina cum postillis Nicolai de Lyra*, vol. III, Venice, 1481, incorporating sewing-guards from early printed indulgences; brought to Dunedin with the Shoults Collection around 1890.

the years or were souvenired by prebendaries or local antiquaries, such as John Twyne (d. 1581), headmaster of King's School in Canterbury. The Boethius, being on music, might have been put among the books of the choristers, for it has an added song in English and several scrawled childish signatures including that of Adam Shakerley, a local name. It is likely that it was still on the premises or not taken far.

The binding of the manuscript is late sixteenth- or probably early seventeenth-century brown calf over pasteboards, re-backed, with the sides stamped in gilt with a Tudor rose below a crown, flanked by the owner's initials 'I' and 'B'. The Quaritch description breaks into capitals in suggesting that this might be for the composer John Bull (*c.* 1562–1628), organist of the Chapel Royal. This is very improbable. He was from the West Country, with no known Canterbury connection, and extant books bound for him (now in London and Cambridge) are nothing like this.

The same stamp of the crowned rose, either identical or with the very smallest of variants, occurs on books dated 1599 and 1600, now in the royal library at Windsor Castle, and, by another of those curious chance connections of New Zealand, on a volume in the Reed Collection in Dunedin, bought in 1955, *An exposition of all the principal Scriptures used in our English liturgie . . . By Iohn Boys Doctor of Diuinitie*, London, 1610, bound with collected works of the same author, 1610–12. It has been exhibited in Dunedin as having belonged to Prince Henry (1594–1612), son of James I. This is not believable either, for it has none of the usual later evidence of books from that library, and an unadorned crowned Tudor rose is not a royal symbol of a Stuart Prince of Wales. However, the Dunedin volume is undeniably an expensive and special copy, perhaps the author's own or for presentation by him. Look at his initials, 'I. B.': I think we have a serious candidate for the Boethius too.

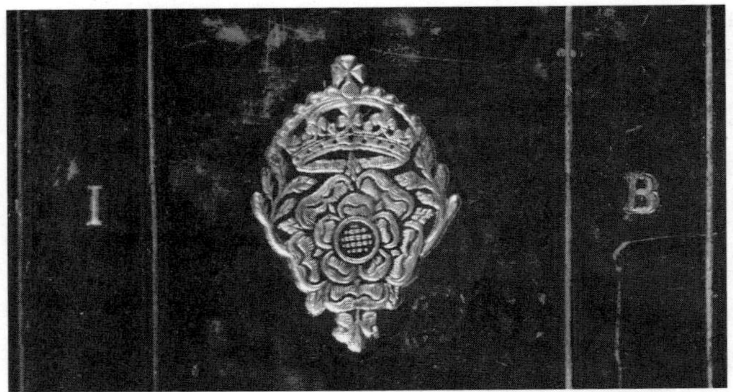

The crowned rose on the binding of the manuscript of Boethius,
flanked by the initials 'I' and 'B', perhaps for John Boys.

John Boys (1571–1625) came up to Corpus Christi College in Cambridge probably on a Parker scholarship from King's School, Canterbury. He was a protégé of Archbishop Whitgift, who gathered up so many of the Canterbury manuscripts. In 1619–25 he was himself dean of Canterbury, where he renewed the musical practices of the cathedral. He is precisely the kind of person to have acquired a manuscript on music from the final remains of the medieval library. 'Boys must have been one of the great book collectors of his time', notes the *Dictionary of National Biography*. It is true that his successor as dean, Isaac Bargrave, shared the initials I. B., but it was Bargrave who put an end to allowing manuscripts to leave the premises and secured what little remained for the restored cathedral library, by which time the Boethius had gone. The fate of Boys' books is unknown. He married but had no children. His younger brother Luke, who might otherwise have been his heir, had migrated to America and died at Cape Charles in Virginia in 1626. Think of it! That would have been a starry adventure for the Boethius, if it could have been carried from Canterbury to colonial America within a year or so of the *Mayflower*.

★

In the last week of July 1972, three weeks after arriving back in England, I set off on a pilgrimage of my own, almost literally, to see Canterbury Cathedral, because of the Turnbull Library manuscript. The plan was to walk the medieval Pilgrims' Way from Winchester to Becket's shrine, 112 miles, with my orange sleeping bag but no tent – a mistake, for even in summer the English nights are dewy, which had not been my experience in New Zealand. The first day I made good time to Alton, and the second through Farnham down into Guildford, already developing blisters. I stayed several days recovering in comfort with my grandmother nearby, setting out again to Albury and Shere and on through Otford, where the archbishops once had a palace. The path was never uniquely for medieval pilgrims, for it meanders along the prehistoric way eastwards across the North Downs, and much of the route is beautiful and timeless. It was a deep immersion in the English countryside, so unlike the straight and dusty roads of rural New Zealand, but it increased my admiration for the stamina of A. H. Reed on his long-distance hikes. When I eventually walked into Rochester I was frankly exhausted, and I accepted a lift for part of the last stretch down the old Watling Street (now the A2), hobbling into Canterbury itself on Monday, 7 August. Medieval pilgrims who left home with little to request from St Thomas might, on arrival, have sought relief from sore feet. I stayed in a bed-and-breakfast that night.

I have been back many times. I am always struck by the immense size of Canterbury Cathedral, probably even more impressive in the Middle Ages when most people lived in houses so low one stooped to pass indoors. The cloister, where the Boethius was kept, is very broad with stone benches on either side where monks might sit for instruction or reading. It is not clear exactly where the teaching books were kept. There are traces of attachments once along the lower level on the south side, up against the church, which might have been cupboards or shelves, and there are shallow Gothic recesses on the north side, just about deep enough for books. The twelfth-century diagram of the cloister in the Eadwine Psalter shows a fountain nearby in the central atrium, which it calls the 'Herbarium', where monks might wash before going into the adjacent refectory, or sensibly in preparation for handling manuscripts. I am always pleased to see the Latin tablet to my former tutor William Urry, 'chartophy-lax' (how he would have loved that word), on the wall beside the Romanesque door on the east side, below where the archive is now. The little medieval wooden door into the slype, where the main manuscript collections were stored until the 1440s, is still there, to the right of the chapter house. It has two small windows above, which would have provided light into the book stacks. It is marked 'Private' these days and kept locked, but once I found it open and pushed in. It has its medieval red floor tiles. You pass through a narrow entrance and up a step where it widens out to the right and upwards in height. It is used now by the cathedral gardeners for storing small equipment such as watering cans, and by the cleaning staff for mops and rubbish bags. I am told the vergers sometimes keep their bicycles there.

Just to the right again is the side door into the cathedral and the (rebuilt) sacred spot just inside where Becket was killed, after being pursued around the cloister. Immediately behind this is what is now called the Chapel of Our Lady Martyr-dom, formerly the Dean's Chapel, reserved for private prayer. This is where John Boys is buried next to the altar. His marble monument on the right-hand side shows him with a beard and ruff, his head dreamily resting on his hand and his elbow on a Jacobean table beside a large book open on a reading stand. Best of all, Boys is immortalized for posterity surrounded by his personal library. I can count about sixty volumes depicted

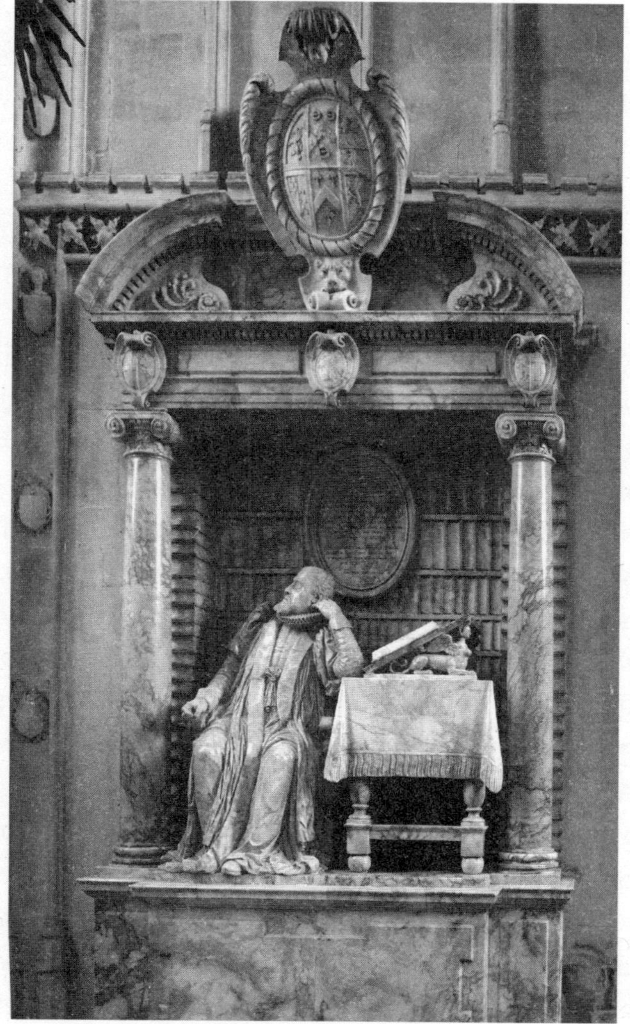

The tomb of John Boys in Canterbury Cathedral, shown seated in his library.

on five shelves behind him on the monument with their fore-edges facing outwards, as was the custom then, between tottering piles of more books carved on either side, each stacked twenty-two volumes high. Somewhere among these wonderful sepulchral representations of his book collection, I hope, is the Turnbull Boethius.

IO

Otago

Once a week, there were what were known as Sex Nights. The name was entirely wishful thinking, for probably nothing salacious or inappropriate ever took place – to our immense regret – in Knox College, the university hall of residence attached to the Presbyterian theological college in north Dunedin. It was then for male students only. In my first year there, 1968, permission for female visitors in student rooms was extended to every Saturday evening up to 11 o'clock; there was a register in the entrance hall, called (by us, at least) the Sex Book, which you had to sign in advance if bringing in a guest. It was eventually abolished as it had no real function except as a focus for ribald humour and invention, for I doubt Raquel Welch and Brigitte Bardot were really in Knox College as often as the book recorded. There is a lesson here that the authority of manuscripts may be fallible. Apart from anything else, most first-year students shared rooms and there was never assurance of privacy. That year, 1968, may be remembered now as the year of the Woodstock festival, the student revolutions in Paris, the Beatles in India, mini-skirts, long hair, flowers, peace marches, nudity, drugs and the pill, but never where we were. In Dunedin we imagined this Eden must be happening in Australia; there they dreamed wistfully of America, where students no doubt thought longingly of swinging London, where they probably supposed it was taking place in Amsterdam (where maybe it did). The nearest we usually got was occasional snuggling or hand-holding on park benches in the botanical gardens after suggested walks by moonlight, achingly romantic, and a formal college dance once a year.

The school and university years in the southern hemisphere follow the calendar, since summer vacations correspond with the New Year. I therefore left school before Christmas of 1967 and, like most of my class from King's High, moved seamlessly across into Otago University at the other end of Dunedin in early 1968. I was just seventeen, still younger than most of them. My parents were on a trip to Britain at the beginning of that year and so it was decided that I should board at Knox College in their absence. In the event, I remained there for four and a half years. Full board with all meals in termtime was $11.90 a week and university tuition was free. I could of course have commuted daily from Macandrew Bay to classes in Dunedin, but the college provided the independence I was ready for and an interaction with others inconceivable from home, especially as my father grew older. My most enduring impression of college life is of conversations. We talked in the dining hall, four to a table so that no one was left out, and in the common room and bathrooms at the end of each corridor and on the staircases and the front steps. Most of all, I remember countless evenings seated on floors of student rooms, our backs up against the wall, far into the night. What we discussed hardly mattered. We had read Dylan Thomas:

> music and poetry and painting and politics; Einstein and
> Epstein, Stravinsky and Greta Garbo, death and religion,
> Picasso, and girls . . .

and then someone made more coffee (alcohol was not allowed in college), communism, symbolism, Bradman, Braque, the Watch Committee, free love, free beer, murder, Michelangelo, ping-pong, ambition, Sibelius, and girls . . .

and more people drifted in,

Augustus John, Emil Jannings, Carnera, Dracula, Amy Johnson, trial marriage, pocket-money, the Welsh sea, the London stars, King Kong, anarchy, darts, T. S. Eliot, and girls . . .

Knox College had been opened in 1909. I was there for its sixtieth anniversary and forty years later gave the address at its centennial dinner. It is a towering and stately red-brick and pale-stone building in Hampton Court Tudor style, looking down over substantial wooded grounds on the steep hillside of what had been named North-East Valley when the imagination of Dunedin's founders ran dry. Knox has been mentioned several

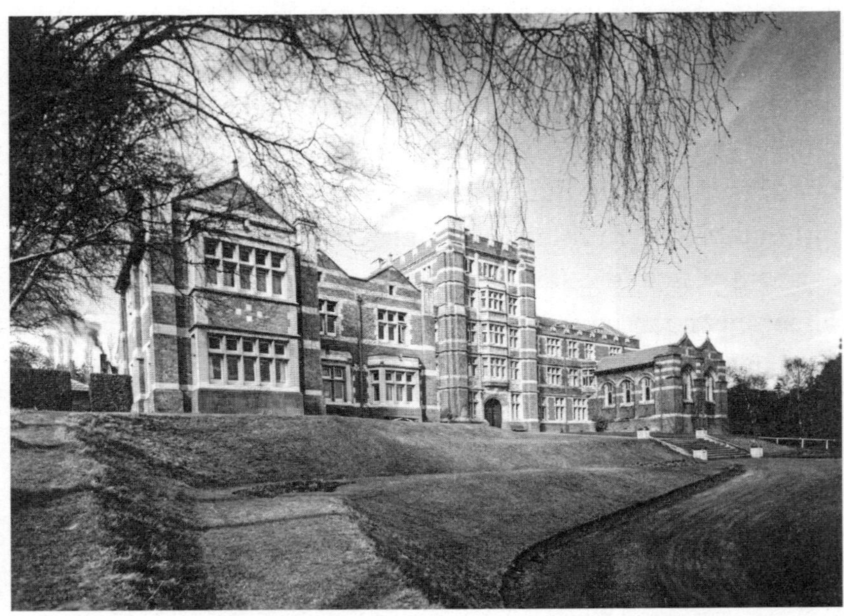

Knox College, Dunedin, theological college
and hall of residence for university students.

times in this book as a theological training college with a library and Lloyd Geering as a professor, but it doubled as a residential college for students of all departments and faculties at Otago University. The theology lecturers formed a Senior Common Room, with a few other chosen postgraduates, dining at High Table each night and providing a notional Christian backdrop. Daily chapel was not at all compulsory, although names were ticked off at the door and it was known who did not attend. In the year I joined, there were 150 students in residence, of whom 17 were theology ordinands. Others were studying law, medicine, dentistry, commerce, science and so on, with those of us unvocationally and loosely classified as 'Arts'. There was also a fictional medical student, one Ollie Alexander Alvidge, who did not exist but who was regularly signed up for exams and events, to the puzzlement and weary vexation of the university administration. His name was always in the Sex Book.

The master of the college was the Very Reverend Jack Somerville (1910–1999). He steered it more-or-less single-handedly, unhurried and genial, with a matron in the kitchens, the large and very Scottish Ella Paterson when I began, and then the bird-like Hazel Sparks in subsequent years. Accustomed now to the huge administrative staffs of colleges of Oxford and Cambridge, I am impressed how it was almost all held together by one man. I learned from Jack Somerville that the oddities and quirks of human nature are to be rejoiced in, not mocked or suppressed. I remained in touch with him until his death. At one remove, he spanned all Dunedin history, for his grandfather, whom he had known, had arrived from Scotland as a child at the city's foundation in 1848, a twenty-week voyage by sailing ship into the unimaginable. Jack had won a Military Cross as a padre in Italy during the Second World War; he was present in May 1944 at the sack of Monte Cassino and used to recount with relish his furtive liberation of an early edition of St John Chrysostom under his cassock – highly illegal. In July 1969, when he returned to Dunedin after receiving an honorary doctorate from the University of St Andrews, our whole college met him at the airport and escorted him out in a sedan chair with bagpipes, back to Knox, where we presented him with our own superior and fictitious doctorate instead, an elaborate document made by me, with illumination copied in part from an Antiphoner leaf in the Reed Collection.

I was never especially good at calligraphy, but I updated the Knox honours boards in gold script and inscribed invitation cards for friends. I decorated my college room with framed manuscript fragments and painted my windows to resemble medieval stained glass. It is quite easy. You use watercolour on the panes and then add outlines in that thick opaque black paint used (then anyway) by photographers to mask out any part of a negative not required in a print.

We larked around. We did silly things, we wasted time, we made speeches and tried to be provocative, and we gate-crashed parties hoping to meet girls. We still had beliefs and causes to fight for: the differences between right and wrong seemed clearer then when we knew less of the world's moral complexities. I was at Knox College when the *Wahine* ferry sank off the heads of Wellington harbour, killing fifty-one people; when Martin Luther King and Robert Kennedy were shot; and when Neil Armstrong walked on the moon. I suppose we took our course work seriously, but certainly in the first years I do not recall it being a priority.

It was about a twenty-minute walk from Knox down to the University through the botanical gardens, a path as soft as carpet with fallen pine needles and bark chips, and over the bridge across the Leith river, a trickle in a ravine. The original Gothic stone university buildings in the central campus date from the late 1870s. There are gables and crenellations and leaded glass in lancet windows. In countries where nothing is medieval, the architecture of higher education still looks back to distant memory of the schools in thirteenth-century Paris, where it all began, and the old buildings of the universities of Yale and Keio and Otago are all descendants of Notre-Dame and the halls of the Sorbonne. My Latin lectures were held in a professorial house here, while others were in modern blocks spread across the university site, towering over north Dunedin streets of tiny nineteenth-century wooden colonial bungalows, where many students shared flats in various states of enviable decrepitude and squalor. Mixed flatting, as it was called, was still not allowed and was a controversial cause with a frisson of wickedness in the air.

I should acknowledge that I now have experience of classes at Otago, Oxford and Cambridge, and I see no difference in the quality of teaching or the rigour of the exams. The way it worked in New Zealand then was by collecting 'units', a course in some subject, examined at the end of the year. Most students began with three or four – in my case, Latin, history, English and French – and maybe two or three units to second-year level and one or two in the third and final year. Eight passes were needed for a degree. If you failed a unit, it was no shame and you could repeat it the next year, or choose another subject, until you had accumulated your total of eight at appropriate levels. There was no time limit; one of my brothers spread it over many years. Because it was easy to get into university, people often took a course or two, failed, and moved on with their lives, without the chip-on-the-shoulder resentment of many in Britain who feel they were never given the chance. It seems a very fair system. You could also, if you wished, apply after reasonable first-year results for a more specialized four-year honours course instead, as I did. I opted for history in a narrow decision over Latin, since both seemed possibly useful for enjoying medieval manuscripts. In my second year, I took a unit in classical Greek and failed it.

I came home to Macandrew Bay in the university holidays. I noticed how small the rooms seemed and how low the ceilings after the spacious dining hall and soaring stairwell of Knox College. Michael had by then moved out and was working first as a floor manager for the new and local television company, and then with a photographic studio of his own in the Octagon. He eventually settled near Christchurch, grew a long beard, now white, and bought and ran the *Akaroa Mail* newspaper for many decades. William was at boarding school in Christchurch; in adulthood he lived north of Auckland and quite late in life spent time back in England. My youngest brothers, Richard and Quentin, were allowed to grow up as unfettered New Zealanders. One became a biologist near Nelson, and the other a lawyer in Rangiora. All my four brothers married New Zealand girls and have children and various grandchildren of their own, as dispersed now throughout the country as the successors of the birds and fruit trees brought out by Grey from Europe to try out colonial life on Kawau Island.

A curious reversal was slowly taking place in the relative assimilations of my parents. My father, initially thrilled by the natural history and adventure of New Zealand, never quite acclimatized or achieved what he hoped. His private experiments in recording native bird song in search of individual avian voices were unsuccessful or overtaken. His colleagues in the Health Department perhaps eventually found his rapid wit and lateral thinking more exasperating than useful. His position there gradually contracted, and no great effort was made to keep him on; he taught, at first part-time and then entirely, in the university Medical School, and he pretended not to care when the professorial chair he so coveted was in time given to an almost exact contemporary of mine from

Knox College half his age. He maintained his jacket and tie and his English accent to the end, and he eventually spent part of his retirement documenting our family history back through British country-house childhoods to the putative village of Hamel in north-west France in the *Ancien Régime*.

My mother, on the other hand, gradually and almost imperceptibly came to love the great expanse of the deep green bushland and the immense throbbing oceans. I recall a typical teenage rant with my parents at about this time. I was saying, as usual, that New Zealand has no part in world history, nothing medieval, nowhere earlier than 1840. My mother replied, 'But where else in the world today can you see a thousand years ago as it really was then? The view out over the bush and the mountains,' she said, 'has not changed the slightest bit since long before the Bayeux Tapestry was ever made, or even Stonehenge was built. No place in England has anything to match that.' It is hard to deny some truth in this. There exist living kauri trees in New Zealand older than the Norman Conquest. By the late 1960s, the uniqueness of the country's ancient landscape was beginning to be recognized and valued, not as something to be bought up and cleared for farming, but worth preserving. We heard the words 'environment' and even 'ecology' for the first time. There was a government scheme to raise the water level of Lake Manapouri in the unpopulated south-west corner of New Zealand and to merge it with the neighbouring Lake Te Anau in order to create a vast modern hydroelectric power station. It would have utterly destroyed a bush-clad landscape untouched since the Creation. A 'Save Manapouri' petition was launched in October 1969 and by 1970 had some 265,000 signatures. My mother later wrote children's books set in the New Zealand wilderness and among the penguins on the beaches of the Otago Peninsula. Because, until that moment, most stories for children there still involved steam engines and wardrobes of Britain, these books captured a new and domestic market. Every school in the country seemed to use them. In her old age, my mother became frankly a famous New Zealander, with the accent and vocabulary, white hair, trousers and trainers, and a plaque commemorating her as a local author proudly unveiled in 1993 in the Octagon by the mayor of Dunedin.

I too had my own first exhilaration of authorship. Towards the end of 1969, doubtless encouraged by my parents, I made a proposal to the Dunedin Public Library that I might write a little monograph on their two manuscript Books of Hours. This was passed to Mr Reed, who wrote to me on Christmas Eve, 'If the collection has in any way inspired you, it makes me very happy', and he agreed that the firm of A. H. and A. W. Reed would publish my text on behalf of the Library. He was then campaigning for the City Council to provide better facilities for his rare book donations, and a publication by anyone other than himself probably seemed godsent armament for his cause, however amateur its probable text.

I experienced in microcosm all those thrills and frustrations known to every author since the dawn of publishing. There was the incomparable triumph of writing the last sentence, tapped out on one finger on my mother's typewriter (forty-nine pages, double-spaced, with a retained carbon copy). By 7 February 1970, Mr Reed had read my text and over several weeks he sent editorial suggestions which so seared my pride that I have never forgotten them. For example, I had opened by saying that Books of Hours were the most common surviving medieval manuscripts. Reed commented: 'This is of course quite correct, but I wonder, seeing that "common" has various shades of meaning, [if] it might be well to change the term, to avoid any possible wrong impression to some readers.' It became 'the most numerous': I could live with that, and many others, some contested, most conceded by attrition and impatience to move forwards. He also, consistent with the refrain of Henry Shaw in 1912 (and himself on earlier occasions), made me insert a sentence at the end on how the financial value of the French Book of Hours had by then risen to maybe ten times the £250 he had originally paid some twenty years earlier.

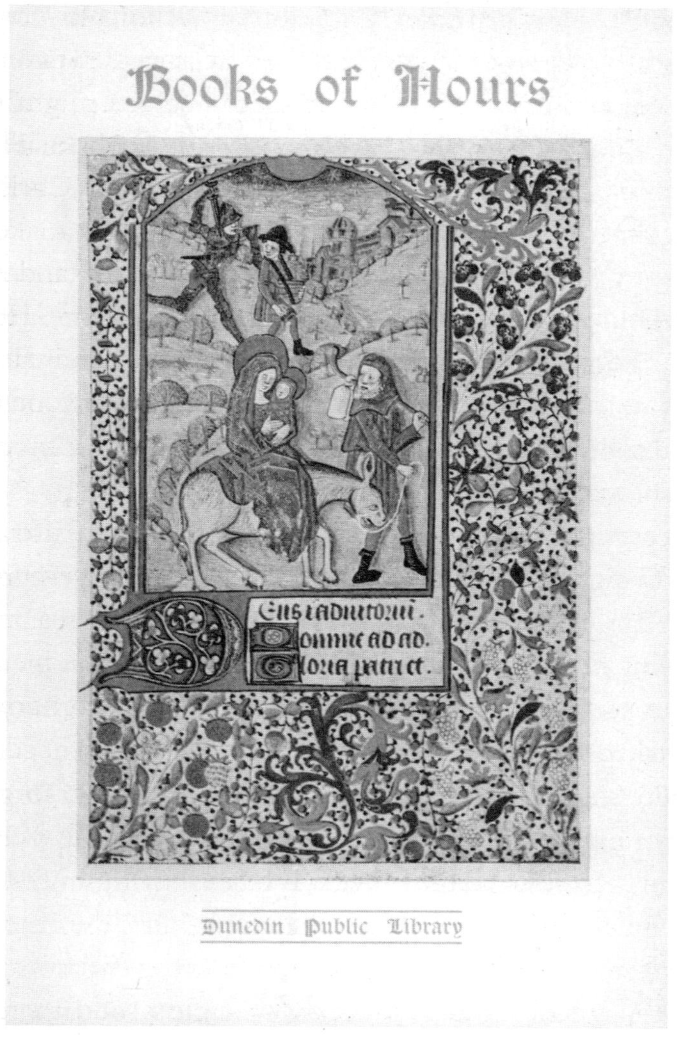

Christopher de Hamel, *Books of Hours*, published in October 1970.

At last he was content. We had galley proofs by 6 March. By 17 April, Reed wrote encouragingly, 'It should be out next month'; and on 30 May, 'It seems it will be another week or two.' And then, and then, ever such, the months edged by at snail's pace, and no impatient author desperate for imagined fame can believe production could ever take so long. The first copy arrived on 10 October. The little *Books of Hours, Notes on Two Illuminated Manuscripts in the Alfred and Isabel Reed Collection, Dunedin Public Library* has seventy-two pages and twelve plates, in laminated covers, and was priced at $1. I cringe now at the juvenile naivety of it all. Mary Ronnie kindly wrote in her Foreword, 'Mr de Hamel has been a member of the Library from his high school years', tactfully concealing that this was not a long memory.

I was right that Books of Hours seemed to be quite common, at least in Dunedin. There was a tiny Dutch example in the library of Knox College, given long ago by A. H. Reed too. I used to borrow the key to the strongroom downstairs. It was silent in there and smelled of old leather bindings, and I could lose all track of time at the small wooden table dreamily turning the manuscript's pages. It has a pencil note on the flyleaf, 'A nice specimen, written in the Flemish language'; it had made £4 at Sotheby's in December 1920. I ordered John Plummer's book on *The Hours of Catherine of Cleves* (1966), my first reference book on manuscripts, and I pleasantly deceived myself that the little Dutch Book of Hours at Knox, with no miniatures, was almost as good.

There were two further Books of Hours in Otago University Library. One was made in France, with twenty small and eleven larger miniatures, and the other was Italian with a single frontispiece which is copied from a printed book and (I think now) is a modern fake. The Library also had a fifteenth-century Breviary, with pretty, coloured penwork decoration, and two small manuscripts of Franciscan texts, all Italian. One of these was

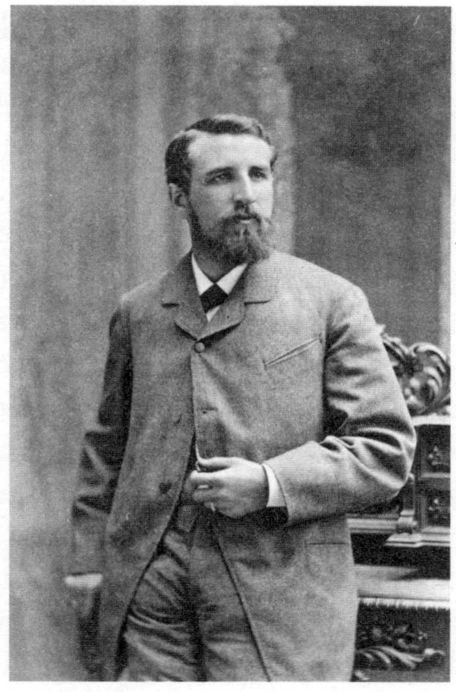

Willi Fels, collector of antiquities and manuscripts.

reproduced as a hazy background to the dust jacket of Taylor's *Oldest Manuscripts in New Zealand*. All five manuscripts were given in 1946 by Willi Fels (1858–1946). This time the motive was not remotely Christian or evangelical, for the donor was Jewish. There is a well-known clothing retailer throughout New Zealand, Hallensteins, founded by Bendix Hallenstein (1835–1905) and his brothers, who migrated from Germany to the gold rushes, initially in Australia in 1857 and then Otago in 1863. They set up their factory in Dunedin in 1873 and their first shop in the Octagon in 1876. Like many Jewish families, their circle was self-contained. Bendix's sister Kötchen married Heinemann Wilhelm Fels, and their son Willi, the collector, married his first cousin, Sara, daughter of Bendix. Willi's grandson was the poet and aesthete Charles Brasch (1909–73), who was a presence in Otago University in my time and once invited me up to his house. Bendix Hallenstein's other daughter, Emily, married Isidore de Beer, and they in turn were the parents of the bibliographer and book collector Esmond de Beer (1895–1990), who lived mostly in Britain.

Willi Fels was primarily a collector over a wide range of antiquities and was a massive benefactor of the Otago Museum, located on the small green park called the Museum Reserve, opposite the University Library. The Italian manuscripts were probably all bought as inexpensive curios, doubtless on one of the Fels' many trips to Italy in 1914 and in the 1920s. The French Book of Hours is of better quality. It was bound in the sixteenth century with the name of its owner, Claude Tribet, stamped in gold on the cover. David Taylor's account of the manuscript regrets that nothing could ever be known about its history before its purchase by Fels in England in 1922: 'Misfortune strikes one owner, and in hiding his trouble from the public gaze, he prevents us from knowing the book's adventures.' Actually, they are not so unrecoverable, and there is no particular misfortune in the story. The manuscript appears in early Quaritch catalogues of 1856 and 1857, priced at £3.10s. It must have been bought at the very end of his life by the Quaker banker Francis Gibson (1805–58), of Saffron Walden, as we can deduce from a faint pencil signature 'F. Gibson' and a bookplate with coats-of-arms which I identified in the margins of my copy of Taylor as those of Gibson and Wyatt. Francis Gibson's mother's maiden name was Wyatt. He married Elizabeth Pease. Like Jewish families, the Quakers often intermarried. Their daughter became the wife of Lewis Fry (1832–1921), of the Quaker chocolate dynasty, a Liberal Member of Parliament and artist, and the Claude Tribet Book of Hours re-emerged in his estate sale at Sotheby's, 22 May 1922, lot 180, bought by bookseller Dobell for £7, in the year Willi Fels acquired it.

There were also three late medieval German theological

manuscripts on long-term deposit at Otago University Library, the property of Selwyn College, the Anglican counterpart to Knox, once intended to train clergy too but soon a hall of residence only. The manuscripts are part of a library which reached New Zealand by no intention whatsoever, either on the part of the collector or the recipient of the benefaction. The Reverend William Arderne Shoults (1839–87) was a supremely undistinguished Victorian High Church curate in south London and a quiet acquisitor of several thousand inexpensive books of intellectual and polylingual theology. These included five manuscripts and thirty-eight incunabula, all minor enough to be within the budget of a clerical stipend. At least two of the manuscripts had come to England with the collection of Georg Kloss (1787–1854), of Frankfurt, who gathered dull books dispersed after

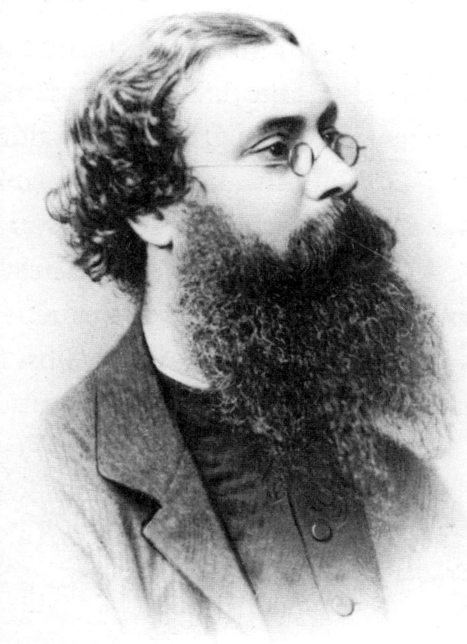

William Arderne Shoults, curate and book collector.

the Napoleonic suppression of German monasteries and sold them in London for negligible prices. There is a photograph of Shoults with tiny round wire glasses and wildly bearded, like an Orthodox monk or Edward Lear's old man with a beard. He died young; his entire estate was valued at under £300. By chance, Samuel Nevill, the Anglican bishop of Dunedin, was in England for the Lambeth Conference in 1888 and persuaded Shoults's widow, Eliza, that the collection would be ideal for the new Selwyn College planned for Dunedin. Nevill wrote enthusiastically that, besides theology and the classics, the Shoults library possessed 'many curiosities of manuscript and printing, the like of which are not to be seen in New Zealand'. (The Grey Collection, unveiled in Auckland the previous year, was evidently unknown to him.) The Shoults books had arrived in Dunedin by 1893. They were looked at by one schoolboy, Esmond de Beer – grandson of Bendix Hallenstein – who as a pupil at the Selwyn College junior school in 1903–10 had untutored access, which he fondly remembered in later life as his earliest and inspirational exposure to rare books. Apart from that glimmer of light, not unimportant, the Shoults bequest was wantonly neglected: it was stored in zinc-lined tea-chests and ritually urinated on by Selwyn students, and used mainly (it is said) as heavy weights for pressing trousers. *Habent sua fata libelli.* Several incunabula and two manuscripts were disposed of in the 1930s. David Taylor inquired about these:

> I am given to understand that they were sent to England and sold in the belief that they were of considerable value, but the price obtained being less than expected, no further experiments in dealing were made. We may be thankful that the prices were low enough to save the remainder of the library for New Zealand.

Once again, there is the concept of 'saving' medieval manuscripts from the dishonour of return to Europe. The two manuscripts were Sotheby's, 1 July 1938, lots 512–13, making £6.10s. and £16 respectively, not so low in those days. The large residue of the Shoults Collection was transferred temporarily from Selwyn College to the University Library in 1951, and more permanently in 1965.

These five Fels manuscripts and three from Selwyn, eight altogether, are actually still the largest number in any university collection in New Zealand. However, there was no particular evidence in the 1960s and 70s that the universities had much use for medieval manuscripts at all. The sole exception was at Canterbury, where Professor Douglas Kidd bought a tiny Renaissance manuscript of Sallust in 1966 to teach students of Latin about the transmission of classical texts. In truth, it might have been better if Willi Fels had left his Books of Hours to the Otago Museum, where at least they could have been exhibited with his other and greater bequests. They were of little value to the Library. In early 1972, I helped set up an exhibition of Books of Hours in the Robert McDougall Art Gallery in Christchurch and we asked to borrow the Claude Tribet manuscript. Otago University Library agreed, on condition of an all-risk insurance figure of $150, even then an undervaluation of quite preposterous absurdity.

There was no university course at Otago in 1968–71 touching in any way on early art or use of manuscripts, or even on medieval history. At best, we had a class on the migrations of Dark Age Germania, taught by Professor Gordon Parsonson, on the barbarian tribes overrunning the Roman empire (without manuscripts); then our curriculum leaped forward by more than a millennium to a paper on the religious Reformation of northern Europe in the sixteenth century. I enjoyed Church history, for it seemed close to Missals and Books of Hours. Most history topics at Otago University were set in the twentieth century. I am amazed that I must have passed exams on the Weimar Republic, for example, and on early Soviet Russia, on which I would be hard pressed to name any facts now. The compulsory final-year course, which included a long essay or mini-thesis, was called 'New Zealand and the United Kingdom to 1902', run principally by Professor Angus Ross, head of department, and Professor Parsonson again. For me, unexpectedly, it proved transformative. Although I might (and probably did) argue that the field was of little intrinsic concern to my interests, it opened my eyes to the nature of historical research. At that time (it is different now), not much had been published on early New Zealand history. Take any topic within the area, anything at all – church spires, mealtimes, electioneering, glass-blowing, literacy, water storage, child mortality, telegraph wire, domestic cats, supply of shoelaces, anything (I have just made these up): where would you go to find information? You have a theory. Let us assume there are no secondary publications. What evidence might reasonably survive to show if your idea is right? I had already watched the Turnbull Library at work, and I loved the infinite variety of source material. Although the documentation is different, exactly the same processes apply to the study of manuscripts of the Middle Ages: an idea, and then where do you begin looking, or what evidence would you expect or need if your theory is sustainable? If something is unknowable, move on. If you find one fact, look for patterns. Is there a story? There is no limit to what is fascinating to know. One thing leads somewhere not expected, and whole paragraphs come tumbling out.

Some of those issues brought up in discussions with Professor Ross and his colleagues in seminars at Otago University are still relevant in this book. There are three big questions which underlie the existence of medieval manuscripts in New Zealand. The first and the most local (and which could have been a long essay in 1971) is what the acquisition of medieval European manuscripts can tell us about New Zealand's own history and the colonial experience of migration and settlement. As we have seen throughout these chapters, some manuscripts, like people, arrived there by merest chance, while others were consciously sponsored and brought out to fulfil roles in an idealistic colony. (This was an aspect of colonial New Zealand: Samuel Butler's utopian *Erewhon* of 1872 was imagined there.) A few never quite acclimatized and returned home. Let us not deny the fascination and joy of handling illuminated manuscripts, a human pleasure which is largely universal and not restricted by boundaries. That apart, however, would Sir George Grey, governor and nation builder, Albert Clemas, in his slippers, survivor of the *Beacon Rock*, or A. H. Reed, campaigner and evangelical, have become manuscript enthusiasts at all if they had remained in Britain? Come to that, would I? It is easy to see a longing for a physically tangible past among people cut off from their roots by the most immense distance on earth – and that too, if true, is something all migrants know and express in different ways.

The second big question is the part played by migration of manuscripts (and maybe people) in the history of Europe in the nineteenth and twentieth centuries. All medieval books in New Zealand, without exception, have been traded in the last two hundred years, which is not at all true of most of the big collections in Europe. Manuscripts can only be sold as they become displaced, even unwanted. They are casualties of events. In Grey's Besançon Missal and other purchases, we see émigrés dislodged into Britain by the French Revolution (as my father believed the de Hamels were); in those of Shoults, the after-effect of Napoleon in Germany; and in the sudden rush of privately owned Psalters and Books of Hours onto the English market, the breaking of entailed estates (1882) and the introduction of death duties (1894). The Victorian Gothic Revival and a passion for all things medieval coincides in date with the European settlement of New Zealand, the last major colony of empire. William Morris and Kelmscott Manor had their furthest outreach in Alexander Turnbull and Sir John Illot. Reed could not have owned his Byszewo Bible without the religious piety which brought it out of Germany to Chicago, or Fels his Claude Tribet Book of Hours without the Quakers. These were manuscripts on the move. Above all, in that hundred years from the mid-nineteenth century, art, for the first time, became public and international. Some people may now deplore the acquisition by European museums of treasure brought back from Easter Island or Benin, or looted from the Forbidden City, or even presented by Māori chieftains to Captain Cook, but the movement of artefacts went the other way too. The diaspora of manuscripts and works of art out from Europe, quite apart from language, architecture, law, sport, religion and commerce, is part of how our modern world was formed.

The third and greatest question is whether European medieval manuscripts have any place at all in a country realigning itself in the twenty-first century as a post-colonial, independent nation, with a Māori and Pacific identity much closer to hand and more obviously relevant to many New Zealanders today than elitist relics from the distant British Middle Ages. There are those who would take this view. The answer partly hinges on whether the span of human history matters at all. The fifteenth-century Maude Roll in Christchurch and the Māori sagas of migration are similar expressions of a fundamental need for tales of origin and infinite ancestry. As a world state, New Zealand is very recent. The first word of its European name is a clue. The time from now back to 1840 is only about twice the length of human memory. I have known older people, including A. H. Reed and Jack Somerville, who had met people who remembered the earliest European settlement. My own experiences of New Zealand already span between a quarter and a third of the length of time since Captain Cook first saw the country's coastline in 1769. Even the original Māori arrivals were quite late in the timeline of the European Middle Ages, perhaps more recently than the date of the Turnbull Boethius. If a nation looks to history no older than itself, it would be a truncated narrative in New Zealand. Some early settlers may have been initially glad to shake off their family past, as my father was on arrival, but maturity often brings reflection on where we come from. Sir Frederic Madden had predicted in 1859 that it would be a century before Australasians cared about medieval manuscripts. He was about right; David Taylor's book of 1955 was a first change of direction. The New Zealand historian J. C. Beaglehole, surveying the holdings of the Turnbull Library in 1970, said that 'Donne's sermons are just as important for us as the journals of Captain Cook'. Even with recent international migration, a majority of established New Zealanders (and most Māori people by now) have at least some genetic ancestors who lived in Britain or Europe at the time of Nicolaus of Byszewo and Margery Fitzherbert and Charles de Neufchâtel. The inhabitants of modern New Zealand are as much the rightful heirs of the Middle Ages as anyone still in the Old World. Otago University now teaches medieval history and literature and has a centre for the history of the book. More-or-less every public collection with medieval manuscripts in New Zealand has been rebuilt since I first knew them, and all serve needs and audiences not so evident in my childhood. The city libraries of Auckland and Dunedin both now define their collections of rare books as

'Heritage' departments, a word much used. Perhaps medieval manuscripts in New Zealand have a story to tell which may sometimes seem more necessary and more resonant under the Southern Cross than if the books had stayed at home.

The Māori had no writing. We can end the chapter with a surprise. One of the earliest written specimens of the Māori language survives in an illuminated manuscript Book of Hours. It belongs to the Catholic diocese of Auckland, in the library of the Pompallier Diocesan Centre in Ponsonby, a suburb of Auckland. The building for the bishop's residence was designed in the 1890s in Gothic Revival style by the firm of Pugin, no less, successors of the architect Augustus Pugin, working remotely from London. A modern extension of 1989 takes one round a

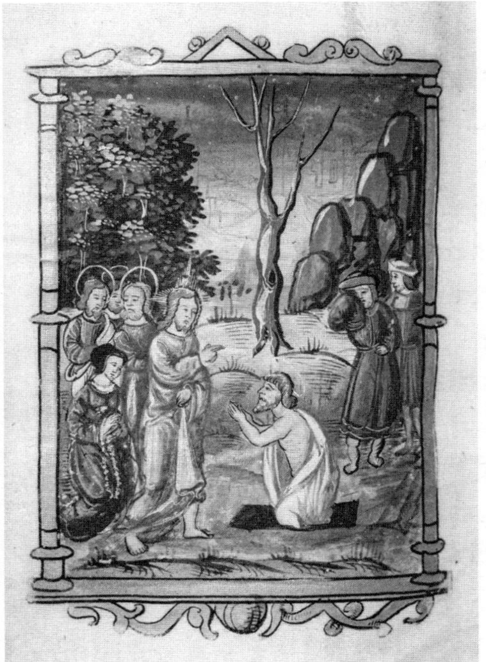
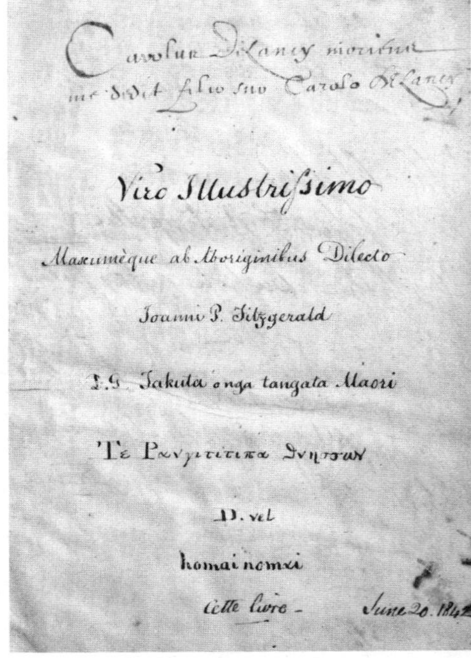

Early sixteenth-century Book of Hours, inscribed by Walter Mantell in Wellington in 1842 in several languages, including Māori.

kind of cloister on the right into a small library filled with books and Catholic images. Here is an early sixteenth-century manuscript Book of Hours, perhaps made in Laon in northern France, with a presentation inscription to Jean-Baptiste-François Pompallier (1801–71), first Catholic bishop of New Zealand, known to Grey, from 'W. B. D. M., June 20 1842, Wellington, New Zealand'. I copied this and the handwriting carefully when I saw the manuscript first in 1970, and later, in the manuscripts department at the Turnbull Library, I showed it to June Starke, who recognized the initials and hand as those of the young Walter Baldock Durrant Mantell (1820–95). He had landed in New Zealand on the *Oriental* on 31 January 1840, a week before the Treaty of Waitangi. This, therefore, is the first documented medieval manuscript in New Zealand and perhaps the first to have crossed the Pacific. The book's spine title, ILLUMIN-ATED MISSAL, as Books of Hours were commonly miscalled, may have suggested its tactful suitability for a Catholic bishop. Mantell's inscription has eight lines in Latin, Māori, French and what looks like Greek. The variety of language was perhaps spur-of-the-moment ebullience of a clever young man meeting a bishop. Latin and French are easy to explain, presenting the manuscript in the languages of Catholic liturgy and of Pompallier himself, who was born in Lyons. However, the recipient is then addressed in Māori, 'Takuta o nga tangata Maori', 'Doctor of the Māori people'. There follows a line in the Greek alphabet, 'Τε Ρανγιτιτιπα θνησσων', which is mostly transliterated Māori again, for there is no real reason why Latin letters are needed for an oral language with no script of its own: in part, 'Te Rangi', 'this day', and 'Ti tipa', Mantell's nickname in Māori, then a word which means 'dead' in Greek (anticipating actuality by fifty years). It ends in Māori once more, 'homai nomai', a vernacular if slightly ungrammatical rendition of 'as a free gift'. Here, then, is the earliest statement of modern New Zealand summed up as Anglican as well as Catholic, English and French, Latin and Greek, European and Māori, one nation under God, from the colony's very beginning, in a medieval Book of Hours.

11

Westminster and Oxford

The European Middle Ages, like childhood, ended imperceptibly as they merged unheralded into what historians now refer to as the early modern period. Three transformative events stand out. One was the fall of Constantinople to Mehmed II in 1453, and the impatient arrival of the armies of Islam in south-east Europe. It caused stark realization in the West that the familiar Christianity of more than a thousand years might not be as secure as had previously seemed. A second and almost exactly contemporaneous occurrence was the invention of printing with movable type by Johann Gutenberg in Mainz in Germany in the first half of the 1450s. It was a defining moment in history, bringing about a gigantic shift in the preservation and transmission of human knowledge. The Gutenberg Bible was produced around 1453–54. The earliest exactly dated pieces of European printing, however, relate to the Muslim encroachments in the eastern Mediterranean, for printed indulgences were run off on the first presses in Mainz in 1454 and 1455 to raise money for the defence of Christendom against the terrifying infidel enemies of the Cross of Christ. A third event, slightly later, which finished the Middle Ages for ever, was the Reformation. This was launched in 1517 with the attack by Martin Luther on the Catholic Church's practice of fundraising by the use of indulgences.

I loved the Gutenberg Bible leaf in the Dunedin Public Library, when I encountered it first. It felt to me like the first properly grown-up manuscript, and I was slightly in awe, like meeting a headmaster or a famous author. I once bravely asked if I might borrow it to take home, as I had with other medieval fragments kept in frames in the Library. They sensibly said no, but did let me have their framed *Golden Legend* leaf printed by William Caxton in 1483, which at different times I hung both on my wall at home and in Knox College. It has a woodcut of St Margaret emerging unperturbed from the side of a dragon which has swallowed her and is still chewing the tip of her robe in its teeth. Her name was familiar in Westminster: when Caxton himself died in 1491, he was buried in the church of St Margaret, adjacent to the Abbey, where his press had operated.

To be strictly truthful, the printed indulgences of this final chapter were not found in my childhood but during a visit back to Dunedin some years later. Like the discoveries of rare birds hidden in the New Zealand bush, once thought extinct, they had been there in Otago University Library all along, but no one knew. It came about in April 1982. I was already working at Sotheby's in London but still with a lingering dream that I might one day update David Taylor's account of all the medieval manuscripts in New Zealand. I had heard that Margaret Manion (1935–2024) and her colleague Vera Vines (1926–2002) at the University of Melbourne were planning a book on the illumination of some of the principal manuscripts in New Zealand libraries, on the model of the volume they were completing for those in Australia (published in 1984). I offered to expand its scope comprehensively by supplying my own descriptions of every medieval manuscript and fragment in the country, whether illuminated or not. I had, I thought, seen all the complete manuscripts, but I took the opportunity of a trip back for family reasons to search through early bindings in rare book collections in New Zealand in the hope of finding further re-used pieces of early manuscripts that had remained unnoticed. By including newly discovered fragments and later acquisitions, the total number of medieval manuscript items known in New Zealand was more than doubled from Taylor's 77, to 181.

In my time as a student (and until its replacement in 2001), the Otago University Library had been a utilitarian, two-storey, white concrete building opened in 1965, connected by a covered walkway to the Student Union where we would meet for coffee between lectures. At the top of an open staircase rising near the Library entrance were several exhibition cases, which sometimes displayed manuscripts and other small rarities or current ephemera. Most of the library was on open shelves, but early books were stored out of sight in an area of closed-off stacks at the far right. These included the uninvited collection of the Reverend William Shoults, brought from England in the 1890s and on deposit from Selwyn College, as recounted, and groups of antiquarian books given more recently by Esmond de Beer and others. The rare book custodian, Elizabeth Tinker, kindly allowed me leisurely trawls along the stacks in 1982, plucking out any early-looking bindings for scrutiny. One of the Shoults books was an odd third volume (of four originally) of a Bible with the commentary of Nicholas de Lyra printed in Venice in 1481, in a chunky and contemporary binding which looked English, made of deeply impressed blind-stamped polished calf over wooden boards (Plate 23). It seemed to have narrow parchment ribbons being used as sewing-guards to strengthen the stitching in the centres of each gathering.

We encountered sewing-guards (or sewing-stays, as they are sometimes called) in Chapter 5. The incunable in Auckland which re-used strips cut from an early ninth-century Bible is a similar workaday text of biblical commentaries very like this, also of around 1480. With the invention of printing, paper (rather than parchment) became the standard medium for the pages of most books. An unjustified concern of late medieval bookbinders was that paper might tear when sewn along the line of a tightly creased central fold, especially in big books, such as these, which were expected to be consulted often. Tiny ribbons of any conveniently available parchment were inserted as lining into the folds, to replicate the strength of stitching through whole parchment pages. In reality, they make very little difference. Handmade fifteenth-century rag paper is extremely robust, and by about 1500 the practice had died out as unnecessary.

Disappointingly, the parchment strips in the binding in the Shoults Collection in Otago University did not seem to be in manuscript but were apparently merely second-hand scraps of printing. One, however, included part of a woodcut initial and the opening of the text in which I could make out the first words in Latin: 'Brother John Kendale, *turcipelarius* of Rhodes . . . .'.

This sounded familiar. Several years earlier, in 1979, Sotheby's had sold the library hoard of Solomon Pottesman (1904–78), tatterdemalion and obsessive Cockney book miser in London,

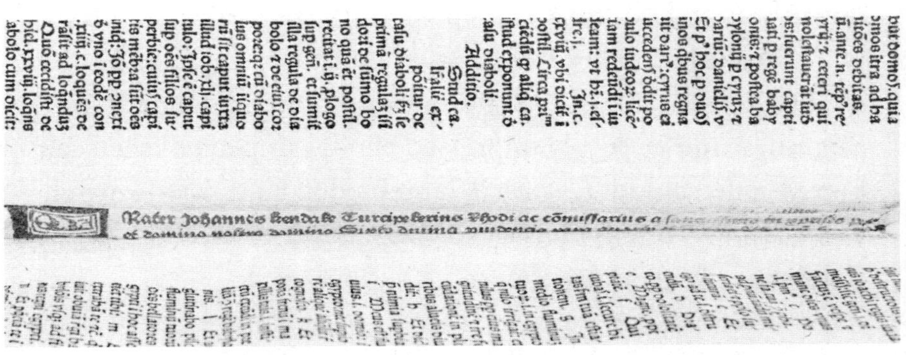

One of numerous strips of an indulgence printed in 1480 by William Caxton, strengthening the sewing folds of an incunable in the Shoults Collection in Dunedin.

whom I had known slightly. His greatest and much-vaunted possession had been a beautiful copy of John Lathbury's commentary on Jeremiah, printed in Oxford by Theoderic Rood in 1482, in its original Oxford binding by the anonymous but so-called 'Rood and Hunt Binder', who is named both after that book's printer and an Oxford bookseller of the time. Mr Pottesman's volume was catalogued for sale by my then colleague at Sotheby's, William Ward (now Lord Bangor), who noticed that the binder had used sewing-guards cut from parchment strips of several indulgences in the name of John Kendale for the relief of the siege of Rhodes in 1480, in printed types recognizable as those of William Caxton, in Westminster, and John Lettou, the first printer in the city of London. The discovery of bits of Caxton typography caused notable interest and the book was bought for £25,000 by the British Library. A few moments with Strickland Gibson's *Early Oxford Bindings* (1903), obligingly conjured up for me in Dunedin by Liz Tinker, showed that the Shoults volume of Nicholas de Lyra (although rather worse for wear) was indeed also bound by that same Rood and Hunt Binder. I carried the book over to a table in the Library, wondering whether this was coincidence. On inspection, it proved to have fourteen pieces of the same indulgence of 1480, twelve printed by Caxton and two by Lettou.

Part of the delight of antiquarianism is that you never quite know where some chance find may suddenly lead you. It resembles migration where one fortuitous arrival brings in a few friends, and within a generation or so has multiplied into an entire colony. When I got back to Europe, I started slowly but systematically checking all twenty-six recorded books bound by that fifteenth-century Rood and Hunt Binder, mostly in libraries in England but also elsewhere. Four of the twenty-six books are written or printed on parchment and so sewing-guards were not necessary. Two had been resewn during later repairs and any parchment strips were discarded. Of the remaining twenty, as many as six – more than a quarter of the total – were found to include multiple fragments from copies of the same printed indulgences for the relief of the siege of Rhodes by the Turks in 1480. As in Dunedin, all are printed on parchment either by William Caxton or John Lettou.

Until the Rood and Hunt bindings started revealing their hidden treasures, there were only three surviving copies of the indulgence by either printer (a fourth has been found since), and four fragments. The latter had been rescued by Henry Bradshaw from Cambridge bindings in the late nineteenth century and their discovery was regarded as important enough to be reported in both *The Times* in London on 8 October 1881, and in the *New York Times* on the 30th. Following the revelations in Dunedin, the Rood and Hunt bindings have now brought to light no fewer than 113 fragments of the Caxton printing alone, not one of which was known before 1979. A single binding at St John's College in Oxford contributed over fifty pieces, which no one knew existed.

A problem with sewing-guards is that they are more-or-less invisible. Especially if the binding is medieval, one may be reluctant to force an entry too far into the fragile central fold. The pieces in the Otago University binding are very hard to see. In 1982 my brother Michael was still working as a photographer in Dunedin. He was (and to some extent still is) known for accumulating pieces of discarded junk which might one day be useful. He happened to have parts of a periscope from a Second World War German tank, including a wedge-shaped prism, which he placed in the centre of each quire of the book and then took pictures through the glass. He printed these out in reverse, and with scissors and paste we shuffled his images on our parents' dining-room table to spell out the complete text.

The indulgence is constructed to resemble a charter, a format familiar to most literate people in the late Middle Ages, to be completed by hand and sealed on delivery. In summary, it says, in Latin:

Brother John Kendale, *turcipelarius* of Rhodes and commissioner of Pope Sixtus IV and his appointed agent throughout the world by virtue of papal licence for the expedition against the perfidious Turks, enemies of the Christian name, for the defence of the island of Rhodes and the Catholic faith, gives greetings to . . . [and here a blank space was left for the name of the recipient]. Since we know that you, out of piety and reverence for the Church, have freely contributed to this holy and necessary expedition and as you especially seek peace and salvation of your soul, and once you have chosen a suitable priest and made contrite confession of all sins (with a few named exceptions, such as laying hands on a bishop, treason against the Roman See, or killing a priest) and have duly received absolution, then in life and at the moment of death you will receive comprehensive and plenary indulgence, in confirmation of which we attach our seal on this . . . [another blank space] . . . day of the month . . . [another again] . . . in the year of the Lord 1480 (some copies also add, 'and in the tenth year of the pontificate of Pope Sixtus IV').

The indulgence is in the name of John Kendale, or Kendall, *turcipelarius* of Rhodes. That is a real word and a good one. The Order of Knights Hospitaller, or Knights of St John, had set up their headquarters on the island of Rhodes following the recapture of Acre by the Muslims in 1291. They had been initially founded to protect and care for Christians visiting the Holy Land. The office of *turcipelarius*, traditionally held by an Englishman, originally meant a military commander of the turcopoles, auxiliary soldiers recruited locally, but it had come simply to mean the international administrator for the protection and defence of the Knights themselves. It has been noted that in 1478–81 one John Kendale rented two tenements in Westminster Sanctuary, almost immediately next door to Caxton's shop, and that in 1482 Kendale co-audited the accounts of St Margaret's Church in Westminster, together with Caxton. The suggestion has been that Kendale involved Caxton in printing his indulgence because they were colleagues and neighbours.

In fact, it was not the same man at all, although they might have been related. The John Kendale of Westminster was dead by late 1482, whereas the *turcipelarius* lived until 1501. We know exactly what he looked like, for he had an Italianate portrait medal of himself struck in 1480, which may be in some way connected with the indulgence campaign, as it is lettered as 'at the time of the siege of the Turks'. It shows a good-looking man in profile with his coat of arms and the date on the verso. He has wavy and shaggy hair down to the collar of his armour, a double chin, small mouth and bags under his eyes, as if exhausted by the cares of office. Kendale became prior of the Order in England in 1489 and appeared on missions to Rome and Venice. It was

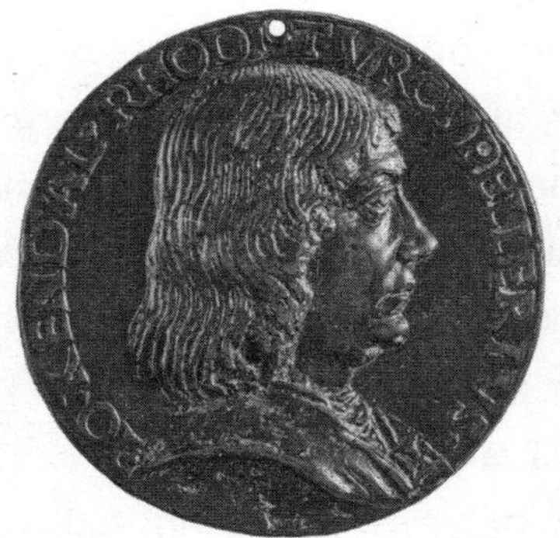

Portrait medal of John Kendale, *turcipelarius* of Rhodes, 1480.

alleged in 1495 that he had been plotting with Perkin Warbeck to assassinate Henry VII by necromancy, but the charge was so obviously preposterous it was dismissed. He would have lived, not in Westminster, but in the priory of St John in Clerken-well, in the city of London. The Order's properties elsewhere in London are remembered today by the placenames of Knights-bridge and St John's Wood.

To Kendale and his colleagues, the defence of Rhodes and of the Catholic faith were indivisible causes. They were planning to send a taskforce from Europe to try to hold back what many saw as an apocalyptic advance of evil. The fear was that the Turks' next target after Constantinople and Rhodes might be Rome itself. History is full of panic about hostile takeover, usually (but not always) unfounded, such as the apparent imminence of a Napoleonic occupation of Britain in the early nineteenth century. As children we used to scramble through overgrown and abandoned gun emplacements on the Otago Peninsula built as defences against a feared Russian navy in the 1880s and an anticipated Japanese invasion of New Zealand in 1943. As his-torians, we must judge not only from what happened, but also from what people did not know would not happen.

By 1480, the island of Rhodes was indeed desperately vulner-able. It was now the frontier of Christendom, and at its closest point is only about fourteen miles off the coast of Turkey. On 23 May that year, after months of very public preparation, the Ottoman forces finally landed on the island with a reported 70,000 troops and laid siege to the citadel. I have been to Rhodes only once, but it was the right way to arrive, by private sailing boat from Greece with a Knight of Saint John on board and a Benedic-tine monk, who later became a chaplain of the Order, a modern *turcipelarius*. Absolutely massive medieval walls and deep baileys still surround the centre of the ancient harbour town. Rhodes was defended in 1480 by six hundred Knights, led by the Grand Master himself, Pierre d'Aubusson, with support from mercenaries and local soldiers. The city was bombarded by the Turks relentlessly day after day. A dramatic account of the siege by Guillaume Caoursin, chancellor of the Order, was translated and circulated round Europe to an avid and outraged audience. A Middle English version was published in London in about 1482–83 by an unidentified printer operating somewhere in the orbit of John Lettou. It describes how 'the Turkes with grete noyse broughte grete bombardes and gonnes toward the walles of Rhodes . . . they putted viii grete instrumentes, which cast grete stones in the cyte'. It was said that the noise of cannons could be heard even from the mainland.

To gather funds for the rescue mission, Kendale issued an indulgence. This was a common medieval method of raising money for any charitable purpose. Indulgences were sometimes for very local causes, such as upkeep of a shrine or even repairing parish roads and bridges, in which case they were mostly sold to pilgrims visiting a particular church. Others had much more international aims, including the defence of Rhodes, and were marketed by pardoners or their representatives travelling from place to place. Like modern crowdfunding, success depended on involving as many participants as possible. Indulgence pedlars needed supplies of identical certificates in very large numbers. Preparing these by hand, over and over again, would have been the greatest drudgery for medieval scribes. Printing offered mass duplication. As Gutenberg and others realized from the outset, indulgence-printing was a quick and profitable sideline, especially in presses newly set up, for payment was upfront on production and required no capital investment, as books did.

Despite the impressive verbiage of salesman's patter, an indulgence does not actually grant or guarantee anything. Recipients still had to confess their sins and receive absolution, which would have applied in any case even without purchase of the document. No one knows precisely when they will die. Images of the Dance of Death impressed the unpredictability of this very strongly on medieval consciousness. Ideally, the confession and absolution invited here should be given just before death, to eliminate opportunity for further lapses, and indulgence documents might be retained by their purchasers to be shown to the priest at that time. If death occurred without the presence of a priest, at least possession of an indulgence in advance probably seemed the next best thing. In that case, the documents would often be buried with the deceased, as potential evidence for use at the Last Judgment. It has been tantalizing to find unknown bits of Caxton printing preserved in half a dozen bindings, but there might in theory be thousands of Caxton indulgences still hidden underground in medieval graveyards and crypts throughout England.

William Caxton (*c.* 1422–92) is one of the most famous non-royal laymen of the English Middle Ages, perhaps matched only by Chaucer and possibly Robin Hood, and even the smallest scraps of his printing are holy grails of typography. As we saw in Chapter 7, he may have had at least a supervisory role in exporting Sarum Books of Hours from Bruges to England in the 1460s. In 1476, he returned to England, renting two premises within the curtilage of Westminster Abbey. This was perhaps because of family connections (a Richard Caxton was a monk of the abbey from 1473 until 1504), but it was also very well placed for business involving both the royal court and the Church. Caxton's first piece of datable printing in England was an indulgence, of which the unique surviving copy was completed with the names of its purchasers on 13 December 1476, also for defence against the Turks. He operated what must have been little more than a stall up against the outside wall of the chapter house, past which potential customers would walk daily from the royal palace of Westminster through to the side door into the south transept of the Abbey. He also rented the 'Red Pale', larger premises that were above or part of the gateway in the western boundary wall of the Abbey's precincts. The name 'pale' was presumably derived from a red wooden gate, but had evidently become a landmark shop sign, like the original red shield of 'Rothschild' in Frankfurt. I have often stood just around the corner from the Abbey in Great Smith Street, waiting for a number 88 bus home, envisaging Caxton's Red Pale shop behind me between what is now the Attorney General's office on the corner of Victoria Street and the back of the Westminster Abbey Choir School. The stone buildings at this point are lower, befitting the site of a former gateway, and there are two rows of neo-Gothic windows. If the lights are on, one can see down into offices on the lower ground floor, with computers and printers. It was somewhere about here that Caxton had his press, and this is where the Kendale indulgence was doubtless printed in multiple copies in 1480.

Printing by John Lettou is not as romantic as work by Caxton but is much rarer. It may be that Kendale's initial choice of printer for his indulgence was not Caxton but Lettou. The first printer in the city of London is enigmatic. He was almost certainly the 'Johannes Bulle', an English-sounding name, who had previously operated in Rome as a jobbing printer, using the same type. At the end of 1479 John Kendale too had been in Rome as procurator of his Order at the papal court, and we know of various bits of business he conducted there, including obtaining a licence from Sixtus IV for the sale of indulgences, dated 12 December 1479. He might easily have met Lettou and brought him back to London in 1480. The indulgence was Lettou's first commission on his arrival. Perhaps he proved not up to the task, or his inexperienced press-work seemed too clumsy. A subsequent decision to transfer part or all of the business to a better and more established English printer seems more plausible than the other way round. This may explain why the crude Lettou indulgences are relatively rare, and the almost simultaneous and better-printed Caxton versions have now yielded over a hundred fragments.

We have no way of knowing how many copies of the Kendale indulgence were printed. It is estimated that an early printer could run off upwards of six hundred impressions a day, and if there were four indulgences to an uncut sheet, which is likely, that is almost two and a half thousand documents. The guild of Our Lady in Boston, Lincolnshire, ordering indulgences from the London printer Richard Pynson in the 1520s, seems to have paid for them in batches of about 2,150 a time, which may each represent one day's work. The involvement of both Lettou and Caxton perhaps had no other reason than to double the speed of output. The numbers may well have been in the tens of thousands, as news of Muslim advances in the Mediterranean caused accelerating panic in western Europe.

In the event, the Ottoman siege of 1480 failed (at least until Rhodes finally fell in 1522). After a brutal defeat in battle on 27 July, the attacking armies were severely repulsed, and they retreated from the island altogether on 17 August. The huge cost of defence and the fear of renewed attack did not necessarily cease, and fund-raising continued. It would in any case have taken some weeks for news to reach England. In fact, the late summer of 1480 seems to have been Kendale's busiest period. Many (not all) of the Rhodes indulgences are dated in their last line of text as being from the tenth year of the pontificate of Sixtus IV, who was elected pope on 9 August 1471 and consecrated on the 25th, and so his tenth year began in August 1480. On 17 August 1480, King Edward IV wrote to the archbishop of Canterbury saying that he was himself contributing to the defence of Rhodes and urging the archbishop to do the same. On 1 September the archbishop extended the indulgence to cover individual members of the clergy (who would otherwise have been exempt); and we know that £60.10s. was raised in the diocese of Worcester alone. Not all of this was necessarily from sale of indulgences, but if they were sold for (say) fourpence each, which was probably about average, that sum would equate to 3,900 indulgences.

Of the huge number probably printed, only four survive intact, sold and completed with dates and inscribed names of their purchasers. Two were printed by Caxton and two by Lettou. The Caxton copies were both filled in by hand on the last day of March, which in each case probably means 1481, in the third week of Lent. One of these was issued to Simon Mountford and his wife, Emma, and was eventually acquired by the British Museum (now Library) in 1846. The second, issued to John Hawardyne, was identified in the Lancashire Record Office as recently as 2004. There are also two used copies of Lettou's printing of the Kendale indulgence, one sold to John Frisden

Kendale's indulgence sold and completed by hand for John Hawardyne in March 1481.

and his wife Katherine, in Oxford, on 18 April, which in 1481 was Wednesday of Holy Week, and the other to Nicholas Dorpeys and his wife Isabelle, on 21 April, Holy Saturday. Both are in the British Library. All four survivals suggest a flurry of sales within a few weeks in mid to late Lent of 1481.

Despite the number of indulgences that must have been issued in late medieval Europe and the high-profile anathema poured on the trade by Martin Luther at the Reformation, we know curiously little about the practicalities of their distribution and sale. One source is an English theological miscellany in the Bodleian Library which includes instructions for selling indulgences in 1489. Much of its detail is on the security of the collecting boxes and on deduction of legitimate expenses. The third clause states that the commissioner should choose suitable and trustworthy people as agents for distribution. Kendale would probably have appointed sub-contractors for each diocese and would have assigned a package of documents to each, doubtless taking some himself. Interestingly, not all of these were printed. There survives in the Essex Record Office in Colchester an identical but hand-written Kendale indulgence, made out to John Prince and his wife Lucy on what must be 10 April 1481, still, like the printed versions, dated 1480 in its text, but in the tenth year of Sixtus IV.

A vivid if entirely fictional picture of the sale of indulgences emerges from the satirical description of the Pardoner in Chaucer's *Canterbury Tales*, a text, incidentally, printed twice by Caxton. Some of the same phrases recur in Heywood's play, *The Pardoner and the Friar*, written in 1519. Chaucer's disreputable indulgence pedlar 'streight was comen fro the court of Rome' (as was Kendale) with 'his wallet . . . bretful of pardoun' on his lap. In the prologue to the *Pardoner's Tale*, he explains how he operates. He preaches in church and sells indulgences during the service:

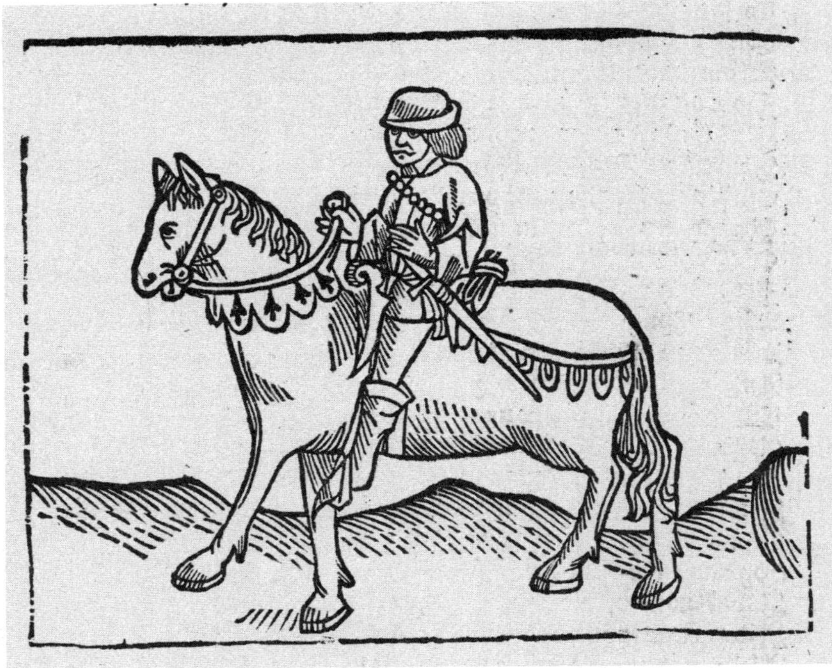

Caxton's woodcut of the Pardoner, from the second edition
of Chaucer's *Canterbury Tales*, 1483.

First I pronounce whennes that I come,
And thanne my bulles shewe I, alle and some.
Oure lige lordes seel on my patente,
That shewe I first, my body to warente.

That is what Kendale might have done. He pronounces where
he comes from (*turcipelarius* of Rhodes, commissioner from
Rome) and he quotes the papal bull, which he had been granted
by Sixtus IV on 12 December 1479. He then shows his authority
from the king with 'our liege lord's seal': Kendale obtained
such a charter from Edward IV on 29 April 1480. He proves
that he is the commissioner mentioned in the document, and
he produces other exhibits, like the Pardoners' dubious relics
described by Chaucer and others. These might have included

the impressive portrait medals, which proclaim Kendale's titles and identity and could also be appropriate gifts for wealthy supporters. In Chaucer's poem, the Pardoner then preaches on the sin of avarice and invites people to come up to give money (Kendale's papal authority specifically mentions a collecting-box in church), and then, says the Pardoner:

> Youre names I entre heer in my rolle anon;
> Into the blisse of hevene shul ye gon.

In theory, one did not buy an indulgence: contributions were voluntary and at the discretion of the donor, who was then freely given a document in return. However, like the 'voluntary donation' required by the Metropolitan Museum of Art in New York before receiving a badge which allows admission, suggested guidelines were usually non-negotiable. The instructions of 1489 recommend two groats (eight pence) a person, or thereabouts (as the Pardoner decided), possibly reduced for more than one subscriber or if the donor was truly poor. Documented sales of indulgences vary from one penny up to 13s. 4d., but, as above, fourpence each was probably about the average.

It would obviously be in the interests of the seller of indulgences to preach on days of especial penance. There are, I think, seven extant indulgences of various kinds printed either by Caxton or by Lettou (and not just for Kendale) which were sold and completed by hand with buyers' names and dates of sale, from 1476 right through to 1490. All seven of these were issued on Fridays, or during Lent, or both.

We should re-visit Dunedin and look again at the volume in Otago University Library. It feels strange to walk back through a campus so familiar to me from long ago and yet at the next moment suddenly unrecognizable. The present students' parents were probably not even born when I was here. The library building is on its former site but is completely new, as vast and spacious as a modern airport. Rare books now have their own reading room in the north-west corner of the first floor, overlooking the Museum Reserve. There are two tangential tables, Venetian blinds to protect books against the piercing and unfiltered sun of the Southern Hemisphere, and a big television screen, presumably for seminars. The Rood and Hunt binding is brought out with great respect, for the unwished-for migrant of about 1893 is now a Dunedin celebrity.

The volume is thick and weighty. Its boards are made of wood, doubtless oak. The covers are of polished leather ruled by double lines around a central rectangle. This is filled with nine rows of neat little deeply impressed and repeating square stamps of dragons and birds, including a double-headed eagle and chickens face-to-face. These stamps are all characteristic of the Rood and Hunt Binder. Inside, the book has a contemporary inscription in Latin recording its gift by Master John Lee, 'late master of this college', who must be the John Lee who was master from 1470 to 1494 of the collegiate church of Maidstone in Kent. He was himself an Oxford graduate. This is one of four surviving books known from the college in Maidstone, which was suppressed in 1546. There are later inscriptions of a Richard Wilson, probably sixteenth century, and 'Bib. Harvin. Cler. Saec.' This is that of the recusant library of the secular clergy at Harvington Hall, Worcestershire, founded in 1696, much of which was eventually transferred to Oscott College, a Catholic seminary in north Birmingham. Oscott still owns another single volume of the same edition of Nicholas de Lyra of 1481, which at one time I hoped might have been part of the same original set. However, this is not the case. The provenance of the book at Oscott is Italian, not English or from Harvington, and it does not contain indulgences. The Nicholas de Lyra in Dunedin was probably simply discarded as an odd volume, and it was doubtless picked up for a negligible sum by Shoults, who inhabited the fringes of Anglo-Catholicism.

The sobriquet 'Rood and Hunt Binder' was devised in the 1890s by the book historian W. H. James Weale. Thomas Hunt was one of the four university stationers in Oxford, documented from 1473 to *c.* 1492. Hunt's shop was in the High Street, just west of St Mary's Church, on what is now part of the street frontage of Brasenose College. It was well placed for the university trade and remains so, for almost immediately opposite is still the bookshop where I bought some early printed leaves on that portentous trip to England in January 1967. Theoderic Rood came originally from Cologne and was a goldsmith and then a printer, living in Oxford from 1480 until about 1483–84. His own premises were also in the High Street, about 170 yards along the road from those of Hunt, approximately where there is now a side gate into the edge of All Souls College, between the warden's lodgings and Queen's, across the street from University College. In the colophon of one book printed in 1481, Rood describes Hunt as his associate (*'atque sibi socius'*) and he was perhaps always Rood's financial backer. The anonymous binder bound five surviving books printed by Rood and also books from Europe which Hunt is independently recorded as importing and selling in Oxford on consignment. The Otago volume was probably one of them, sold by Hunt. Those with publication dates were all printed between *c.* 1472 and 1482, corresponding almost exactly with the known dates in the Oxford archives of a bookbinder called Nicholas, who rented premises on the north side of Catte Street and a storeroom in New College Lane, all nearby. The identification is extremely probable but not absolutely proven.

The Rood and Hunt bindery appears to have worked largely for institutional clients, although this may be the chance of survival. Five of its bindings belonged to monks of Durham Cathedral or to Durham College, which represented them in Oxford. (It was on the site of what is now Trinity College, behind Blackwell's.) Two Rood and Hunt bindings were acquired by All Souls College, probably bought new; a third, listed in the college's possession by 1494, was given by Richard Gaunte, a fellow (d. 1518). Others were owned by Magdalen College in Oxford; Abbot John Newland of the Augustinian abbey in Bristol; and Shelford Church, near Cambridge.

Sewing-guards can be made from any old waste parchment that the binder happened to have at hand. Like my brother Michael, the Rood and Hunt Binder clearly saved discarded items which might come in useful one day, perhaps in his storeroom in New College Lane (if he is rightly identified as Nicholas the bookbinder). In my search for Caxton strips, I have noticed that he also snipped sewing-guards from pieces of twelfth-century liturgy, fifteenth-century polyphony, and from documents including what seems to be part of a cartulary mentioning York. Best of all, a Rood and Hunt binding at Winchester College uses strips of saints' lives in a beautiful mid-eleventh-century English hand, almost certainly pre-Conquest, and the former Pottesman volume in the British Library also includes two ribbons of liturgy in a large insular set minuscule of the second half of the eighth century (or possibly early ninth), with a decorated initial which is unknown to scholarship. Obsolete books can get discarded at any moment in their lives, even before the Reformation, and these hidden strips give us a tantalizing glimpse of the random contents of a wastepaper basket in the Oxford book trade in the early 1480s. Since Durham Cathedral and its college in Oxford were the largest known clients of the Rood and Hunt bindery, the very early pieces might have been monastic discards from the far North, the oldest perhaps even from Lindisfarne.

The big question, then, is how this store of re-usable parchment in Oxford came to include quantities of unsold indulgences printed over fifty miles away in London and Westminster. The usual explanation of printed waste being used in binding books is that the binder's workshop was in the same place as that of the printer. However, it is not feasible that either Lettou or Caxton ever had presses in Oxford. In one feature the indulgence fragments differ from other parchment waste used by the Rood and Hunt Binder: they are all horizontal strips along the length of the lines of text, whereas most of the binder's other sewing-guards were made from manuscript leaves cut vertically, to furnish longer pieces of parchment. If the indulgences were still in multiple sheets, straight from the press, we would expect at least some upright strips, and there are none. It is one clue that the fragments were taken from oblong documents already separated for sale by an indulgence seller.

The crucial piece of evidence is the papal bull authorizing John Kendale to issue his indulgence. As mentioned, it was granted to him in Rome on 12 December 1479, and the text is published in the *Calendar of Entries in the Papal Registers*. Sixtus IV says that he has been informed of the advance of the Turks and their threatened attack on the castle of St Peter on the island of Rhodes, and that he has learned this from three orators, John Quindal (that is Kendale, through the ears of a papal clerk), *turcipelarius* and lieutenant-general of the Master in Italy, England, Flanders and Ireland, and procurator of the Order in the court of Rome, supported by two other members of the Order of the Knights of St John, Pedro Fernandi de

Heredia, from the diocese of Saragossa, and Gui de Blanchefort, from the diocese of Limoges. Kendale is clearly in charge. The pope agrees to grant remission of sins to all faithful people who give alms for the defence of the Church and, being penitent, make confession in an appropriate church, at any time from first vespers on Palm Sunday next until Easter Day 1481. He instructs the three orators (that is Kendale and his two colleagues), or their agents, to designate appropriate churches and to provide suitable collecting boxes, and, the bull iterates in its conclusion, 'The present letters shall not hold good after Easter Day in the said year 1481.'

By the fortunate fact of one surviving indulgence having been issued to John Frisden and his wife Katherine in Oxford during Holy Week in 1481, we now know that Kendale or his agent were in Oxford for Easter that year, which was the day the papal licence ran out, on Sunday 22 April. By the next morning, any remaining indulgences were unsaleable. If the Pardoner's church was St Mary's, he had only a few yards to walk to Thomas Hunt's shop in the High Street, or to Nicholas the bookbinder's house in Catte Street. The newly expired indulgences could now be disposed of only as parchment scrap. This makes complete sense. That is why 124 fragments of unused Lettou and Caxton indulgences for the relief of Rhodes survived in sewing folds of the Rood and Hunt bindery of Oxford.

The migration of the printed indulgences from London to Oxford was probably in a saddlebag on horseback. I myself took the same journey in July 1972. I landed from New Zealand at Heathrow airport and made my way to Oxford. I recall walking from the station up to the High Street, off to the left past St Mary's into Catte Street, along by the Bodleian, turning right under the bridge linking the two parts of Hertford College into New College Lane, where Nicholas the binder's storeroom had

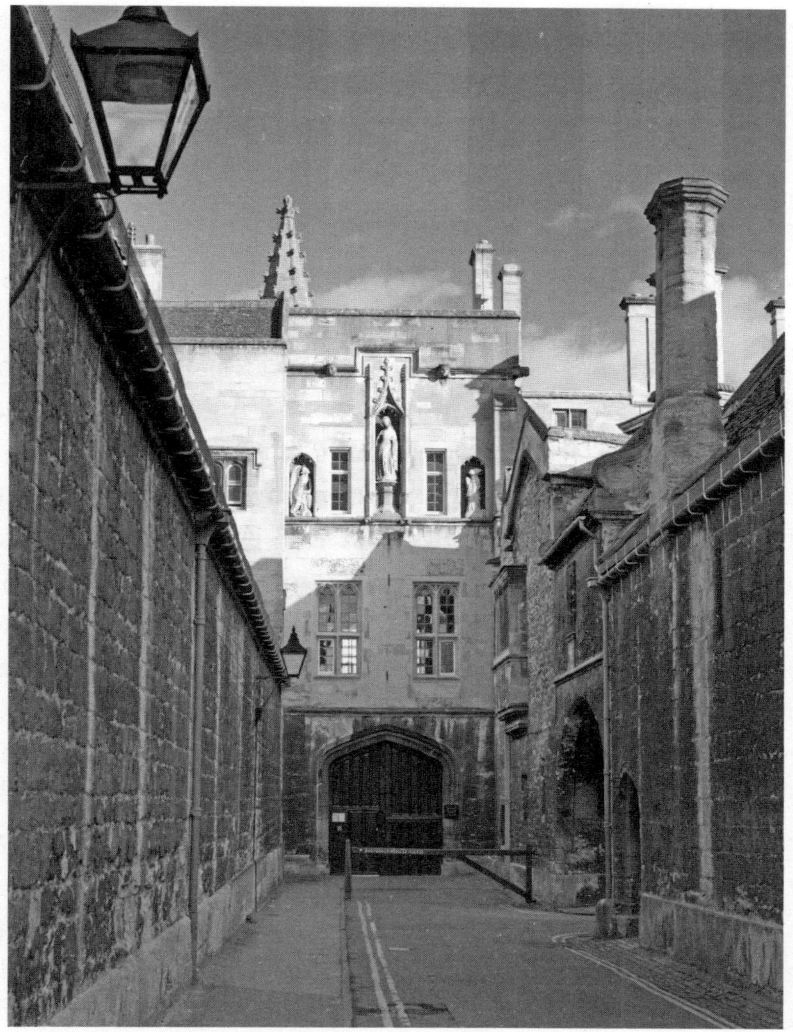

The medieval gateway into New College, Oxford, in New College Lane.

once been. I ducked through the small door in the medieval wooden gate at the end into New College itself, where I announced myself to the porter on duty. He gazed at me with supreme indifference and gave me a room key.

Epilogue

This has been a book about people and manuscripts on the move. Migrants become settlers and attract others to follow their example, and they begin to multiply. This applies to manuscripts as much as to people. When my parents disembarked with three small children from the *Rangitoto* on 17 June 1955, they had no known relatives in New Zealand. By the late 1960s, by which time we were reasonably established, our house in Macandrew Bay seemed to have become a destination for restless younger family members from Britain, who knew our address and drifted through eventually with their own rucksacks and a spirit of adventure. Some were merely friends of relations, whom my parents referred to wearily as the 'You-don't-know-who-I-am-buts' and grimly tolerated, up to a point, as they settled in for free meals and laundry. Three of my eight first cousins came out too because we were there and then remained, marrying New Zealanders, two Maclarens and one Fergusson. The pattern was repeated, which is how the chairman of the Mansion House Foundation on Kawau could be my relative by marriage through my father's sister's son then living in Auckland. My brothers all had children of their own and most now have grandchildren too, or soon will. Counting wives, there are about twenty de Hamels currently scattered through New Zealand, where once there were none, including my own son

Alexander and my eldest granddaughter, Bella. In fifty years, there may be hundreds. Like the proliferating descendants of plants and animals brought out experimentally by Sir George Grey to test their acclimatization, there will probably be at least some of my parents' posterity in New Zealand for centuries or even millennia, so far as that is imaginable – all because my mother once chanced on a discarded issue of a medical journal lining the gumboot box in Holly Cottage near Guildford in the mid-1950s.

The manuscript migrants too have become part of New Zealand. They arrive as individuals and they join with others to form libraries. Once there, some move together, like the Shoults books at Selwyn College to Otago University Library, or the collection of Albert Clemas in Masterton to the Bible Society and then across to the Turnbull. Others strike out alone. The Bible from Koronowo Abbey which migrated in 1925 is, quite literally, dispersed throughout the country. The presence of some arrivals in a new country can enable kinsmen to emigrate too and settle, as with humans. One becomes established and others follow. The early books brought out by Benjamin Hibbard almost certainly inspired the collections of both his neighbour Percy Watts Rule and of his grandson's father-in-law Albert Clemas, whose acquisitions in turn sparked David Taylor to survey the country's resident manuscript population. Sir George Grey's shelves of medieval manuscripts caused Henry Shaw to bring out more to join the expatriate community of early books in Auckland. Sir John Ilott chose suitable manuscripts to be companions for the lonely Boethius of Alexander Turnbull. I began my own purchases of medieval single leaves entirely by observation of A. H. Reed's acquisitions.

When manuscripts leave New Zealand again, their departure is often considered fickle and disappointing. The term in

Australia is 'boomerang Poms'. Sales back in London of the Books of Hours privately owned by Mrs Norris and Dr Heine were seen as regrettable losses to the nation, as was even the disposal of two manuscripts in 1938 from the unsolicited and never used (or even ever wanted) collection of William Shoults. If a manuscript has once been in the country, this may be sufficient reason to bring it back. When a second Book of Hours once owned in New Zealand by Walter Mantell (see above, p. 235) came through Sotheby's in London in 1987, it was bought at the sale by the Dunedin Public Library and was underbid by the Turnbull Library in Wellington. In recent years the Turnbull has acquired several medieval manuscripts for the national collections from the local auctioneers Dunbar Sloane for no especial reason beyond loyalty to manuscript inhabitants of New Zealand. One, secured in 2022, had been bought at Christie's in London as recently as 2008, but its short sojourn in New Zealand since then was already enough to confer local status. This resembles the characteristic and very appealing attitude towards human immigrants into New Zealand: once you are there, you are one of us, mates together, whether you arrived recently or years ago. This may be a feature of any society once made up almost entirely of settlers, and it is not necessarily true in Europe. People who move to English villages tell you it can take fifty years before locals stop treating you as an outsider. It is the same with manuscripts, for British heritage laws state that any manuscript imported into the United Kingdom in the previous half-century cannot have its export licence stopped, for arrival is too recent for it to have become national patrimony. In New Zealand, however, people and manuscripts are all fellow citizens on arrival. 'They have chosen to make New Zealand their home, and it is their home,' said the Prime Minister memorably of the migrants affected by the shootings in Christchurch in 2019.

Immigrants settle and reproduce. One New Zealand student of French literature in the 1960s, Glynnis Cropp, worked on the conveniently accessible manuscript of the anonymous translation of Boethius, *Le livre de consolacion*, among the treasures exhibited to Grey's guests on Kawau and now in the Auckland Central Library. She later edited the text, reproducing the opening miniature of the Grey manuscript on the front cover of her edition (2006). In the meantime, another fifteenth-century manuscript of the same rare translation emerged in a sale in Heidelberg in 1981, acquired by a bookseller in New York. I forwarded his subsequent catalogue to Glynnis, and in 1983 the manuscript was bought with a subsidy from the New Zealand University Grants Committee for Massey University in Palmerston North, in honour of Professor Cropp, who taught there. It is an instance of an endangered manuscript suddenly breeding. One copy begets another. There was a manuscript birth in Dunedin with two parents. A. H. Reed had several collecting interests beyond the Middle Ages, including Samuel Johnson. In 2009 a little Flemish Book of Hours of the mid-fifteenth century was offered at Sotheby's. It has the signature of Alexander Boswell (1707–82), who had bought it in Brussels in 1729, and it was at Auchinlech House in East Ayrshire when Dr Johnson stayed there with his biographer, the owner's son, James Boswell, in 1773. On 2 November it rained all day, and 'my father showed Dr Johnson his library', as recorded in Boswell's *Journal of a Tour to the Hebrides*. The Book of Hours, which they may well have looked at together, is now in the Reed Collection (and Dunedin is still Scottish and raining).

It is obvious that students, like Glynnis Cropp initially, will tend to study whatever material is available in their local libraries. Late medieval Books of Hours are not so prominent in early European research collections, where even now they are regarded as hardly serious or academic manuscripts. The fashion for collecting Books of Hours began only in the late nineteenth century, by which time most of the national libraries of Europe were more-or-less fully formed. It was, however, precisely when the bibliophiles and libraries of the New World were acquiring illuminated manuscripts and people were migrating. There are far more Books of Hours in New York and Baltimore, for example, and now in Perth in Western Australia, than in any city in Britain or Europe with the possible exception of Paris. There are more in New Zealand than any other text. Sir George Grey's collection, given to Auckland in 1887, had only one, but A. H. Reed, two generations later, owned four, and Willi Fels two. The modern scholars of Books of Hours, as one might expect, have been mostly from America or, in the case of Margaret Manion, from Australia, simply because that is where the manuscripts are.

My own passion too as a late teenager was naturally Books of Hours, the manuscripts I had seen most of in New Zealand, with Bibles second. That was why I applied to Oxford, since for a short period Books of Hours were being studied there by a Belgian, L. M. J. ('Bob') Delaissé (1914–72), of All Souls College, with a research group of graduates, mostly, in fact, Americans. I had spirited correspondence with him from Dunedin. He agreed to take me on and I was granted admission to New College. (The choice had a certain appropriateness, since my parents had first met each other in the New College dining hall.) Then, shortly before I was to leave for England, Delaissé suddenly died. For a few terrible and uncertain weeks, my acceptance by Oxford was cancelled. Eventually, I was taken up instead by Richard Hunt (1908–79), of the Bodleian Library, who edged me back into the twelfth century, a much more British subject, and New College re-opened their offer of a place. I now became exposed to manuscripts of wondrous variety. Over the next three years I travelled with rucksack and notebooks through the little libraries of Europe looking at Romanesque biblical manuscripts. However, it was childhood familiarity with Books of Hours which got me through my interview and into Sotheby's in 1975, for those were (and are) still the most frequent manuscripts on the art market. I eventually saw and wrote catalogue descriptions of dozens of Books of Hours every year, sometimes more. Some were of a class and a quality infinitely beyond anything I knew in New Zealand, such as the extraordinary early sixteenth-century Spinola Hours, which once shared a shelf with the *Très Riches Heures* of the duc de Berry. We sold that at Sotheby's in London in July 1976, only eight years after I left King's High School.

Cause and effect are never simple in history. There are no alternative universes, and directions taken at any moment may be brought about by chance or countless little but cumulative factors in a complex world. One thing I do know is that I owe an enormous debt to A. H. Reed, and especially to the Dunedin Public Library and its staff. The City Librarian when I first encountered medieval manuscripts was Ada Fache (1918–94) with Mary Ronnie (1926–2023) as her deputy, supervising the Reed Collection and tactfully handling visits from Mr Reed himself. On Miss Fache's retirement in 1968, Miss Ronnie succeeded to the librarianship, and Ngaira Mercer (1909–90) took over the rare book reference duties. Mary Ronnie is the outstanding figure of that exceptional trinity. She was born in Glasgow, migrating with her parents in 1937 and never losing her precise Scottish accent. I realize now that she was only in her late thirties when she let the little fair-haired English schoolboy touch his first medieval manuscript, trembling with excitement. Miss Ronnie went on to be National Librarian in Wellington,

1976–81, and Auckland City Librarian 1982–87, and eventually retired back to Dunedin, where she lived almost as long as A. H. Reed, dying aged ninety-six. Public libraries have many duties and roles in society. I still dream of the little, long-demolished mezzanine gallery in Dunedin, with its Book of Hours and some thirteenth-century Vulgates and a framed leaf of the Gutenberg Bible, quiet from the world outside. If I could choose a corner of paradise, a tiny Kawau Island for myself, that would do.

Bibliographical Sources

Michael King, *The Penguin History of New Zealand*, Auckland and London, 2003: most uncredited facts throughout on New Zealand and Māori history are from here. I have used extensively *Papers Past*, the online archive of New Zealand newspapers, 1839–1989. On the medieval manuscripts, the principal source is still Margaret M. Manion, Vera F. Vines and Christopher de Hamel, *Medieval & Renaissance Manuscripts in New Zealand Collections*, Melbourne, London and New York, 1989 (all physical descriptions and provenances were by me), henceforth cited as *MRMNZC*.

I. KAWAU ISLAND

On Grey and Kawau, James Rutherford, *Sir George Grey, K. C. B.: A Study in Colonial Government*, London, 1961; Keith Sinclair in the *Dictionary of New Zealand Biography*, Wellington, 1990, now online; Edmund Bohan, *To Be a Hero: Sir George Grey, 1812–1898*, Auckland, 1998; and for nineteenth-century excursions to Kawau, numerous accounts and announcements from *Papers Past*, 1870–84. For his library, above all, Donald Kerr, *Amassing Treasures for All Times: Sir George Grey, Colonial Bookman and Collector*, New Castle, Del., and Dunedin, 2006; and also Wynne Colgan, *The Governor's Gift: The Auckland Public Library*, Auckland, 1980; Carol Steyn, *The Medieval and Renaissance Manuscripts in the Grey Collection of the National Library of South Africa*, 2 vols., Salzburg, 2002 (*Analecta Cartusiana* series, no. 180: the Petrarch of 1455 is vol. I, pp. 200–204, MS 3.c.14); and *Migrations: Medieval Manuscripts in New Zealand* (ed. Stephanie Hollis and Alexandra Barratt), Newcastle, 2007, esp. Christopher de Hamel, 'Medieval Manuscripts and New Zealand', ch. 1, pp. 33–48, and Donald Kerr, 'Sir George Grey and Henry Shaw: Antipodean Collectors of Medieval Manuscripts', ch. 2, pp. 49–71. Quotations from Kerr's *Amassing Treasures* are 'a kind of . . .'

(**p. 14**), p. 187, citing J. G. Grey, *His Island Home*, Wellington, 1879, p. 61; 'I sit here . . .' (**p. 19**), pp. 167–8; 'some 300 . . .' (**p. 24**), p. 200; and 'Let them consider . . .' (**p. 27**), p. 208. Madden's 'of course . . .' (**pp. 18–19**) is Oxford, Bodleian Library, MS Eng. hist. c. 172, entry for 28 September 1859; 'But why a MS . . .' (**p. 20**) is Roslyn Russell, 'Travel Writers, Museums and Reflections of Empire, 1770–1901', doctoral dissertation, University of New South Wales, Canberra, 2011, p. 226, citing Trollope, *South Africa*, London, 1878, in the reprint, Cape Town, 1973, p. 81; 'old illuminated . . .' (**pp. 24–5**) is James Grattan Grey, *Australasia, Old and New*, London, 1901, p. 301, partly cited by Kerr, *Amassing Treasures*, p. 199; 'In the evening . . .' (**p. 25**) is J. A. Froude, *Oceana, or England and her Colonies*, London, 1886, p. 91, frequently cited later; 'from a Monastery . . .' (**p. 26**) is cited by me in *MRMNZC*, p. 46; 'They did no harm . . .' (**p. 26**) is Froude, *Oceana*, p. 316; 'penetrated unbidden . . .' (**p. 27**) is E. W. Wilson, 'Kawau – Island of Dreams, Memories of Sir George Grey', *The New Zealand Railway Magazine*, 10, 1935, pp. 33–7, at p. 35; and 'The people here . . .' (**p. 28**) is Colgan, *The Governor's Gift*, p. 48, and Kerr, *Amassing Treasures*, p. 251.

2. CHRISTCHURCH

'Exactly like . . .' (**p. 35**) is from *The Press*, Christchurch, 11 February 1958. The Maude (or Canterbury) Roll is *MRMNZC*, p. 79, no. 53. See also Arnold Wall, *Handbook to the Maude Roll*, Auckland, 1919; Rebecca Hayward, 'Prestige and Pedagogy: The Ownership of Medieval and Renaissance Manuscripts by New Zealand Universities', in Hollis and Barratt (eds.), *Migrations*, ch. 4, pp. 89–107; Robert Allen Rouse, 'Inscribing Lineage, Writing and Rewriting the Maude Roll', *ibid.*, ch. 5, pp. 108–22; Chris Jones, 'A Warning to the Curious: Medieval and Early Modern Collections in Aotearoa New Zealand', *Parergon, Journal of the Australian and New Zealand Association for Medieval and Early Modern Studies*, 32, 2015, pp. 1–16; and Maree Shirota, 'Royal Depositions and the Canterbury Roll', *ibid.*, pp. 39–61. The Roll is now digitized with commentary online, edited by Chris Jones and others, December 2017.

3. BESANÇON

The Missal is Auckland Central City Library, Med. MSS G. 138-139: *MRMNZC*, pp. 55–8, no. 18; see especially Vera F. Vines, 'Reading Medieval Images: Two Miniatures in a Fifteenth-Century Missal', in *Medieval Texts and Images: Studies of Manuscripts from the Middle Ages*, ed. Margaret A. Manion and Bernard J. Muir, Reading and Sydney, 1991, pp. 127–47, which introduces both St Antidius and the black attendant of the Magi; and Vera F. Vines, 'A Centre for Devotional and Liturgical Manuscript Illumination in Fifteenth-Century Besançon', in *The Art of the Book: Its Place in Medieval Worship*, ed. Margaret M. Manion and Bernard J. Muir, Exeter, 1998, pp. 195–223; Kate de Courcy and Georgia Prince, 'The Besançon Missal: 125 Years in the Auckland Central City Library', in Hollis and Barratt (eds.), *Migrations*, pp. 72–88; and Margaret Manion in *The Medieval Imagination: Illuminated Manuscripts from Cambridge, Australia and New Zealand*, ed. Bronwyn Stocks and Nigel Morgan, Melbourne, 2008, pp. 60–61, no. 14. For the flight of St Antidius, see Sabine Baring-Gould, *The Lives of the Saints*, vol. 6, London, 1897, p. 352; the cuttings from an Italian Missal, one apparently dated 1525, had been given to the Art Gallery by Moses Davies (1847–1933). On the two cathedrals, see Bernard de Vregille *et al.*, *La Cathédrale Saint-Jean de Besançon*, Besançon, 2006; on the liturgy for 6 January, Karl Young, 'La procession des Trois Rois à Besançon', *The Romanic Review*, 4, 1913, pp. 76–83; on Charles de Neufchâtel, Claude Fohlen (ed.), *Histoire de Besançon*, Paris, 1964, pp. 507–53, and J. T. de Mesmay, *Dictionnaire historique, biographique, généalogique des anciennes familles de Franche-Comté*, II, Versailles, 2006, pp. 499–500. His secular manuscripts are Paris, Bibliothèque nationale de France, mss lat. 7945 and 8455 – both Virgil – and Perth, Kerry Stokes Collection, LIB.2024. 172, Boccaccio (previously K. V. Sinclair, *Descriptive Catalogue of Medieval and Renaissance Western Manuscripts in Australia*, Sydney, 1969, pp. 427–9, and Christie's, New York, 23 April 2001, lot 6). The term 'Master of Charles de Neufchâtel' was originally used in relation to a Book of Hours, New York, Morgan Library and Museum, M 28 (first associated with the Auckland manuscript in John Plummer with Gregory Clark, *The Last Flowering: French Painting in Manuscripts, 1420–1530*, New York, 1982, pp. 57–8, no. 75); the Book of Hours in Besançon is Bibliothèque municipale, ms 125. Others there which belonged to Charles de Neufchâtel are mss 115–117 (Pontifical), ms 69 (large Breviary) and ms 138 (thirteenth-century Pontifical); he also owned

Porrentruy, Bibliothèque cantonale jurassienne, ms 10 (small Pontifical). For his borrowing a Missal for presumed use as an exemplar in 1469, see Sandrine Legendre, ' *"Nos decanus et capitulum ecclesie Bisuntine"*. Le chapitre cathédral de Besançon: Un corps social et son insertion dans l'état bourguignon (1404–1477)', doctoral dissertation, Université de Franche-Comté, II, 2021, p. 39; I am grateful to Laurence Delobette for this, as I am, even more, for a copy of the summary of the archbishop's will, Archives départementales du Doubs, G.531, fols. 315v–316r. Through introduction from David Skegg and Anthony Pincott, Jacques Laget identified the Scherer bookplate for me, no. S0803 in the Germaine Meyer-Noirel database at the Association française pour la connaissance de l'ex-libris.

4. DUNEDIN

A. H. Reed, *An Autobiography*, Wellington, Auckland and Sydney, 1967 – 'The Bible has been . . .' (**p. 91**) is from p. 259 – and his little booklets on the collection, especially *A XV Century MS of the Wyclif-Purvey Gospels: An Introduction to the Dunedin Public Library's Copy*, Wellington, 1956, and *Rare Books and Manuscripts: The Story of the Dunedin Public Library's Alfred and Isabel Reed Collection*, Wellington, 1968; also Ian Dougherty, *Books and Boots: The Story of New Zealand Publisher, Writer and Long Distance Walker, Alfred Hamish Reed*, Dunedin, 2005; Mary Ronnie, *Freedom to Read: A Centennial History of Dunedin Public Library*, Dunedin, 2008; and Anthony Tedeschi, *Early Bibles, Liturgies & Prayer Books from the Alfred & Isabel Reed Collection: A Catalogue*, Dunedin, 2011. 'Pray, Sir . . .' (**p. 80**) is from *A Noble Fragment, being a Leaf of the Gutenberg Bible, with a Bibliographical Essay by A. Edward Newton*, New York, 1921, p. [4], partly cited in Michael Visontay, *Noble Fragments: The Gripping Story of the Antiquarian Bookseller who Broke Up a Gutenberg Bible*, Melbourne, 2024, p. 24. Reg Graham, *Click! Portraits of New Zealanders*, Dunedin, 2006, includes a photograph of my mother, p. 121, mentioning me.

5. KORONOWO

The Bible is Dunedin Public Library, Reed MS 4a (*MRMNZC*, p. 83, no. 59; other portions are pp. 76–7, no. 49, p. 110, no. 119, and p. 113, no. 126).

On evangelical breaking up of Bibles and, in turn, on the format of Bibles until the thirteenth century, see my own 'The Leaf Book', in *Disbound and Dispersed: The Leaf Book Considered*, Chicago, 2005, pp. 6–23, and *The Book: A History of the Bible*, London, 2001, esp. chs. 1, 3 and 5. The Gregory *Moralia* in Auckland is Med. MS G. 132 (*MRMNZC*, pp. 49–50, no. 12). On the ninth-century leaves in Dunedin, Richard Gameson, 'The Oldest Manuscript in New Zealand (Dunedin Public Libraries, Reed Fragment 1)', in Hollis and Barratt (eds.), *Migrations*, as above, pp. 147–64; on the strips in Auckland, Alexandra Barratt, 'Waste not, Want not: Manuscript Fragments in the Sir George Grey Special Collections, Auckland', *Parergon*, as above, pp. 19–37, esp. pp. 27–30 (also Elizabeth Mullins, 'Carolingian Bible Fragments in Dublin', *Fragmentology*, 6, 2023, pp. 67–87, and Sotheby's, 10 July 2012, lot 32). The Bible of 1446 from Benediktbeuern is Munich, Bayerische Staatsbibliothek, Clm 4501a. The Holme Cultram Bible is *MRMNZC*, pp. 121–2, no. 138, and Shaw's early one-volume Bible, *ibid.*, pp. 70–71, no. 41 (Med. MS S. 1590). Andrew McPherson helped me in the Hewitson Library at Knox College and told me of the College minutes of 1928–29; on the white mice, Alison Clarke, *A Living Tradition: A Centennial History of Knox College, Dunedin*, Dunedin, 2009, p. 180; 'but I wouldn't . . .' (**p. 104**) is a letter from Reed to David M. Taylor, Reed archive, Dunedin Public Library; Paulien Martens helped search in the Canterbury Museum and Anna Tovey in the Carey Baptist College; 'manuscript copy . . .' (**p. 104**) was reported in both the *Dominion* and the *New Zealand Herald*, 26 February 1931; Judith Bright has always been hospitable in the Kinder Library. On the scribe Nicolaus at Koronowo, Dariusz Karczewski, 'Z dziejów wewnętrznych klasztoru cystersów w Byszewie (Koronowie) w okresie przedtrydenckim', *Nasza Przeszłość*, 96, 2001, pp. 11–32, esp. p. 13, nn. 7–8; for wider context, Józef Dobosz, *The Church and Cistercians in Medieval Poland: Foundations, Documents, People*, Turnhout, 2023. The five-volume Bible probably from Morimond is Chaumont, Bibliothèque municipale, mss 1–5; the little Bible once at Koronowo is Kórnic, PAN (Polish Academy of Sciences) Biblioteki Kórnickiej, BK 2.

6. DUNEDIN

For the Sturt reprints, **pp. 120–21** here, A. T. Hazen, 'J. Sturt, Facsimilist', *The Library*, ser. 4, 25, 1944, pp. 72–9. 'A collection worth . . .' (**p. 129**) is *Otago Daily Times*, 28 July 1966; 'will probably be doubled . . .' (**p. 129**) is Reed, *Autobiography*, p. 266. 'There are literally . . .' (**p. 130**) is cited from A. N. L. Munby, *Connoisseurs and Medieval Miniatures, 1750–1850*, Oxford, 1972, p. 160. The confrontation over the Wycliffite Bible, Ronnie, *Freedom to Read*, pp. 185–6, and I have also heard her tell the story. 'I wonder Mr Jarman . . .' (**p. 132**) is from Janet Backhouse, 'A Victorian Connoisseur and His Manuscripts: The Tale of Mr Jarman and Mr Wing', *British Museum Quarterly*, 32, 1968, pp. 76–92, at p. 78, with more now in my own *The Medieval World at Our Fingertips*, London and Turnhout, 2018, pp. 135–42; the Jarman miniature in Dunedin is *MRMNZR*, pp. 103–4, no. 98, and the leaf with a beaver, p. 96, no. 77. The letter to Geering from Reed (not named but easily recognizable) is Lloyd Geering, *Wrestling with God: The Story of My Life*, Wellington, 2006, p. 153; at the time of writing, Professor Geering is almost 108, the oldest man in New Zealand. Our Latin class with the Carmina Burana is described in my *Meetings with Remarkable Manuscripts*, London, 2016, pp. 330 and 333.

7. NORBURY

The Fitzherbert Book of Hours is Dunedin Public Library, Reed MS 5: *MRMNZC*, pp. 84–6, no. 61; also Michael Orr, 'The Fitzherbert Book of Hours (Dunedin Public Libraries, Reed MS 5) and the Iconography of St Anne Teaching the Virgin to Read in Early Fifteenth-Century England', in Hollis and Barratt (eds.), *Migrations*, pp. 216–46; Christopher de Hamel in Stocks and Morgan (eds.), *The Medieval Imagination*, pp. 150–51, no. 47; and Alexandra Barratt, 'Keep it in the Family: Researching Women and their Books of Devotion', in *Imagination, Books & Community in Medieval Europe: Papers of a Conference held at the State Library of Victoria, Melbourne, Australia, 29–31 May 2008*, ed. Gregory Kratzmann, South Yarra, 2009, pp. 152–61; I am grateful, as always, to Professor Barratt for advice on this chapter. The French Book of Hours, Mr Reed's favourite, is Reed MS 8 (*MRMNZC*, pp. 87–8, no. 64). On Books of Hours used in England, Eamon Duffy, *Marking the Hours:*

English People and their Prayers, 1240–1570, New Haven and London, 2006, and Nigel Morgan, 'English Books of Hours, *c*.1240–*c*.1480', in *Books of Hours Reconsidered*, ed. Sandra Hindman and James H. Marrow, London and Turnhout, 2013, pp. 65–95; on those imported from Flanders, Nicholas Rogers, 'Patrons and Purchasers: Evidence for the Original Owners of Books of Hours Produced in the Low Countries for the English Market', in *Als ich can, Liber Amicorum in Memory of Professor Maurits Smeyers*, ed. Bert Cardon *et al.*, Louvain, 2002, pp. 1165–82, citing his own M. Litt. dissertation, Cambridge, 1982, and referring to University of Durham Ushaw College MS 10 and the citation of a Book of Hours in 1446 as 'cum ymaginis . . . ad modum Flandr', for each of which, see Richard Gameson, 'Exporting Private Prayer', in *Treasures of Ushaw College, Durham's Hidden Gem*, ed. James E. Kelly, London and Durham, 2015, pp. 58–61, and James Raine (ed.), *Testamenta Eboracensia, A Selection of Wills from the Registry at York*, II, Durham, 1855 (Surtees Society, XXX), pp. 116–18. The Rossdhu Hours is *MRMNZC*, pp. 61–2, no. 25 (now also Anne McKim, 'The Rossdhu Book of Hours: Tracing Connection', in Hollis and Barratt (eds.), *Migrations*, pp. 202–15); the Mildmay Hours is Chicago, Newberry Library, Case MS 35; the register of the guild of St John the Evangelist is Bruges, Stadsarchief, Oud Archief, Librariërsgilde 76 (after I had seen it, Evelien Hauwaerts kindly sent me scans). For the parallel with the Luton Guild Book (Luton Art Museum), see Kathleen L. Scott, *Dated & Datable English Manuscript Borders, c. 1395–1499*, London, 2002, pp. 98–9; on the cleft hennin, Anne H. van Buren with Roger S. Wieck, *Illuminating Fashion: Dress in the Art of Medieval France and the Netherlands, 1325–1515*, London and New York, 2011, pp. 174–7. The reference to Margery Kempe (**p. 157**) is from Duffy, *Marking the Hours*, p. 58, and on the royal proclamations of 1534–35, *ibid.*, pp. 149–52. On the Hours at Berkeley Castle, citing the Fitzherbert manuscript in Dunedin, Kathleen L. Scott, *Later Gothic Manuscripts, 1390–1490*, catalogue (*A Survey of Manuscripts Illuminated in the British Isles*, IV), London, 1996, II, pp. 92–7, no. 23. 'In the Church . . .' and 'my best prymer . . .' (**pp. 162–3**) are from R. H. C. FitzHerbert, 'Will of Elizabeth Fitzherbert . . . of Norbury, Derbyshire, dated 20th October 1490', *Journal of the Derbyshire Archaeological and Natural History Society*, 20, 1898, pp. 32–9, at p. 35; on the Fitzherberts at Norbury, Bede Camm,

Forgotten Shrines, An Account of Some Old Catholic Halls and Families in England and of Relics and Memorials of the English Martyrs, London, 1910, pp. 1–74.

8. WELLINGTON AND AUCKLAND

David M. Taylor, *The Oldest Manuscripts in New Zealand*, Wellington, 1955 (New Zealand Council for Educational Research, Educational Research Series, 36); 'Indeed, I may say . . .' (**p. 167**) is p. 76, and 'a magnificent specimen . . .' (**p. 169**) is p. 60. Professor Volker Heine of Cambridge University has told me about his father, of the same name. For Hibbard, Watts Rule and Clemas, see Ruth Lightbourne, 'Where Did They Come From? Incunabula in the Special Printed Collections of the Alexander Turnbull Library', *Turnbull Library Record*, 41, 2008, pp. 1–24. My account of Clemas (and his newly realized family connection to Hibbard) is constructed from very numerous newspaper references searched through *Papers Past*, including the *Ashburton Guardian*, 17 November 1932, for his part on the *Beacon Rock*, which is supplemented by the *New Zealand Times*, 13 July 1902 and Australian papers during the voyage, such as the *Launceston Examiner*, 23 November 1900, the *Australian Town and Country Journal*, Sydney, 8 December 1900, and *The Advertiser*, Adelaide, 3 January 1901. Quotations, **pp. 172–4**: 'a fair attendance', *Wairarapa Age*, 12 July 1932; 'All of us . . .', ibid., 23 September 1936; 'relics of . . .', *New Zealand Truth*, 4 October 1928; 'The volume had been . . .', *Wairarapa Age*, 7 June 1929; 'CLEMAS COLLECTION SOLD . . .', *ibid*, 5 November 1932; and 'bought by my people . . .', 'bought many years ago . . .' and 'and was considered . . .', all Taylor, *Oldest Manuscripts*, p. 77. Anthony Tedeschi sent me scans from the Clemas correspondence in the Bible Society archives in the Turnbull Library, parts of ref. 80-179-21; Scott Gwara told me of the American Federation of Arts exhibitions; see also Peter J. Lineham, *Bible & Society: A Sesquicentennial History of the Bible Society in New Zealand*, Wellington, 1996, esp. pp. 193–4. The Bible Society's Book of Hours and Psalter are *MRMNZC*, pp. 119–21, no. 136, and pp. 118–19, no. 135; 'As a work of art . . .' and 'quite different . . .' (**p. 175**) are Taylor, *Oldest Manuscripts*, pp. 85 and 80. On the Shirley Psalter, Margaret Connolly, *John Shirley: Book Production and the Noble Household in Fifteenth-Century England*, Aldershot and Brookfield, Vt, 1998, pp. 113–14, and her 'A London Widow's Psalter: Beatrice Cornburgh and Alexander Turnbull Library MSR-01', *Trivium*, 31, 1999, pp. 101–16, and 'Another Medieval London Widow: The story of Beatrice Cornburgh', *The Ricardian*, 13, 2003, pp. 148–58. The Sarum Missal is *MRMNZC*, pp. 128–9, no. 147, and now also, Christine McCarthy, 'Making Significance: Historiated Initials and the Donation of the Sir John Moody Albert Ilott Illuminated Manuscripts to the Alexander Turnbull Library', in Hollis and Barratt (eds.), *Migrations*, pp. 123–43. 'Mr Henry Shaw served . . .' (**p. 181**) is Taylor, *Oldest Manuscripts*, p. 159; 'tastefully illuminated . . .' (**p. 181**) is Henry Shaw, *A Guide to the Principal Man-uscripts, Early Printed Books, Autograph Letters, etc., contained in the Auckland Free Public Library*, Auckland, 1908, p. 23, and 'Books of hours . . .' is p. 18; while 'the finest illuminated . . .' (**p. 52**, in Chapter 3) is also *ibid.*, p. 17. For Shaw, Kerr, 'Sir George Grey and Henry Shaw', as above, in Hollis and Barratt (eds.), *Migrations*, pp. 49–71, esp. pp. 60–67, and Kerr in the *Dictionary of New Zealand Biography*, III, Wellington, 1996 and now online; I supplemented these considerably by quarrying *Papers Past*, including 'SHAW LIBRARY WORTH . . .' (**p. 183**) from the *New Zealand Herald*, 4 October 1913, and 'which would be valued highly . . .' (**p. 184**), *ibid.*, 4 May 1928; 'put into exile . . .', is from 'ART AND GOLD' in the *Sun*, Auckland, 4 February 1929.

9. CANTERBURY

The Boethius, *De musica*, is *MRMNZC*, pp. 122–4, no. 140, and now Fiona McAlpine, '*Concorditer Dissonant*: From Consonance to Polyphony (Alexander Turnbull Library, MSR-05)', in Hollis and Barratt (eds.), *Migrations*, pp. 165–201, and McAlpine in Stocks and Morgan (eds.), *The Medieval Imagination*, pp. 204–5, no. 67. For the collector, E. H. McCormick, *Alexander Turnbull: His Life, His Circle, His Collections*, Wellington, 1974: Turnbull's will, 'to His Majesty . . .' (**pp. 189–90**) is described on p. 286 and 'Dear Sir . . .' (**pp. 192–3**) is p. 195. Neil Ker's review of Taylor, identi-fying the Canterbury provenance, is in *Medium Ævum*, 28, 1959, pp. 874–5; his letters to the Turnbull are TL 3/1, dated 10 May and 8 June 1956; the manuscript is listed in the Canterbury library catalogues of the twelfth century and then the early fourteenth in M. R. James, *The Ancient Libraries* *of Canterbury and Dover*, Cambridge, 1903, pp. 3 and 8, no. 40, and p. 55, no. 438. The two Alexander Staples are now in Joan Greatrex, *Biographical Register of the English Cathedral Priories of the Province of Canterbury, c. 1066–1540*, Oxford, 1997, pp. 290–91. The Juvencus is James, *Ancient Libraries*, p. 11, no. 152, now Cambridge, Corpus Christi College, Parker Library MS 304; the Eusebius is MS 51. On the library of Christ Church, Nigel Ramsay, 'The Cathedral Archives and Library', in *A History of Canterbury Cathedral*, ed. P. Collinson, N. Ramsay and M. Sparks, Oxford, 1995, pp. 341–407; the Canterbury 'ice-cream cone' marks were first described by N. R. Ker, 'Membra Disiecta, II', *British Museum Quarterly*, 14, 1940, pp. 79–86, p. 85, n. 1; the Watts Rule leaf is now *MRMNZC*, p. 135, no. 154 (b). The Boethius *De musica* in the State Library of Victoria is pp. 202–3, no. 66, in Stocks and Morgan (eds.), *The Medieval Imagination*; the *De consolatione* in the Turnbull is *MRMNZC*, pp. 127–8, no. 146, and the French translation among Grey's manuscripts is *ibid.*, p. 43, no. 3. The Trinity College Boethius with Guido is R. 15. 22 there (cat. 944). The Wellington manuscript was ascribed to possibly Normandy by Jonathan Alexander in his review of *MRMNZC* in *Burlington Magazine*, 132, 1990, p. 719, and by François Avril to Normandy or Maine, perhaps Le Mans, in correspondence with me, for which I am very grateful. The lectionary associated with Le Mans or Tours is Paris, Bibliothèque nationale de France, ms lat. 5323: Walter Cahn, *Romanesque Manuscripts: The Twelfth Century (A Survey of Manuscripts Illuminated in France*, III), London, 1996, pp. 30–31, no. 19, esp. ill. 42. The other Canterbury manuscripts of musical texts now in Cambridge are University Library, Ii. 3. 12 (Boethius), and Corpus Christi College, Parker Library, MS 260 (*Musica Hogeri*). On Becket's library, see my own *The Book in the Cathedral: The Last Relic of Thomas Becket*, London, 2020; his quick cramming of monastic learning and trip through Le Mans is described by Herbert of Bosham in *Materials for the History of Thomas Becket, Archbishop of Canterbury*, III, ed. James Craigie Robertson, London, 1877 (Rolls Series), pp. 204 and 253–5; the Canterbury or Eadwine Psalter in the cloister is ascribed by default to Becket's patronage by Margaret Gibson in *The Eadwine Psalter*, ed. Margaret Gibson, T. A. Heslop and Richard W. Pfaff, London and University Park, PA, 1992, pp. 211–12. Examples of the binding stamp of a Tudor rose below a crown are listed on the British Armorial Bindings website of the University of Toronto

Libraries, including Windsor Castle 1076104 (Camden, 1600) and 1121305 (*Emblemata*, 1599); the one in Dunedin on their copy of Boys (1610) is in their online exhibition catalogue, 'Our Will and Pleasure, Royal Autographs, Letters & Memorabilia of the British Monarchy', 2011, case 17; despite claims, none of these can be royal bindings.

10. OTAGO

This chapter has been read by Charmian Smith, née Dod, with whom I shared much time in my first year. For Knox College, see Clarke, *Living Tradition*, as above; 'music and poetry . . .' (**pp. 215–16**) is from Dylan Thomas, 'Return Journey to Swansea', radio performance, 1947, widely published; on the master, J. S. Somerville, *Jack in the Pulpit, An Autobiography*, Dunedin, 1987. The Dutch Book of Hours at Knox is *MRMNZC*, pp. 109–10, no. 118; the manuscripts given by Fels to Otago are *ibid.*, pp. 110–13, nos. 120–124; 'Misfortune strikes . . .' (**p. 226**) is Taylor, *Oldest Manuscripts*, p. 26. The Shoults manuscripts from Selwyn College are *MRMNZC*, pp. 114–15, nos. 128–130; on that collection, Donald Jackson Kerr, *Awakening a Curate's Library, The Rev. William Arderne Shoults (1839–1887): His Life, his Book Collection, and his Legacy to New Zealand* [Melbourne], 2022; 'many curiosities . . .' (**p. 228**) is from p. 293; de Beer's childhood access is Michael Strachan, *Esmond de Beer (1895–1990), Scholar and Benefactor: A Personal Memoir*, Norwich, 1995, pp. 13–14; 'I am given . . .' (**p. 228**) is Taylor, *Oldest Manuscripts*, p. 56. Recent revivals of medieval studies are the subject of Anna Czarnowus and Janet M. Wilson (eds.), *New Zealand Medievalism, Reframing the Medieval*, Abingdon and New York, 2024, not much of it comprehensible or relevant, but including Victoria Condie, 'Between Worlds: The Afterlife of Medieval Manuscripts in the Alfred and Isabel Reed Collection', pp. 101–15, which cites 'Donne's sermons . . .' (**p. 233**) on p. 104, from J. C. Beaglehole, 'The Library and the Cosmos', *Turnbull Library Record*, 3, 1970, p. 65. Mantell's Book of Hours in Auckland is *MRMNZC*, pp. 74–5, no. 46; Robert Rouse, 'Indigenising the Medieval; or How Did Māori and Awabakal Become Inscribed in Medieval Manuscripts?', *Parergon*, 32, 2015, pp. 233–50.

11. WESTMINSTER AND OXFORD

The book is Otago University Library, Shoults/Ic/1481/B; cf. Kerr, *Awakening a Curate's Library*, p. 227. A version of this chapter was the fourth of my unpublished Lyell Lectures, Oxford, 2009. On the binder, Strickland Gibson, *Early Oxford Bindings (Illustrated Monographs Issued by the Bibliographical Society*, X), Oxford, 1903, pp. 4–6; Mirjam Foot, 'English Decorated Bookbindings', in *Book Production and Publishing in Britain, 1375–1475*, ed. Jeremy Griffiths and Derek Pearsall, Cambridge, 1989, pp. 65–86, at pp. 77–8; Isabelle Pingree, 'A Catalogue of the Bindings of the Fifteenth-Century Bookbinder Called the Rood and Hunt Binder', *The Library*, 7 ser., 4, 2003, pp. 371–401. For the printed Kendale indulgences, R. N. Swanson, 'Caxton's Indulgence for Rhodes, 1480–81', *The Library*, 7 ser., 5, 2004, pp. 195–201; *Printing in England in the Fifteenth Century: E. Gordon Duff's Bibliography with Supplementary Descriptions, Chronologies and a Census of Copies by Lotte Hellinga*, London, 2009, pp. 53–5, nos. 204–208; and Lotte Hellinga, *Catalogue of Books Printed in the XVth Century now in the British Library (BMC, XI, England)*, 't Goy-Houten, 2007, pp. 114, 118–19 and 245–6; I am indebted to Dr Hellinga for reading an early (and more complex) draft of this chapter and much advice over many decades; for this narrative, I have simplified the variants, treating singular and plural versions as one, and assuming no necessary chronological difference between them or between issues that do or do not cite the tenth year of Sixtus IV. The Pottesman binding was Sotheby's, 15 October 1979, lot 253, and is now British Library, IB 55317a. Fragments of Kendale indulgences occur in Rood and Hunt bindings (as numbered by Pingree), 3, Oxford, All Souls College, Bartolomaeus Montagnana, 1476, five pieces by Caxton; 8, British Library, Voragine, 1482, seventeen pieces by Caxton and seven by Lettou; 9, British Library (formerly Pottesman), Lathbury, 1482, twenty-one pieces by Caxton and two by Lettou; 20, Christie's, 20 November 2002, lot 6 (formerly Otto Schäfer, Sotheby's New York, 1 November 1995, lot 172, and Helmut Friedlaender, Christie's, New York, 23 April 2001, lot 11), Pierre d'Ailly, *c.* 1480, three pieces by Caxton; 21, Dunedin, as throughout, twelve pieces by Caxton and two by Lettou; and 22, Oxford, St John's College, Alexander Carpentarius, 1480, fifty-five pieces by Caxton. On the different Kendales, Anne F. Sutton, 'John Kendale: A Search for Richard III's Secretary', *Richard III*,

Crown and People, ed. J. Petre, Gloucester and London, 1985, pp. 224–38. 'the Turkes . . .' (**p. 246**) is from 'The Delectable Newesse of the Glorious Victorye of the Rhodyans agaynest the Turkes', *Medieval English Travel: A Critical Anthology*, ed. Anthony Bale and Sebastian Sobecki, Oxford, 2019, pp. 427–8. On indulgences in England, Paul Needham, *The Printer & the Pardoner: An Unrecorded Indulgence Printed by William Caxton for the Hospital of St Mary Rounceval, Charing Cross*, Washington, 1986, and R. N. Swanson, *Indulgences in Late Medieval England: Passports to Paradise?* Cambridge, 2007. On Caxton's premises in Westminster, Hellinga, *BMC* XI, pp. 8–10, based partly on Howard M. Nixon, 'Caxton, his Contemporaries and Successors in the Book Trade from Westminster Documents', *The Library*, 5 ser., 31, 1976, pp. 305–26. The Bodleian Library instructions for indulgence sellers are MS Bodley 123, fol. 149r–v; the manuscript indulgence in Colchester is Essex Record Office, D/DCe/Q2 (Swanson, 'Caxton's Indulgence', p. 198). The inscription in the Dunedin book is 'Ex dono magistri Johannis lee quondam magistri huius Collegii' (cf. A. B. Emden, *Biographical Register of the University of Oxford to A. D. 1500*, Oxford, 1957–59, p. 1123). Paul Meller kindly checked the Oscott Nicholas de Lyra for me. For the bookseller Hunt, M. B. Parkes, 'Thomas Hunt and the Oxford Book Business in the Late Fifteenth Century', *The Library*, 7, 2016, pp. 28–39, and his consignments from Europe, Paul Needham, 'Continental Printed Books Sold in Oxford, *c.* 1480–3: Two Trade Records', in *Incunabula, Studies in Fifteenth-Century Printed Books Presented to Lotte Hellinga*, ed. Martin Davies, London, 1999, pp. 243–70; on Rood, Hellinga, *BMC* XI, pp. 13–15. On the binder's possible identification with Nicholas, Graham Pollard, 'The Names of Some English Fifteenth-Century Binders', *The Library*, 5 ser., 25, 1970, pp. 193–218, at p. 209. Provenances cited here of Rood and Hunt bindings, using Pingree numbers again, are Durham or Durham College (12–14, 20, 25), All Souls College (1–3), Magdalen College (10), Abbot John Newland of Bristol (24) and Shelford Church (15). Kendale's papal licence of 1479 is J. A. Twemlow *et al.* (ed.), *Calendar of Entries in the Papal Registers, Papal Letters*, 13, i, 1471–84, London, 1955, pp. 254–5; the copy of the Lettou printing of Kendale's indulgence issued in Oxford to John and Katherine Frisden is British Library, IA 55403.

EPILOGUE

The second Mantell Book of Hours is *MRMNZC*, pp. 142–3, no. 180, bought by the Dunedin Public Library, Sotheby's, 1 December 1987, lot 54. The Turnbull Library bought Dunbar Sloane, Wellington, 11 August 2022, lot 254, Sermons, *c.* 1200, which had previously been Christie's, London, 12 November 2008, lot 17. The Massey University Boethius is *MRMNZC*, p. 116, no. 132; the Boswell Book of Hours was Sotheby's, 7 July 2009, lot 47; 'my father . . .' (**p. 263**) is James Boswell, *The Life of Samuel Johnson, LL.D. including a Journal of a Tour to the Hebrides*, III, London, 1831, p. 72.

Index of Manuscripts and Incunabula